Accounting Fundamentals for Non-Accountants

Accounting Fundamentals for Non-Accountants

Stephen A. Moscove, Ph.D.
University of Nevada, Reno

Reston Publishing Company, Inc.
A Prentice-Hall Company
Reston, Virginia

Library of Congress Cataloging in Publication Data

Moscove, Stephen A
    Accounting fundamentals for non-accountants.

    Includes index.
    1.   Accounting. I.   Title.
HF5635.M875   657   80–18561
ISBN 0–8359–0071–1
ISBN 0–8359–0070–3 (pbk.)

(also published as *Accounting Fundamentals:
A Self-Instructional Approach, Second
edition*)

657   c.1   16 95
Moscove, Stephen A.
Accounting fundamentals for
non-accountants /

© 1981 by
Reston Publishing Company, Inc.
A Prentice-Hall Company
Reston, Virginia   22090

All rights reserved.
No part of this book
may be reproduced in any way,
or by any means,
without permission in writing
from the publisher.

10 9 8 7 6 5 4 3

Printed in the United States of America

*To my wife Linda,
son Justin Seth,
and daughter Jodi Samantha*

Contents

Preface

Book Objectives

After teaching elementary accounting for several years at the university level, the author believes that many students have difficulty understanding the textbook material. This is often caused by the failure of the book to adequately explain the accounting principles and procedures. Students may become too involved with all the small details presented in the textbook. As a result, they lose sight of the important underlying accounting concepts.

This book has been written in a simplified, self-instructional manner to explain the basic principles and procedures of financial accounting. The author has attempted to present logical explanations of the subject matter so that the reader will better understand and thereby appreciate the dynamic accounting field. It is hoped that this approach will enable the reader to grasp the many accounting principles and procedures without the need for teacher explanations. The majority of the illustrations and problems discussed in the book have small numbers in order that the accounting principles can be emphasized rather than the mathematics.

Book Organization

The eleven chapters in this book present the basic principles and procedures of financial accounting in a logical order. The first part of Chapter 1 sets the stage for the readers' subsequent study by analyzing the important business communication function that accounting performs. The remainder of this chapter discusses the techniques utilized when an organization's financial statements are prepared. Clear explanations are given of the various monetary items appearing in such financial statements.

Chapters 2 and 3 give logical explanations of the accounting cycle steps that should be followed so that financial statements are accurately prepared. After discussing the accounting cycle and its importance, Chapters 4 through 8 provide analysis of the specific monetary items that typically appear in the financial statements. Both the "how" and "why" are discussed for the many accounting computations presented in Chapters 4 through 8. Additional topics within these chapters include internal control and specialized journals.

Chapters 9 and 10 cover important topics that the reader should be able to understand based on his or her comprehension of the previous book material. The former discusses the basic principles and procedures of partnership accounting, while the latter does the same for corporation accouning.

Chapter 11 analyzes an important financial statement called the "Statement of Changes in Financial Position." The objectives of this financial statement along with a step-by-step approach to its preparation are discussed. This chapter also gives a practical illustration of a matrix accounting system for a small business.

A few short multiple-choice questions testing the readers' understanding of the book material are provided (along with the correct answers) at various intervals throughout each chapter. In addition, a comprehensive problem requiring computational analysis is included at the end of every chapter. Each problem covers the major concepts developed within the particular chapter.

A unique presentation appears in this book's appendix. It includes a step-by-step logical solution and explanation for each chapter problem.

Acknowledgments

There are many people to thank. In particular, the following stand out in my mind: Dr. Charles Spencer (former chairman of the accounting and finance department at the University of Hawaii) for his guidance and positive encouragement contributing to my professional development as both a college professor and an author; Mr. Frederic K. Easter (assistant vice president and executive editor of Reston Publishing Company) for his patience, understanding, and constructive suggestions throughout the writing of this book; Miss Carol Jardin (instructor at Chaminade College, Honolulu, Hawaii) for her many hours spent editing this book; Mrs. Joan Karimoto (secretary of the accounting department at the University of Hawaii) for her excellent work in typing this book; and Linda Bogle (my wife) for her warm love and understanding, and also, to my children, Justin Seth and Jodi Samantha.

Stephen A. Moscove

Accounting
Fundamentals for
Non-Accountants

1

Financial Statements

The End Product of Financial Accounting

People without a knowledge of accounting may find themselves facing one of these real-life situations:

> "I don't understand! My business earned a large income this year. However, the amount of cash within my business organization significantly decreased."

> "I borrowed $1000 cash from the bank this month to purchase some equipment for my business and have not yet paid the bank any interest on my loan. However, the accountant told me today that my company has $10 worth of interest expense this month on the $1000 loan. I am confused!"

> "My company made a $10,000 sale to a customer in December 1982. The customer paid the $10,000 he owed my company on January 15, 1983. I was pleased because I thought this $10,000 cash collection would cause my company's 1983 income to increase. However, I was informed today by my accountant that the $10,000 cash collection has no effect whatsoever on by business organization's 1983 income. I wish the accountant would explain this to me!"

1

"My company purchased a piece of machinery last year which cost $50,000. I met an accountant last night at a party and he told me that my company could have paid a much smaller amount of income taxes to the federal government last year if I would have chosen a different depreciation method for the new machinery. Why didn't somebody tell me this last year?"

"Here I am in court having my family home sold in order to pay my business debts. If somebody had only told me three years ago when I started my business that it would be smarter for me and my associates to form a corporation rather than a partnership!"

With an understanding of accounting, each of the individuals in the above situations could have avoided the confusion that existed. The comprehension of accounting that you will obtain from reading this book will enable you to face such business situations in a knowledgeable manner.

The first section of this chapter analyzes the purpose of accounting followed by a discussion regarding the preparation of a company's two major financial statements: the income statement and the balance sheet. Finally, the theoretical framework of accounting and the major types of business organizations that people may choose to form are briefly examined.

The Communication Function of Accounting

The major purpose of an accounting system is to communicate relevant information to interested parties as an aid in decision making. In order that the reader may better understand the nature of accounting and its role as an information system, this purpose will be analyzed in depth.

A large quantity of data is continually flowing into the typical business organization of today. Moreover, these data may be in a quantitative or nonquantitative form. Accounting is mainly concerned with converting the quantitative data into useful decision-making information through the process of *interpretation* and *communication.* For example, the symbols *XS150* represent data. By taking these data and interpreting them to mean, "The X Company bought supplies for $150," the accountant has converted the data into an understandable form called *information.* The symbols *XS150* would already be information if they were thoroughly understood by the recipient. However, if the symbols do not communicate an understandable message, then they are just data and not information.

Accounting has a difficult task in attempting to communicate information. The quantitative data, which are the input of an accounting system, must be converted into an understandable message in order for accounting to fulfill its function. One major problem that accounting faces is the wide variety of interested parties who need accounting information. These interested parties require different types of information for making business decisions. The task of accounting is to attempt to satisfy these needs. Furthermore, people with dissimilar backgrounds tend to interpret the same information in different ways. Accounting faces the problem of adequately communicating information to this variety of users.

In an attempt to solve this information communciation problem, the field of accounting has developed along two major lines—*financial accounting* and *managerial accounting.*

Financial Accounting

The purpose of financial accounting is to communicate relevant information to *external* parties as an aid in decision making. "External party" encompasses anyone who is not directly involved in the day-to-day operating activities of a particular business organization. There are a great many external parties who need financial accounting information to make decisions.

If a business organization is short of cash, it may go to a bank to negotiate a loan. Since the bank has no involvement in the day-to-day operating activities of the business organization, it is considered an external party. Before the bank will grant a loan to the organization, it will require some information from the loan applicant. A large amount of the information that the bank requests will come from the company's financial accounting system. The bank wants to be reasonably sure before granting a loan that the recipient will be able to pay it back plus interest at a later date. The final decision on the loan application will be based on the information supplied by the financial accounting system.

An individual may have $5000 that he wants to invest in some corporation stock. This individual is another example of an external party. In order to make an investment decision, he would want financial information about various corporations. The financial accounting system would be called upon to provide the information to the potential investor. He would then attempt to make a decision concerning in which corporation it would be most advantageous to invest his $5000.

Instead of an individual's analyzing the financial information himself prior to making an investment decision, he may go to a professional security analyst. Security analysts (who make investment recommendations) are another external group that uses financial accounting information for decision making.

A final example of an external party who is provided financial accounting information is the various taxing authorities—the federal government, the state government, etc. Individuals and corporations must pay taxes to governmental agencies based upon their earned incomes. A financial accounting system enables them to determine their income upon which they will pay taxes. Thus, federal and state taxing authorities require financial accounting information to make decisions about taxes that are due them.

As the preceding discussion has indicated, there are various external parties that require information from financial accounting. Furthermore, each of these groups requires different types of financial information. These differing demands place a large responsibility on financial accounting. In other words, a financial accounting system has to be developed so that it is sufficiently flexible to meet the needs of the varying external parties. In addition, the *communication* of financial accounting information must be in an understandable manner to achieve proper interpretation by the recipients. The backgrounds and experiences of the recipients should be considered by the financial accounting system when decision-making information is communicated to external parties.

Managerial Accounting

The purpose of managerial accounting is to communicate relevant information to *internal* parties as an aid in decision making. "Internal party" encompasses anyone within an organization's system who is directly involved in the day-to-day operating activities of that organization. *Management* is the major internal group who utilizes the output from managerial accounting.

During the past several years the field of managerial accounting has increased in importance. Menial tasks such as recording business transactions, adding columns and rows of figures, etc., that used to require a good portion of the accountant's time are now being handled by electronic data processing (i.e., computer) equipment. As a result, the accountant can devote more time to creative and dynamic activities within an organization. Accountants are becoming more intensively involved in the decision-making aspects by helping management plan and control business operations.

Management requires numerous types of information for decisions that affect its short-range (one year or less) and long-range (over one year) planning. The managerial accountant has become one of the major sources of management's decision-making information. For example, management may be attempting to decide whether to purchase a particular manufacturing component from an outside company or to produce the component within its own organization. The managerial accountant may be called upon to perform a cost analysis of both alternatives and to make a recommendation to management. As another example, management may be considering the feasibility of eliminating a specific product line and adding another product line. Again, the managerial accountant can provide a cost analysis as a basis for the decision.

The field of managerial accounting is "wide open" in terms of its realm of activity. Whenever management needs information for a decision, the managerial accountant may be called upon to furnish the needed inputs. Because the major users of financial accounting are external parties without access to an organization's internal functionings, numerous principles and procedures for preparing and reporting financial accounting information are required for their protection. Without these guide lines, the external parties would face the risk of misleading and inaccurate information. However, since managerial accounting is directed toward the people within an organization rather than outsiders, the same degree of methodology is not required. Flexibility and creativity in preparing managerial accounting information is more important than fixed principles and procedures. The managerial accountant should analyze the needs of management in a particular decision-making environment and use his creative abilities to help management reach a decision.

Financial Statements

As discussed previously, the purpose of financial accounting is to communicate relevant information to external parties as an aid in decision making. This communication process is achieved largely through two major analyses prepared by the accountant—the *balance sheet* and the *income statement* (also called financial statements). The object of the subsequent discussion is to develop the basic concepts and procedures involved in the preparation of the balance sheet and the income statement.

Balance Sheet (Statement of Financial Position)

If an individual wants to start his own business, a cash investment is typically required. With this money he may buy office equipment, inventory, machinery, land, and a small building in which to operate his business. In buying these various items, the individual may run short of cash. As a result, he may go to a bank and arrange to borrow money. Upon receipt of the loan, he can then buy any additional business items needed.

The above simplified example illustrates what is included in an organization's statement of financial position (a *balance sheet*). The three major financial items included in a balance sheet are *assets, liabilities,* and *owners' equity*. These financial items can be expressed by the following relationship, called the balance sheet equation:

$$\text{Assets} = \text{liabilities} + \text{owners' equity}$$

The logic behind this relationship is now discussed.

Assets are economic resources of an organization that are of value to the organization. In the previous example, the cash invested, the office equipment, the inventory, the machinery, the land, and the building are all examples of assets. Anyone starting a business must have various types of assets to perform the necessary organizational operating activities. When we talk about something having value to qualify as an asset, we are basically considering value as a "bundle of service potentials (or benefits)" that can be received from an object. For example, cash is considered an asset because it has a service potential to us. We can use the cash to buy things needed in our business. A piece of machinery is an asset, since we can receive *benefits* from the machine in the present and future by using it to produce products (i.e., inventory) that will eventually be sold to customers.

As an example of something that would not qualify as an asset, assume that you buy a 1950 Ford for $200 from a used car dealer. As soon as you get the car home, it completely breaks down. You try to sell the car, but nobody will buy it. As a result, the car just sits in your driveway. This car does not fit our definition of an asset, because it has no value (service potential) to you. The car is unsalable and you are not able to receive any present or future benefits from it. This may be an extreme example, but it illustrates a purchase that does not result in an asset. In effect, you made a bad purchase. In most cases, individuals and business organizations are considered to be rational; they would not buy something unless they thought it had value to them. However, individuals and organizations occasionally buy an item that they feel at the time of purchase is an asset. Subsequently, it turns out that the item purchased has no service value whatsoever. When this happens, the item that was originally thought to be an asset is, in effect, a loss. Of course, if a business organization makes too many bad purchases, the organization may not survive for long.

If we accept the premise that all organizations need assets, it follows that these assets must come from somewhere. In other words, assets do not suddenly appear from thin air. One major *source* of an organization's assets is the owner's (or owners') investment. In the original example at the beginning of this section, the individual started his own business by investing cash (an asset) into his business. Owners may also invest some of their personal noncash assets (for example, a piece of land or equipment). The concept "owners' equity" represents the owners' interests in a business organization. When the owners invest assets into an organization, their interest in the organization *increases*. Conversely, when the organization's assets are withdrawn by the owners, their interest in the organization *decreases*. The other major activity which causes the owners' interests in a business organization to change will be discussed in the next section of this chapter when the income statement is analyzed.

Thus, a major source of an organization's assets is from the owners themselves. However, the owners may not have sufficient personal assets to completely operate their organization. They may have to find an additional source of assets. The other major source of assets to an organization is from "liabilities." In our example, the individual who started his own business organization ran short of cash and obtained a bank loan. Upon granting the loan, the bank became another source of assets to the organization. That is, the cash received from the bank increased the organization's assets. The bank is an example of a *liability* source of assets. Liabilities typically represent "debts owed to parties *external* to an organization." (However, a company can have a liability to an internal party; for example, the salaries owed to its employees for work performed.) The bank from which the loan was obtained had no involvement with the business organization prior to granting the loan and is thus considered an external source of assets. When owners invest assets into an organization, they are considered an *internal* source of assets, since the owners are involved in the internal operating activities of the company.

Regardless of the size of a business organization, the two major sources of assets are *external* sources (causing the incurrence of liabilities) and *internal* sources (the owners of the business organization). We come back to the relationship (that is, the *balance sheet equation*) that we presented earlier:

Assets = liabilities + owners' equity

Another way of stating the above relationship would be

Assets = equities

In other words, for every business organization asset, someone must have an interest (equity) in the asset. One of the interests is an external interest called *liabilities*, and the other is an internal interest called the *owners*. Conventionally, the word "equity" is not attached to the term "liabilities." However, we should think of the liabilities as being the other major equity source of an organization's assets.

Exhibit 1-1 is a simplified example of a *balance sheet* for the Super X Company on January 1, 1983, before the start of a new business organization (but after the acquisition of various assets). (Note: dollar signs normally appear only by the first dollar items in a column and by the first dollar items below a column line [e.g., the $1800].)

Exhibit 1-1

The Super X Company
Balance Sheet
January 1, 1983

ASSETS		*LIABILITIES & OWNERS' EQUITY*	
Cash	$ 100	Liabilities:	
Merchandise inventory	500	Loan from bank	$ 600
Office supplies	200	Owners' equity:	
Machinery	600	Investment by the owners	1200
Land	400		
		Total liabilities and	
Total assets	$1800	owners' equity	$1800

There are several observations to be made from this balance sheet. The title of the statement includes the name of the company, what kind of statement it is (a balance sheet), and the specific date of preparation. The left side of the balance sheet shows the economic resources of value to the Super X Company, the *assets*. The asset called "merchandise inventory" represents the wholesale cost to the Super X Company of the merchandise that it has purchased and plans to sell to customers at retail prices. The right side of the balance sheet shows the *sources* of the Super X Company's assets. You can think of the right side as indicating the various *interests* in the assets. Parties outside the organization (the *liabilities*) have a $600 interest in the $1800 total assets, and internal parties (the *owners' equity*) have a $1200 asset interest. Percentage relationships can also be used to analyze the asset interests. The *owners* have a 66-2/3 percent interest in the total assets (owners' equity/total assets = $1200/$1800 = 66-2/3 percent), and *outside parties* have a 33-1/3 percent interest (total liabilities/total assets = $600/$1800 = 33-1/3 percent). Since the total interests in the assets must be 100 percent, the liability *plus* owner interests must total 100 percent (66-2/3 percent owner interest + 33-1/3 percent liability interest = 100 percent).

As soon as you determine that the assets are *equal* to the liabilities plus the owners' equity, double lines are drawn under the $1800 figures to indicate that the statement balances. Upon completion of the balance sheet, if you have made no errors, both sides will always be equal, since this financial statement is based upon the balance sheet equation

Assets = liabilities + owners' equity

It is important to keep in mind that the balance sheet presented here is simplified in order to present the basic concept and format. In later chapters, more complicated balance sheets will be examined. Also, companies vary the format in which they present their balance sheets, as will be illustrated in future text chapters.

The purpose of the balance sheet is to give interested parties *relevant information* about the financial condition of a company at a specific date. In other words, one can analyze a company's financial condition if he has information about its *assets* and the sources of these assets, the *liabilities* and the *owners' equity*. We shall now examine the second major financial analysis, the income statement, and demonstrate how this statement is directly related to the balance sheet.

Income Statement

A major reason why individuals start a business is to *increase* their assets. Initially, assets are invested into a new business organization. Through subsequent operating activities, the owners hope to increase their assets. For example, the operating activity of a clothing store is to purchase clothing goods at wholesale prices and then to sell these goods at retail prices. The income statement gives *relevant information* regarding an organization's success at increasing its assets or failure to increase them.

The two major financial items included in an income statement are *revenues* and *expenses*. Revenues, *increases* in a company's assets, are earned through selling a product or providing a service to someone. Earned revenues are *positive* occurrences to the owners of an organization, since the organization's assets are increased as a result of the revenue earning function. The earning of revenues causes an "inflow of assets" into an organization. If you walk into a department store and purchase some merchandise, the department store earns revenue at the time that it makes the sale to you. The revenue is earned by the department store when the sale is made whether you immediately pay cash or charge your purchase on a credit card. At the point of sale, you receive a service from the store of being able to buy and utilize its merchandise. Some individuals in the accounting profession favor the recognition of revenue prior to a sales transaction. However, only at the point of sale when an individual agrees to purchase an organization's product at a specific price does *objective evidence* exist concerning the actual dollar amount of revenue earned.

Revenue recognition in a service industry is illustrated by the television repairman who earns revenue through fixing customers' TV sets. Upon repairing someone's television set and billing the customer (for example, a $25 service bill), the repairman earns the $25 even if the cash is not immediately received. It is the act of providing the service that earns the revenue for the repairman.

As discussed previously, earned revenues represent *increases* in an organization's assets and are thus positive events to the owners. Earned revenues can be thought of as the *accomplishments* of an organization. However, in order to have these accomplishments, certain *efforts* must be put forth. The efforts that a business organization puts forth in attempting to earn revenues are called *expenses*. Expenses represent a decrease in an organization's assets (either currently or at a future time). They are caused by receiving benefits from someone or something as an aid in earning revenues. Ideally, a business organization would like to incur no expenses, since they eventually result in an *outflow* (decrease) of assets. Thus, expenses are a *negative* activity from the owners' point of view. It is impossible, however, to operate a business organization without incurring expenses. An organization receives different types of benefits, which cause different types of expenses. For example, the benefits received from leasing building space to operate your business results in "rent expense." The benefits received from having employees work for you results in "salaries expense." Organizations incur expenses upon receiving benefits from someone or something, regardless of whether cash is immediately paid for the benefits received. If an individual provides a company benefits by working as an employee but has not yet been paid, then the company has a *liability* to eventually pay the employee cash. In this case, the asset cash is not immediately decreased as a result of the expense. However, as soon as the company pays the employee, its assets decrease.

If we think of revenues as *accomplishments* and expenses as *efforts,* the objective of an organization is to have the accomplishments *exceed* its efforts (that is, the revenues *exceed* its expenses). When this happens, the organization earns a net income. An organization's net income causes an overall increase in its assets from business operations, as shown below:

Revenues (accomplishments)—
    increase in assets from business operations
Less: *Expenses* (efforts)—
    decrease in assets from business operations
Equals: Net income (accomplishments exceed efforts)—
    overall increase in assets from business operations

Net income does not represent an increase in just the asset *cash*. Rather, any or all of a company's assets may increase from earning a net income. The important point to remember is that net income represents an overall increase in a company's assets and this increase can be reflected in various assets. For example, a portion of an organization's net income may be used to purchase additional *equipment* (which is an asset). Conversely, if more efforts (expenses) are put forth than accomplishments (revenues), a company has a *net loss*. The effect of an organization's net loss is to cause a decrease in its assets. An organization attempts to perform its operating activities in a manner to avoid a net loss.

An organization's *net income* is the reward to the owners from successful operation of their business organization. Thus, the increase in assets caused by earning a net income goes to the owners and *increases* their equity in the organization. The balance sheet classification called *owners' equity* is increased as a result of a company's earning a net income. On the other hand, if a company incurs a *net loss* (a decrease in assets), the owners must absorb the loss. Therefore, the effect of a net loss from business operations is the reduction of the owners' equity.

Continuing the example of the Super X Company (see Exhibit 1-1), Exhibit 1-2 reflects the company's income statement for January 1983, the first month of business.

The heading of the income statement indicates the name of the company, the title of the statement, and the period of time for which the analysis is prepared. The first major category on the income statement is the *revenue earned*, which represents the increase in the company's assets from the sale of its merchandise at retail prices.

The second major category indicates the efforts (*expenses*) put forth to earn the revenues. As previously discussed, expenses represent decreases in a company's assets as a result of receiving benefits from someone or something. The $2920 "cost of merchandise sold" is the wholesale cost to

Exhibit 1-2

The Super X Company
Income Statement
For the Month Ended January 31, 1983

Revenues
Retail price of merchandise sold $5000*

Less: *Expenses*

Cost of merchandise sold	$2920	
Salaries to employees	1400	
Rent on the store and office facilities	500	
Advertising in the newspaper	75	
Interest on cash borrowed from the bank	5	
Total expenses		4900
Net income		$ 100

*Note: dollar signs normally appear only by the first dollar items in a column and by the first dollar items below a column line (e.g., the $100).

the Super X Company of the merchandise that was sold. The retail price of this merchandise was $5000, the revenue item reported on the income statement. The "salaries expense" of $1400 represents the benefits received by the Super X Company from the employees that worked for the organization during January. The $500 rent is an expense, since the Super X Company received benefits during January from using the rented store and office facilities to operate its business organization. The Super X Company has $75 "advertising expense" from announcements in the local newspaper publicizing the company's products. The $5 "interest expense" is caused by the company's bank loan. Interest on a bank loan is an expense resulting from the privilege of being able to borrow money for a designated time period.

Since the Super X Company's revenues are $100 greater than its expenses during January, the resultant $100 net income causes the owners' interests (represented by the "owners' equity" on the balance sheet) in the company's assets to increase by $100. Thus, the income statement gives interested parties relevant information concerning the success of an organization in increasing its assets from operating activities.

Relationship of Income Statement to Balance Sheet

Exhibit 1-3 is the Super X Company's statement of financial position (balance sheet) on January 31, 1983, after the January net income of $100 was determined from the company's income statement (Exhibit 1-2).

Exhibit 1-3

The Super X Company
Balance Sheet
January 31, 1983

ASSETS		LIABILITIES & OWNERS' EQUITY		
Cash	$ 200	Liabilities:		
Accounts receivable	150	Accounts payable	$ 400	
Merchandise inventory	200	Loan from bank	200	
Office supplies	300			
Machinery	650	Total liabilities		$ 600
Land	400			
		Owners' equity:		
		Investment by the		
		owners, January 1,		
		1983	$1200	
		Plus: Net income		
		for the month of		
		January	100	
		Owners' equity		
		January 31, 1983		1300
		Total liabilities and		
Total Assets	$1900	owners' equity		$1900

    The Super X Company's total assets increased from $1800 on January 1 (see Exhibit 1-1) to $1900 on January 31. This $100 increase was caused by the $100 earned net income. The $100 increase in total assets is also reflected as a $100 increase in the "owners' equity," since the owners receive the net income. As a result of both the *assets* and the *owners' equity* increasing by $100, the balance sheet equation (Assets = liabilities + owners' equity) and the balance sheet (which is based upon the equation) will continue to "balance." Before the net income is formally computed at month's end on the income statement, it is already included among the company's various assets. For example, a portion of the net income may have been used during the month to buy additional machinery, causing an *increase* in the asset "machinery." However, the total net income is not reflected as an increase in the *owners' equity* until it is computed on the income statement and then transferred to the balance sheet. After this is accomplished, both the assets and the owners' equity will have the net income included in their total monetary figures, and the statement of financial position (balance sheet) will "balance." Thus, the connecting link between the income statement and the balance sheet is through the net income figure. The income statement must be prepared first. Then, the computed net income is *added* to the owners' equity section of the balance sheet in order to complete the financial statements.

Two new items illustrated on the Super X Company's January 31, 1983 balance sheet are the asset "accounts receivable" and the liability "accounts payable." An *account receivable* means that somebody owes the Super X Company cash. Receivables result from the sale of the company's products without immediately collecting the cash. For example, if you go into a department store, buy a $25 radio, and use your credit card to make the purchase rather than paying cash, the department store has a $25 account receivable against you. Since some individuals to whom sales have been made have not yet paid for the products purchased, the Super X Company has a $150 asset claim against these customers for the cash that will eventually be paid to the company.

The $400 *accounts payable* on the balance sheet means that the Super X Company bought something and did not immediately pay cash for the items purchased. The Super X Company thus has a liability to eventually pay for the purchased goods. As soon as the company makes payment, its liability will be eliminated. As can be seen, an account receivable and an account payable are opposites. An *account receivable* means that somebody owes the Super X Company cash and is thus an asset, whereas an *account payable* means that the Super X Company owes somebody cash and is thus a liability. In the previous paragraph's example of your buying a $25 radio from a department store and charging the purchase, the store has a $25 account receivable against you. However, from your point of view as the buyer of the radio, you have a $25 account payable (a liability) to pay the store $25 cash.

A comparison of the Super X Company's balance sheets on January 1 (Exhibit 1-1) and January 31 (Exhibit 1-3) reveals that the bank liability for the $600 loan was *reduced* to $200 by January 31. In other words, the Super X Company decreased its bank debt during January by paying the bank $400. The only asset that did not change from January 1 to January 31 was the "land," which remained at $400 during the entire month.

In summary, a large amount of valuable information can be obtained from the income statement and the balance sheet. The former provides useful information about a company's operating activities; the latter discloses relevant information concerning the company's financial position.

Projected Financial Statements for Management Decision Making

A company's management needs information concerning the success or failure of its operating activities and the adequacy of its current financial position. A technique often used by management is to project the future operating activities (a projected income statement) and financial position (a projected balance sheet) for the coming year. Projecting future financial results, called *budgeting*, is a very helpful planning and controlling tool. When projected financial statements are prepared (the planning function), management can subsequently evaluate the effectiveness of its operating performance by comparing the information accumulated in the *actual* financial statements against the information contained in the *projected* financial statements (the controlling function). Any significant variations between the actual and the projected financial results can then be investigated by management to determine the causes for the variations.

For example, assume that a company's projection of January sales revenue is $5000. If actual January sales are $4000, a $1000 unfavorable budget variation exists, since the actual revenues are $1000 less than the budget projection. Management should investigate the $1000 variation and attempt to discover its cause so that future sales revenue will improve.

Some Basic Accounting Concepts

The field of financial accounting is based upon an underlying conceptual framework. A few major concepts will be discussed at this point to give the reader a better understanding of financial accounting. Additional accounting concepts will be discussed in later parts of the book.

Entity Concept

An entity is a specific unit of accountability. The "entity concept" as used in accounting refers to maintaining business records for specific organizations. For example, Linda Bogle decides to open a small dress shop. She invests cash into the business and obtains a loan from the bank to help finance her company. Miss Bogle rents a store and buys various styles of dresses at wholesale prices to build up an inventory of merchandise that will eventually be sold to customers. Finally, she commences business operations. Two weeks later Miss Bogle buys a new automobile for her personal use. In maintaining accounting records and preparing financial statements for her dress shop, Miss Bogle should not include the automobile in her business records and financial statements. Miss Bogle's other activities (investing cash into the business, obtaining a business loan from the bank, renting a store, and buying merchandise for resale) are all events which affect her business entity, the dress shop. However, the car purchased by Miss Bogle represents a personal activity separate and distinct from her business entity and should not be included in her dress shop's financial data. Furthermore, if Linda Bogle should start a gourmet food shop in a few years and also continue to operate her dress shop, the entity concept would require Miss Bogle to maintain separate records for each of her business operations.

Cost Concept

The cost concept utilized in financial accounting is based upon two subconcepts, the monetary unit concept and the stable measuring unit concept. Discussing these subconcepts will lead into the rationale behind the *cost concept*.

The monetary unit concept says that we are able to measure business activities on a *monetary basis* in accounting. In the United States, the monetary unit is the *dollar*. Thus, balance sheets and income statements of organizations are presented in terms of dollars of assets, dollars of liabilities and owners' equity, and dollars of revenues and expenses. In France, for example, financial statements would be based upon its monetary unit, the *franc.*

Once the need for a monetary measurement unit is accepted, the assumption is then made that this measuring unit does not change significantly in value over time (the stable measuring unit concept). In other words, accounting assumes that the purchasing power of the monetary unit is relatively stable from one year to the next and over a number of years. Although actual experience would probably cause us to question the stability of the dollar, accountants still perform their work under the assumption that an organization's dollar measurements do not have to be adjusted for inflationary trends. (However, this assumption is gradually changing.)

The need for accounting data to be measured in a monetary unit and the assumption that this monetary unit is stable leads us into the *cost concept* of financial accounting. In essence, the cost concept says that when an organization has completed a measurable monetary activity, this activity can then be included in the accounting records at its actual cost. Furthermore, the actual cost at which the activity was originally recorded should continue to be used within the accounting system even if the purchasing power of the dollar subsequently changes. For example, assume that a company bought a piece of land fifty years ago for $25,000. The $25,000 original cost of the land would have appeared as an asset on the company's balance sheet for each of the past fifty years. In other words, under the cost concept, the land should continue to be shown on the balance sheet at its original cost to the company even though the purchasing power of the dollar may have changed significantly in the past fifty years. The cost concept is sometimes called the *historical* cost concept, because the original cost of something is the basis used in the accounting records during the historical life of a company.

Major Types of Business Organizations

The three major types of business organizations are

1. Proprietorships
2. Partnerships
3. Corporations

As an illustration of the differences between these three organizational types, consider the following.

Harry Portwood decides to start a small business organization that sells stereo equipment. He invests some money into the organization and also obtains a loan from the bank. Mr. Portwood's stereo equipment store is an example of a *proprietorship*, a business organization owned by *one* individual. During the next two years Harry's business is very successful. The sales of stereo equipment continue to increase, and Harry decides to expand his business organization by opening another store across town. However, he lacks sufficient assets of his own to open a second store, and he does not want to borrow additional cash from the bank. Harry has a friend, Joe Ellis, who wants to invest in Harry's company. Through discussions, Harry and Joe decide to join together as co-owners of the stereo equipment business and open an additional store. Mr. Ellis invests some cash into the business, and a *partnership* is formed by Ellis and Portwood. Thus, a partnership is a business organization owned by *two or more* individuals. As this example has shown, a partnership form of business organization may come into existence when a proprietorship owner needs additional assets. The single proprietor then looks for another person who has sufficient assets to invest, and a partnership is organized.

Five more years pass, and the partnership of Ellis and Portwood has become highly successful. They decide to open several stereo equipment stores in other cities. This major expansion will require a large investment, so the partners agree to obtain additional cash by forming a *corporation*. A corporation is an organization whose owners are called *stockholders*. The ownership interest of each stockholder is represented by the quantity of stock he has purchased. Ellis and Portwood each receive shares of stock for their ownership interests in the new corporate organization. They then sell the remaining shares of stock to other individuals who are interested in purchasing an ownership interest in the company.

The sequence of proprietorship, partnership, and corporation is not always the way in which a business organization develops. It was presented only for the purpose of discussing the three major types of business organizations. For example, an individual starting a new business may initially decide to form a corporation rather than a proprietorship.

One major advantage of forming a corporation is the "limited liability" of the corporate owners (stockholders) compared to the "unlimited liability" of proprietorship and partnership owners. If a corporation has insufficient assets to pay its *creditors* (the *liabilities*) and the creditors thereby force the corporation into bankruptcy, each stockholder's liability is basically *limited* to the dollar amount invested in the corporation through buying stock. Creditors cannot claim the stockholders' personal assets (for example, their homes or automobiles) if the corporation's assets are insufficient to pay creditor debts. However, if a proprietorship or a partnership is forced into bankruptcy by its creditors, the proprietor or the partners have *unlimited* liability. The personal assets of the proprietor or the partners can be claimed by the creditors if there are not sufficient business assets to pay the debts. Individuals often incorporate to avoid the risk of their personal assets being claimed should the organization develop financial trouble and end up in bankruptcy.

Legally, a corporation is a *separate entity* from its owners. As a result, the stockholders' personal assets are considered to be separate and distinct from the corporation and cannot be claimed by corporate creditors in bankruptcy proceedings. A proprietorship and a partnership are not separate legal entities from their owners. Therefore, creditors can claim the personal assets of the proprietor or the partners in bankruptcy cases.

There are variations of the three major types of business organizations discussed in this section. For example, individuals starting a business organization may form a "limited partnership." In a limited partnership, some of the partners can have the advantages of *limited liability* rather than the normal unlimited liability of all partnership owners.

Review Questions

At this point, answer the following multiple-choice questions to test your knowledge of the previous reading material. The solutions are given below.

1. The major objective of financial accounting is
   a. To communicate relevant decision-making information to a company's internal parties.

b. To communicate relevant decision-making information to a company's external parties.

c. To analyze nonquantitative data for management decision making.

d. To convert accounting information into relevant data for management decision making.

2. Which financial item is an asset?
   a. Accounts payable.
   b. Cost of merchandise sold.
   c. Office supplies.
   d. Rent expense.

3. Which concept prevents an individual from including his personal assets within his business accounting records?
   a. Monetary unit concept.
   b. Stable measuring unit concept.
   c. Cost concept.
   d. Entity concept.

4. Which type of business organization is a separate legal entity from its owners?
   a. Corporation.
   b. Proprietorship.
   c. Partnership.

5. Included among the X-ray's financial statement items at the end of June 1983 are: cash, $5000; expenses, $8000; land, $7000; revenues, $12,000. What is the X-ray's June 1983 income (or net loss)?
   a. $4000 net income.
   b. $5000 net income.
   c. $1000 net loss.
   d. $8000 net loss.

Answers

1. b

2. c

3. d

4. a

5. a ($12,000 revenues − $8,000 expenses)

Chapter Summary

Accounting's function in the business community is to provide relevant decision-making information to interested parties. The two major areas of accounting are *financial* and *managerial* accounting. Financial accounting provides useful information to external parties, whereas managerial accounting provides valuable information to internal parties. Financial accounting is built around certain principles and procedures of analysis that make this area of accounting less flexible than managerial accounting.

Financial statements are the principal means by which external parties obtain relevant information about a business organization's monetary activities. The balance sheet shows a company's financial condition on a specific date by disclosing its assets and the two sources of the assets, the liabilities and the owners' equity. The income statement shows operating results by comparing the revenues earned against the expenses incurred. Analysis of a company's income statement gives financial statement readers an indication of the company's success or failure to increase its assets through earning a net income. The income statement and balance sheet are linked together, because the net income computed on an income statement is added to the "owners' equity" section of the balance sheet.

Two important concepts in financial accounting are the entity concept and the cost concept. The entity concept is concerned with maintaining accounting records and preparing financial statements for specific business organizations. The cost concept means that the original historical costs of monetary items are reflected on an organization's financial statements.

A *proprietorship* is a business organization owned by one individual, whereas a *partnership* is an organization owned by two or more individuals. A *corporation* is a form of organization whose owners are called stockholders. The "limited liability" of corporation owners is a major advantage of a corporate business organization compared to proprietorship and partnership organizations.

Chapter Problem

The solution to the following problem is given in the appendix. However, the reader is urged first to attempt to work the problem on his own and then check his work against the given solution.

In all the problems presented in this book, the *objective* (or *objectives*) of the problem and the solution approach will be indicated. Stating the objective of each problem should give the reader a better understanding of the computations necessary to reach a solution.

Problem Situation

The River Company began business on November 1, 1983. The company sells various types of household appliances. During November the River Company earned some revenues from the sale of household appliances and incurred several expenses in operating its business. On November 30, the River Company wants to borrow money from the local bank. The bank indicates that it will not consider granting the loan until the company's financial statements have first been examined by the bank's accountants. Presented below are the monetary items (except for accounts receivable) of the River Company on November 30, 1983:

Cash	$ 200
Cost of merchandise sold	$1550
Merchandise inventory	$1300
Rent on the store and office facilities	$ 275
Office supplies	$ 100
Retail price of merchandise sold	$2500
Accounts payable	$ 450
Salaries to employees	$ 625
Owners' equity, November 1, 1983	$1300
Accounts receivable	(?)

Problem Requirements

Using the information provided, complete the following requirements.

1. As requested by the bank, prepare financial statements for the River Company on November 30, 1983.

2. In order to provide the bank with additional information regarding the River Company, compute the percentage relationships indicated below:
   a. The percentage interest of the outside parties (that is, the *liabilities*) in the company's total assets.
   b. The percentage interest of the internal parties (that is, the *owners*) in the company's total assets.

Problem Objectives and Solution Approach

Objectives:

1. To correctly classify monetary items on a company's income statement and balance sheet.

2. To utilize knowledge of the balance sheet equation in order to determine the "accounts receivable" dollar amount.

3. To compute relevant percentage relationships from a company's balance sheet.

Solution Approach:

1. Prepare the income statement.

2. Using the income statement result, prepare the balance sheet. (You must compute the "accounts receivable" monetary amount.)

3. Using the balance sheet information, compute the required percentage relationships.

2

The Accounting Cycle
Part I

In order to obtain the monetary amounts for a company's financial statements, a system of records must be maintained on a day-to-day basis. The accounting cycle is the process by which financial information is accumulated for an organization's financial statements. The first four steps of the accounting cycle are presented in this chapter, and the remaining steps are analyzed in Chapter 3. The discussion presented in Chapters 2 and 3 illustrates a generalized accounting cycle that an organization may incorporate into its total business information system. It is important for the reader to recognize, however, that each company's information system should be designed to satisfy its own specific decision-making needs. Consequently, the accounting cycle utilized by various organizations will differ somewhat from the generalized cycle discussed in these two chapters. Many organizations today have mechanized systems (for example, a computerized data processing system) to aid in the accumulating, processing, and analyzing of their financial data. However, to enable the reader to understand thoroughly each of the accounting cycle steps, the following discussion will assume that the accounting cycle activities of the business organizations analyzed are all performed using a manual data processing system (that is, employing pencil and paper rather than mechanized techniques).

The Use of *Accounts* In a Business System

A business organization has various types of assets, liabilities, revenues, expenses, and owners' equity items. In order that their individual dollar quantities may be known, a separate *account* is maintained for each monetary item. For example, an account would be kept for the asset "cash." In most business organizations, cash comes in every day from completed sales, and cash goes out daily to pay expenses. By maintaining a separate cash account, a company will be able to determine how much cash it actually has at any specific time. The same is true for all other types of financial items in a company. By having a separate account for each type of monetary item, the company is able to ascertain at any time the dollar amount of its many financial items.

Exhibit 2-1 shows the basic format of an account.

Exhibit 2-1

An Account

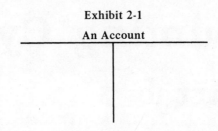

An account looks like the letter "T," resulting in its often being called a "T" account. Furthermore, the left side of an account is called the *debit side,* and the right side is called the *credit side.* Whether you are talking about *asset, liability, owners' equity, revenue,* or *expense* accounts, the left side is always the *debit* side, while the right is the *credit.* By having two sides for an account, it enables you to maintain a mathematical record of "increases" and "decreases" in each account and thereby to determine each account's dollar amount.

Asset Accounts

For all types of assets in an organization, the *debit* side (left side) of an account is used for increases and the *credit* side (right side) for decreases, as illustrated in Exhibit 2-2.

Exhibit 2-2

All Asset Accounts

Debit side for Increases	Credit side for Decreases

Exhibit 2-3 gives an example of how the "office furniture" account of the Rotary Music Shop would look on October 31, 1983.

Exhibit 2-3

Office Furniture

1983			1983	
Oct. 1 Balance	5000		Oct. 20	2000
Oct. 10	1000			
	6000			
Oct. 31				
	(4000)			

An analysis of the account indicates that as of October 1, the Rotary Music Shop owned furniture costing $5000. The word "balance" written by the $5000 indicates that this dollar amount is carried over from previous months and at the beginning of October, there is a $5000 balance in the office furniture account. Since office furniture is an *asset*, and for all assets, increases are shown on the *debit* side (left side), we would expect this account to have a *debit* balance. If an asset such as office furniture had a *credit* balance (the *credit* side of the account exceeding the *debit* side), it would indicate a "negative" amount of furniture, which would be rather unusual, if not impossible. In general, all assets will have *debit* balances in the normal course of business. On October 10, additional office furniture costing $1000 was purchased by the Rotary Music Shop. Following our rules, the office furniture account is *debited* for the asset increase resulting from the purchase. On October 20, the Rotary Music Shop sold a portion of its office furniture which had originally cost $2000. Whenever an asset is sold, you are naturally *decreasing* the amount of the particular asset. Following the rules for decreases in assets, we *credit* the office furniture account $2000 to recognize the asset reduction.

There was no other activity in the office furniture account during October, and the account *balance* at the end of the month is $4000. In order to compute the balance of an account, you *add* separately the debit side and the credit side. If the debit or credit side has more than one number, you can place a small pencil figure below the last number indicating the total of the column (in our example, the $6000 pencil figure for the *debit* side of the office furniture account). Finally, to compute the account balance, you then *subtract* the dollar amount of the smaller side from the larger side, and the resultant difference indicates the "dollar balance" of the account. Since the office furniture account's debit side exceeds its credit side by $4000 ($6000 *minus* $2000), this account has a $4000 *debit* balance. For information purposes, the $4000 balance (and, if desired, the Oct. 31 date) can then be written at the bottom of the account. It should also be noted that dollar signs are not written by the amounts within the "T" accounts. It is automatically understood that quantitative amounts appearing in accounts represent dollars and cents.

Liability and Owners' Equity Accounts

The rules for increasing and decreasing liability and owners' equity accounts are the *same* and are just the opposite of the rules for increasing and decreasing asset accounts (see Exhibit 2-4).

Exhibit 2-4

All Liability Accounts		All Owners' Equity Accounts	
Debit side for Decreases	Credit side for Increases	Debit side for Decreases	Credit side for Increases

Exhibit 2-5 illustrates how the accounts payable liability account of the Rotary Music Shop would look on October 31, 1983.

Exhibit 2-5

Accounts Payable

1983		1983	
Oct. 12	400	Oct. 1 Balance	800
		Oct. 21	100
			900
		Oct. 31	
			500

An "accounts payable" means that a company owes cash to someone. On October 1, the balance of the accounts payable account from previous months is $800. The Rotary Music Shop paid $400 of its liability on October 12. Following the rules for *decreasing* liability accounts, we show the $400 on the *debit* side. On October 21, an additional $100 liability was incurred by the company as a result of purchasing something but not immediately paying cash. Following the rules, we show the $100 on the *credit* side to indicate an *increase* in the liability account. The balance of the accounts payable account at month's end is therefore a $500 *credit* balance ($900 total credit side *minus* $400 total debit side), indicating that the Rotary Music Shop still owes $500 to creditors. As with assets, to determine the balance of any liability or owners' equity account, you add the total *debits* and the total *credits* and then subtract the smaller total from the larger total. The resultant figure is the account balance. This balance appears on the side of the account that has the largest dollar amount.

Since the same rules apply for increasing and decreasing owners' equity accounts as for increasing and decreasing liability accounts, a specific example of an owners' equity account will not be given at this point in the chapter. However, it is important to understand that since both liability and owners' equity accounts are increased on the credit side and decreased on the debit side of the account, these two types of accounts *normally* have *credit* balances. If, for example, a liability account has a *debit* balance, it would indicate that instead of a company owing cash to a creditor, the creditor actually owes cash to the company. Although it could happen in some cases, such a situation would be rather unusual.

The owners' equity accounts represent the monetary interests of the "owners" in their company's assets. Because owners' equity accounts are increased by *credits*, the larger the credit balance in the owners' equity accounts, the greater the owners' interests. If, however, a business organization has been extremely unsuccessful in its operating activities, it would be conceivable to have *debit* balances in the owners' equity accounts. This would indicate that the owners, in effect, have negative interests in the assets of their organization.

Revenue and Expense Accounts

Revenues represent the accomplishments of an organization, and expenses represent the efforts put forth to earn the revenues. If revenues exceed expenses, the difference is called a *net income* (or *net profit*). This income reflects a "net inflow of assets" into a company. If expenses exceed revenues, the difference is called a *net loss* and reflects a "net outflow of assets" from a company. The net income or net loss of an organization belongs to the organization's owners. From their point of view, a net income is a *positive* event, while a net loss is a *negative* occurrence.

Most organizations have several different revenue and expense items; therefore, separate accounts are maintained for each type of revenue and expense. The purpose of having separate accounts is to provide *information* to a company's management and other interested parties regarding the monetary amounts of the various revenues and expenses. However, since a company's revenue and expense items actually belong to its owners, we can think of the individual revenue and expense accounts as being subdivisions of the owners' equity accounts. Exhibit 2-6 emphasizes the relationship between owners' equity accounts and individual revenue and expense accounts, incorporating the *debit* and *credit* relationship:

Exhibit 2-6

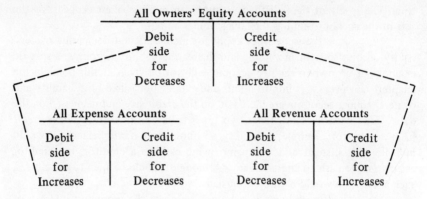

Since the earning of revenue represents a *positive* event from the owners' point of view, *revenue accounts* are increased by *credits* in the same manner as the *owners' equity accounts.* It would be rather unusual to have a *debit* to a revenue account because that would basically indicate *negative* revenues.

The incurrence of an expense, in effect, represents a *negative* activity from the owners' point of view and a resultant decrease in their equity in the company. Since an owner's equity account is decreased on the *debit* side, an incurred expense is thus shown on the *debit* side of the individual expense account. Except for certain rare situations, it is very unusual to have a *credit* to an expense account (which would imply a *negative* expense).

Basically, all revenue accounts and all expense accounts are *subdivisions* of the owners' equity accounts. Conceivably, it would be possible for a company not to establish any separate revenue and expense accounts. Each time revenue was earned, the dollar amount of the revenue could be *credited* directly to the owners' equity accounts to indicate the increase in the owners' interests. Whenever a company incurred an expense, the monetary amount of the expense could be *debited* directly to the owners' equity accounts to indicate the owners' decreased interests in their company's assets. However, if this were done, it would be difficult for most companies to maintain good information on the various dollar amounts of revenues earned and expenses incurred. The owners' equity accounts would become quite messy and difficult to interpret if all the revenues earned and expenses incurred were entered directly into the owners' accounts. By establishing separate accounts for each type of revenue and expense, relevant information about the dollar quantity of the various revenues and expenses is much easier to maintain. Furthermore, information regarding the dollar balances of individual revenue and expense items is highly useful to management in helping to operate a business. For example, management may look at the specific expense account set up for advertising and discover that it is quite large. As a result, management may decide to take action to reduce the money spent on future advertising. This type of information would be more difficult to obtain if a separate account for advertising expense had not been established.

Review Questions

At this point, answer the following multiple-choice questions to test your knowledge of the previous reading material. The solutions are given below.

1. An accounting record maintained for every financial item in a company is called a (an);
   a. List.
   b. Balance sheet.
   c. Income statement.
   d. Account.

2. A company sold a piece of land for $1000 cash. This land had originally been acquired by the company for $1000 cash. Which statement is *true* on the land sale date?
   a. The asset account "land" is *debited* for $1000.
   b. The asset account "land" is *credited* for $1000.
   c. The liability account "accounts payable" is *debited* for $1000.
   d. The liability account "accounts payable" is *credited* for $1000.

3. To increase a revenue account, what must be done?
   a. *Debit* the revenue account.
   b. *Credit* the revenue account.
   c. *Debit* the owner's equity account.
   d. *Credit* the owner's equity account.

4. Which of the following accounts are subdivisions of the owners' equity accounts?
   a. Asset accounts.
   b. Liability accounts.
   c. Revenue and expense accounts.

Answers

1. d

2. b

3. b

4. c

Steps in the Accounting Cycle

A *cycle* is a recurring time period within which certain specific activities (or events) occur in a definite sequence. Those specific activities performed by accountants in order to accumulate the relevant information for business organizations' financial statements (which are the income statement and the balance sheet) are called the *accounting cycle.* The accounting cycle's length varies in different enterprises. For example, some enterprises complete the entire accounting cycle monthly, whereas other enterprises go through the cycle only once a year. As will be emphasized in Chapter 3, the length of a company's accounting cycle is basically determined by how often the company prepares its financial statements. By studying the accounting cycle in this chapter and in Chapter 3, the reader will have a good understanding of how an organization logically accumulates accounting information for inclusion in its income statement and balance sheet. The remaining pages of Chapter 2 will discuss steps 1-4 of the accounting cycle, and the additional cycle activities, steps 5-9, will be analyzed in Chapter 3.

Step 1. Preparation of Original Records

A *business transaction* results from any monetary event which causes a change in an asset, liability, owners' equity, revenue, or expense account. Transactions can occur from business activities between a company and either some external party to the company (for example, when an organization sells some of its products to a customer), or an internal party within the company (for example, when an organization pays its employees their weekly salaries). For a business transaction to enter an organization's accounting information system, the transaction must be of a quantitative nature and also be measurable in monetary terms.

For example, John Simkin walks into the Rotary Music Shop and purchases a stereo tape for $5.95. At the time of the purchase, a sales invoice would be prepared by the clerk who made the sale. The sales invoice represents an *original record* (also called a transaction source document), which is the basis for the entry of this transaction into the Rotary Music Shop's accounting system.

Exhibit 2-7 is the Rotary Music Shop's sales invoice after the sale to John Simkin has been completed.

The Rotary Music Shop may want to prepare four copies of the sales invoice by using carbon paper. One copy is given to the buyer. A second copy of the invoice is kept on file in the sales department for its information. Another copy is sent to the inventory department so that it can update the inventory files for the various types of stereo tapes in stock. The inventory stock number shown on the sales invoice is the basis for the inventory department's updating of its files. If the quantity of a certain stereo tape in inventory gets too low, the inventory department can then request the purchasing department to place an order for additional tapes. The last copy of the sales

Exhibit 2-7

		Rotary Music Shop 1835 South King Street Honolulu, Hawaii 96813		Invoice Number ___785___ Date ___November 10, 1983___		
		SALES INVOICE		How paid		
Sold to :	John Simkin			__XXX__ Cash		
	8311 Dole Street			____ Credit		
	Honolulu, Hawaii 96822			Credit terms _____		
			Salesclerk	*Paul Smith*		

Description	Inventory Stock No.	Quantity	Selling Price Per Unit	Total Price Before Sales Tax	Sales Tax at 4%	Total Price After Sales Tax
Hits of the 50's— Volume II	X5675	1	$5.95	$5.95	$.24	$6.19

invoice is sent to the accounting department for entry of this monetary event (transaction) into the company's accounting records.

Original records, as the previously discussed sales invoice illus-trated, represent visual evidence regarding the occurrence of business trans-actions. A common policy existing in many organizations today is that a financial transaction is not subject to entry into their accounting information system until proper original records are first prepared and approved. The types of original records utilized by business organizations will vary depend-ing upon each organization's own special operating characteristics. A few of the more common original records (or source documents) used by business organizations, in addition to the already discussed *sales invoices,* are as follows:

Purchase orders	— reflect a company's desire to purchase a specific quantity of inventory items or other assets (such as office supplies) from another company.
Purchase invoices	— reflect the bills received from another company for the quantity and cost of inventory items or other assets pur-chased from that company.
Receiving reports	— reflect the actual quantity of inventory items or other assets delivered to a com-pany from another company.
Bills of lading	— reflect the freight charges on physical goods shipped to a company.
Employee time cards	— reflect the number of hours worked by a company's employees during a specific pay period (the time card is the basis for computing an employee's salary).

Step 2. Recording Monetary Transactions in a Journal

Accounting cycle after step 2:

Preparation of original ———→ RECORDING MONETARY TRANSACTIONS
records   IN A JOURNAL

What is a journal? The daily newspaper is often called a journal, since a journal is a *chronological* listing of activities. For example, the news activities of January 15 are reported on that date in the newspaper, the news events of January 16 are reported on January 16, etc. This same idea is true for an accounting journal. The purpose of having a journal in accounting is to enable a business organization to keep a chronological record of the monetary activities that occur over the life of the organization. If a managerial executive within a company wants to know what monetary activities took place on February 26, 1983, he can turn to the page of the company's journal for February 26 and obtain the necessary information.

Assume that the following two business transactions occurred on November 20, 1983 for the Rotary Music Shop:

1. Purchased office furniture from John Watson by paying cash of $5000.

2. Returned $1000 of equipment purchased from Browning Manufacturing Company because the equipment was defective.

Exhibit 2-8 presents how these two transactions would be recorded in the Rotary Music Shop's *journal* (explanations will follow):

Exhibit 2-8

Rotary Music Shop
Journal   Page __25__

DATE		DESCRIPTION	POSTING REFERENCE	DEBIT	CREDIT
1983 Nov.	20	Office furniture		5000	
		Cash			5000
		(Purchase of furniture from John Watson— Purchase Invoice #131)			
	20	Accounts payable		1000	
		Equipment			1000
		(Return of defective equipment to Browning Manufacturing Co.— Debit Memorandum #X124)			

The purpose of the column labeled "posting reference" is discussed in step 3 of the accounting cycle and may be ignored at this point. Any additional transactions occurring on November 20 would also be recorded in the journal to complete the day's activities. The monetary transactions of the following day, November 21, are recorded as a group in the journal after all the transactions of November 20 are recorded. This is the idea of the chronological sequence concept.

Each page of the journal is numbered for ease of reference at a later date and for *posting* purposes. One column is provided for the date of each transaction followed by a column for the description of each transaction. The description column indicates the accounts that are *debited* and *credited* for the particular transaction. Conventional format in preparing journal entries is to place the *debit* part of the entry first and the *credit* part second. The *credit* in an entry is indented slightly from where the *debit* is listed. You can have more than one *debit* or *credit* making up a single entry; when this occurs, we call the entry a *compound entry*.

Two columns are also provided in the journal for entering the dollar amounts of the *debits* and *credits*. Dollar signs are not used, since the numbers in the debit and credit columns are always in terms of dollars and cents. An important concept to understand from the two entries illustrated in the journal is that for every entry, the total dollar amount of the debit and credit parts are *always* equal to each other. If, for example, you have a compound entry consisting of debits to three different accounts and a credit to only one account, the total monetary amount of the three debits should still equal the total of the one credit. This requirement of equal monetary amounts for the debits and credits recorded in every accounting transaction is the basic idea behind *double entry accounting*. Double entry accounting does *not* mean that only two accounts are involved in a business transaction, since more than two accounts may be affected by a particular transaction. Rather, double entry accounting refers to the requirement that the total debits and total credits of every journal entry must always be *equal*. The double entry accounting concept results from the balance sheet equation,

$$\text{Assets} = \text{liabilities} + \text{owners' equity}$$

This equation must always be satisfied after each transaction is recorded in the journal. Therefore, any time that you record a certain dollar quantity of *debits* in a journal entry, you must also record an equal dollar quantity of *credits* in that same journal entry. Otherwise, the balance sheet equation will not be in balance. For example, if you increase an asset by $500 (a *debit*) and depending on what the increase was caused by, you must either increase a liability account (a *credit*) by $500, or an owners' equity account (a *credit*) by $500, or decrease another asset account (a *credit*) by $500, or a combination of the three possible "credit" situations that total $500. Thus, with total *debits* equal to total *credits* after each journal entry, the balance sheet equation relationship will continue to be "in balance."

Beneath the *debits* and *credits* of the individual entries is a brief explanation based on a reference to the *original record*. Remember, in following the steps of the accounting cycle to this point, an original record (purchase order, sales invoice, etc.) is first prepared when a monetary transaction occurs. After the preparation of the original record, an entry is then made in the journal to record this transaction in the accounting system. Information concerning the original record prepared is usually placed in the journal entry explanation for ease of reference at a later date.

The *debit* and *credit* rules discussed previously for "T" accounts are utilized in recording these transactions in the journal. The first entry (see Exhibit 2-8) is for the purchase of office furniture by paying cash. The "office furniture" account is *debited*, since the music shop increased its office furniture asset. Another type of asset called "cash" is *credited* because the company's cash decreases as a result of paying for the purchased furniture.

In the second entry illustrated in the journal, the liability account called "accounts payable" is *debited* since the company is decreasing its liability to Browning Manufacturing Company (thus, the original record prepared for this transaction is called a *debit memorandum*) by returning defective equipment purchased at an earlier date. When the equipment was originally purchased, an entry would have been recorded in the Rotary Music Shop's journal *debiting* the equipment account to show the increase in this asset. Also, the accounts payable account would have been *credited* to show the increase in the company's liability for the amount owed on the equipment purchase. Before paying the cash owed, the Rotary Music Shop discovered that the equipment was defective. Consequently, the Rotary Music Shop returned the equipment to Browning Manufacturing Company and does not have to pay the liability it previously recognized. The accounts payable liability account is *debited* to reflect the elimination of the music shop's liability to Browning Manufacturing Company. In addition, the return of the equipment caused the Rotary Music Shop to *credit* its equipment asset account in order to reduce this account.

The journal which we have been discussing in step 2 of the accounting cycle is often called the "general journal." The reason for adding the word "general" will be understood in Chapter 4 when the topic of journals is expanded briefly to discuss various "specialized journals" that may be utilized by a business organization.

Step 3. Posting Monetary Transactions From the Journal to the General Ledger and Determining Individual Account Balances

Accounting cycle after step 3:

| Preparation of original records | → | Recording monetary transactions in a journal | → | POSTING MONETARY TRANSACTIONS FROM THE JOURNAL TO THE GENERAL LEDGER AND DETERMINING INDIVIDUAL ACCOUNT BALANCES |

In accounting, a *ledger* (often called the *general ledger*) is a book in which information is maintained detailing the dollar quantities of a business organization's various assets, liabilities, owners' equity, revenues, and expenses. As discussed at the beginning of this chapter, a "T" account (also called a general ledger account) is established for each type of monetary item in an organization. Without information regarding the dollar quantity of a company's various assets, liabilities, etc., it would be difficult to successfully operate a business, since management decisions are often made on the basis of specific account balances.

Within the general ledger a separate "T" account would be kept for each asset, liability, owners' equity, revenue, and expense account. If management, for example, wishes to know the dollar quantity of wages paid to its employees after the first six months of the year, it can refer to the page in the general ledger where the "T" account for wages (or salaries) expense is located. It is common practice to have a separate page in the ledger for each type of business account. Since every organization is somewhat different, each should determine the types of accounts needed on the basis of the specific operating requirements of the business. Each account that a business organization maintains within its general ledger is given a number (called an *account number*) for ease of reference, and the numbering system utilized depends upon the organization's personal preference. A document typically maintained within a company's accounting system which lists its specific types of accounts, describes the purpose (or purposes) of each account, and shows the reference numbers of individual accounts, is called a *chart of accounts*.

Exhibit 2-9 illustrates the chart of accounts used by the Bill Hunt Law Firm. Two of the accounts reflected in Exhibit 2-9, the liability account "wages payable" and the owner's equity account "Bill Hunt, capital," require a brief explanation. The account called "wages payable" discloses the law firm's liability to its employees for wages that are *owed* as a result of their performing work services for which they have not yet been paid. The account called "Bill Hunt, capital" is the law firm's owner's equity account (in our example, Bill Hunt is assumed to be the sole owner of the Bill Hunt Law Firm). Since the word "capital" is often used in business to mean *assets,* the owner's equity account "Bill Hunt, capital" indicates Mr. Hunt's interest in the Bill Hunt Law Firm's assets.

Step 2 of the accounting cycle discussed the recording of monetary transactions in a journal. The journal provides a chronological record of the various monetary events in an organization and indicates the accounts and amounts of the *debits* and *credits* for each transaction. However, the journal does not provide information concerning the individual dollar quantities for the various items in a business organization. For example, if a company's management wanted to know the monetary amount of its organization's cash, the individual "T" account maintained for cash within the company's general ledger would provide this information. The journal would not provide information concerning the specific dollar balance of cash. Rather, the journal would show only the many *debits* and *credits* that were entered to the

Exhibit 2-9

Bill Hunt Law Firm
Chart of Accounts*

BALANCE SHEET ACCOUNTS		INCOME STATEMENT ACCOUNTS	
ACCOUNT NUMBER	*ACCOUNT TITLE*	*ACCOUNT NUMBER*	*ACCOUNT TITLE*
	1. Assets		4. Revenues
10	Cash	40	Revenue from legal
11	Accounts receivable		services
12	Office supplies		
13	Land		5. Expenses
		50	Rent expense
	2. Liabilities	51	Utilities expense
20	Accounts payable	52	Wages expense
21	Wages payable	53	Office supplies expense
	3. Owner's Equity	54	Insurance expense
30	Bill Hunt, capital		

*The number and types of accounts assumed to exist in the Bill Hunt Law Firm have intentionally been kept small so that the basic format of a chart of accounts could be emphasized without attempting to introduce various additional accounts that the reader has not yet been exposed to at this stage in the text. If the law firm should need to include some new accounts at some future date, these accounts can be added to the proper chart of accounts category and given specific numbers. For example, if the law firm eventually bought a small building in which to operate its law service activities, an account titled "Building," with an account number of 14, could be included under *assets*.

cash account during a particular time period. Therefore, to enable the company to determine its cash balance at any particular time, the various debits and credits recorded in the journal for cash must be transferred to the "T" account for cash in the general ledger. This process of transferring debits and credits from entries in the journal to their proper accounts in the general ledger is called *posting*.

Assume that the two business transactions in Exhibit 2-10 were recorded in the journal of the Hook Company during December 1983.

Exhibit 2-10 shows how the journal would look after these two entries were recorded but before the journal entries were posted to the general ledger. Exhibit 2-11 is a portion of the Hook Company's general ledger before the two entries from the journal have been posted. Only the accounts needed to post the above two entries are shown. (The "check marks" in the posting reference columns will be explained shortly.)

Exhibit 2-10

Journal   Page __30__

DATE		DESCRIPTION	POSTING REFERENCE	DEBIT	CREDIT
1983 Dec.	2	Office furniture		500	
		Cash			500
		(Purchase of furniture from Packard Co.— Purchase Invoice #88)			
	3	Cash		100	
		Accounts receivable			100
		(Received payment from Wilson Co. of amount due from November sale— Sales Invoice #1712)			

Exhibit 2-11

General Ledger*

Account: _Cash_   Account No. __10__

DATE	ITEM	POSTING REFERENCE	DEBIT	DATE	ITEM	POSTING REFERENCE	CREDIT
1983 Dec. 1	Balance	✓	1000				

Account: _Accounts Receivable_   Account No. __11__

DATE	ITEM	POSTING REFERENCE	DEBIT	DATE	ITEM	POSTING REFERENCE	CREDIT
1983 Dec. 1	Balance	✓	500				

Account: _Office Furniture_   Account No. __25__

DATE	ITEM	POSTING REFERENCE	DEBIT	DATE	ITEM	POSTING REFERENCE	CREDIT
1983 Dec. 1	Balance	✓	800				

*The accounts shown here are the same type of "T" accounts as illustrated earlier in the chapter. The only difference is that the *debit* and *credit* sides of each account include descriptive column headings for date, item, posting reference, and debit (for the left side) and credit (for the right side).

The word "balance" is written in the *item column* of each account to designate the account balance carried over from the previous month. After the posting of the two journal entries, the Hook Company's journal and general ledger would appear as shown in Exhibits 2-12 and 2-13. (Explanations of the posting process are provided below.)

The numbers in the "posting reference" columns of the journal and the ledger accounts are for *cross reference* between the journal and ledger. In the example of the *debit* to the office furniture account on December 2, the $500 debit in the journal is transferred to the debit side of the office furniture account in the general ledger. The number 25 is then placed in the journal posting reference column to indicate that the $500 was transferred to account number 25 (the account number of office furniture) in the general ledger. Within the posting reference column of the general ledger office furniture account, the number 30 was written to indicate that this $500 debit came from page 30 of the journal. Thus, by the process of placing the proper numbers in the posting reference columns of the journal and the ledger, a cross reference between the journal and the ledger is achieved. Posting makes it possible for someone at a later date to look at a debit or credit in a particular ledger account and immediately know the journal reference of the original transaction. The individual can then turn to the particular journal page and obtain additional information about the transaction.

The check mark placed in the posting reference column of each account in the ledger (next to the item called "balance") is used to indicate that the balance of each account was not specifically posted from the journal. The *balance* is merely the mathematical total of the account computed from the previous month and carried over to the next month. If desired, brief de-

Exhibit 2-12

Journal   Page 30

DATE		DESCRIPTION	POSTING REFERENCE	DEBIT	CREDIT
1983 Dec.	2	Office furniture	25	500	
		Cash	10		500
		(Purchase of furniture from Packard Co.— Purchase Invoice #88)			
	3	Cash	10	100	
		Accounts receivable	11		100
		(Received payment from Wilson Co. of amount due from November sale— Sales Invoice #1712)			

Exhibit 2-13

General Ledger

Account: __Cash__   Account No. __10__

DATE	ITEM	POSTING REFERENCE	DEBIT	DATE	ITEM	POSTING REFERENCE	CREDIT
1983 Dec. 1 3	Balance *(600)*	✓ 30	1000 100 *1100*	1983 Dec. 2		30	500

Account: __Accounts Receivable__   Account No. __11__

DATE	ITEM	POSTING REFERENCE	DEBIT	DATE	ITEM	POSTING REFERENCE	CREDIT
1983 Dec. 1	Balance *(400)*	✓	500	1983 Dec. 3		30	100

Account: __Office Furniture__   Account No. __25__

DATE	ITEM	POSTING REFERENCE	DEBIT	DATE	ITEM	POSTING REFERENCE	CREDIT
1983 Dec. 1 2	Balance *(1300)*	✓ 30	800 500 *1300*				

scriptions for posted transactions can be placed within the *item columns* of the general ledger accounts. For example, the $100 credit posted to accounts receivable on December 3 could include a comment within the item column such as "payment received from Wilson Company." After all the individual entries in the journal are posted to their proper accounts in the ledger, a company can then determine the dollar balances of its accounts. For example, after the posting of the Hook Company's two transactions, the account balances are: cash, $600; accounts receivable, $400; and office furniture, $1300. These balances are written in small pencil figures in the item column of each account.

       Let's assume for a moment that no further activity other than what is shown in Exhibit 2-13 took place in the Hook Company's "accounts receivable" account during December 1983. At month's end, the balance of the "accounts receivable" account (which would still be $400) is carried over to the subsequent month and thus becomes January 1, 1984 balance. This process of carrying over the end of the month's account balance as the beginning of the next month's balance is called "balancing-down an account." The balancing-down process for the Hook Company's "accounts receivable" account at the end of December 1983 is illustrated in Exhibit 2-14.

Exhibit 2-14

Balancing-Down Process Illustrated

Account: _____Accounts Receivable_____   Account No. __11__

DATE		ITEM	POSTING REFERENCE	DEBIT	DATE		ITEM	POSTING REFERENCE	CREDIT
1983 Dec.	1	Balance	✓ (400)	500.	1983 Dec.	3		30	100.
				___		31	Balance	✓	400.
				500.					500.
1984 Jan.	1	Balance	✓	400.					

This balancing-down process is solely a "bookkeeping technique" which enables a company to start its new accounting period (assumed to be January 1, 1984 in our example) with the beginning of the period's individual account balances clearly disclosed. On December 31, the Hook Company's "accounts receivable" account has a $400 *debit* balance. By entering a $400 *credit* to this account at month's end, the debit and credit sides will now be equal to one another. Double lines are then drawn under the $500 on each side of the account, thereby signifying the end of December's transaction activity for accounts receivable. The $400 end-of-month account balance is now carried over to January and reflected as the beginning balance of this month.

It should be pointed out here that some companies prefer to use a format for their general ledger accounts which is slightly different from the "T" account format discussed and illustrated in this chapter. Using the same monetary data as shown in Exhibit 2-13 for the Hook Company's "accounts receivable" account, an alternative format that could be used in the company's general ledger to reflect this account's activity is illustrated in Exhibit 2-15. (Incidentally, this alternative account format eliminates the need for the "balancing-down" process.)

Exhibit 2-15

Alternative Account Format Illustrated

Account: _____Accounts Receivable_____   Account No. __11__

DATE		ITEM	POSTING REFERENCE	DEBIT	CREDIT	DR (CR) BALANCE*
1983 Dec.	1	Balance	✓			500.
	3	Payment Received	30		100.	400.

* "Dr" is a common abbreviation for *debit* and "Cr" is a common abbreviation for *credit*. Since an asset account (such as "accounts receivable") normally has a *debit* balance, "Cr" is shown in parentheses to indicate that if a *credit* balance existed in this account, parentheses would be placed around the dollar balance.

This account format (commonly called the "running balance" form of general ledger account) provides a separate "balance" column so that the new account balance can be reported each time a debit or a credit occurs. Thus, after recording the $100 *credit* on December 3, the new $400 balance of the company's accounts receivable account is written in the "balance" column. To recognize a debit in the accounts receivable account, the dollar amount would be recorded in the "debit" column and then *added* to the previous balance shown in the "balance" column.

Both the journal and the ledger are needed as part of an organization's accounting system. The major advantage of a journal is that it gives a complete chronological listing of a company's monetary transactions. The journal tells the "full story" of each transaction, since the debit and credit parts of the transaction are shown together along with a brief explanation. However, if a company decides to use a journal without a general ledger, it will be rather cumbersome to determine the dollar balances of the individual accounts. The general ledger takes over where the journal leaves off by providing information concerning the monetary balances of a company's accounts. If a company maintains only a ledger without a journal the company thereby sacrifices useful information, because a ledger does not show in one location the complete picture of a business transaction. For example, the debit side of a transaction may be in account number 15 of the ledger, while the credit side of this same transaction may be in account number 32 of the ledger. Consequently, the parts composing a specific transaction become separated, since they go to different accounts within the ledger. Working together in a company's accounting system, the journal and ledger provide useful information about the monetary transactions that have occurred. Through the process of posting, a cross reference between the journal entries and the general ledger accounts is achieved.

Step 4. Preparing a Trial Balance

Accounting cycle after step 4:

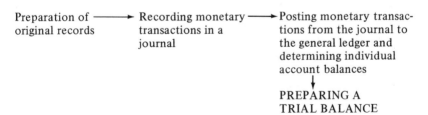

The time interval over which companies prepare financial statements (monthly, quarterly, semi-annually, or yearly) depends upon individual company policy. Because taxes must be paid to the government each year, an organization must prepare financial statements at least once a year to determine its tax liability. However, many companies prepare financial statements more frequently than once a year in order to provide useful information concerning the business activities of their organizations to interested individuals.

When a company is ready to prepare financial statements, all of the posting work must be completed so that the various ledger accounts, which are used in the preparation of the financial statements, are updated with their current balances. Assume that the Justin Company (which sells stereo albums) prepares monthly financial statements. By the end of each month, all of the posting from the journal to the individual ledger accounts should be finished. Upon completion of the posting, the balance of each ledger account is determined so that the company will know the monetary amounts of its individual accounts. After the determination of these account balances, a schedule called a trial balance is prepared. A trial balance lists all the account balances within the ledger to ascertain if the total debits and total credits are *equal*. Exhibit 2-16 is the Justin Company's trial balance for the month of November 1983.

The order in which the accounts appear in the general ledger is typically used when the accounts are listed on the trial balance. The accounts that appear on a company's balance sheet (assets, liabilities, and owners' equity) are listed first on the trial balance, followed by the accounts that appear on the income statement (revenues and expenses). This order of listing the accounts on a trial balance facilitates the preparation of financial statements.

Those accounts that have *debit* balances are listed in the first dollar column of the trial balance, and those accounts with *credit* balances are listed in the second dollar column. It is common practice to place a dollar sign by the first dollar item in a column and also by the dollar items that represent the total of a column. As indicated earlier in this chapter, each time

Exhibit 2-16

The Justin Company
Trial Balance
November 30, 1983

	DEBIT	CREDIT
Cash	$1000	
Accounts receivable	500	
Merchandise inventory	1000	
Office equipment	800	
Accounts payable		$ 400
Wages payable		300
Harry Worthley, capital		2400
Revenue from album sales		2300
Cost of the albums sold*	1000	
Rent expense	200	
Wages expense	800	
Utilities expense	100	
	$5400	$5400

*The "cost of the albums sold" account is an *expense* account representing the whole-sale cost to the Justin Company of the stereo albums that were sold at retail prices.

an entry is recorded in the journal, the total debits and the total credits of that entry must be equal in order to maintain the equality of the balance sheet equation. Therefore, after all entries have been recorded in the journal and posted to the general ledger accounts, and after the balances of each ledger account have been determined, the total of the accounts with debit balances should be equal to the total of the accounts with credit balances. The trial balance is just what the title implies; that is, it represents, in essence, a "trial run" to ascertain the equality of a company's accounts with debit and credit balances before the company's financial statements are formally prepared.

It is important to understand, however, that certain errors may still have been made in a company's accounting work which would not be disclosed by a trial balance. For example, a bookkeeper may have completely omitted the recording of a transaction in the journal; therefore, this omitted transaction will not appear anywhere in the accounting records. This type of error will not be disclosed in a trial balance, since the error resulted from the bookkeeper's failure to record an equal dollar amount of debits and credits. Consequently, the error would not cause the *total* of the debits and credits that were recorded within the accounting system to be unequal. An error of this type may be discovered by a general review of the accounting work completed for a particular time period, or the error may never be detected. The important point here is that the equality of a company's accounts with debit and credit balances gives some assurance that the accounting work is correct but does not guarantee the absence of errors.

Review Questions

At this point, answer the following multiple-choice questions to test your knowledge of the previous reading material. The solutions are given below.

1. The accounting book with a chronological listing of financial transactions is called a (an):
   a. Journal.
   b. Ledger.
   c. Trial balance.
   d. Original record.

2. A $100 liability was paid by a company. What is the correct journal entry?
   a. Owner's equity account   100
        Cash   100
   b. Cash   100
        Owner's equity account   100
   c. Cash   100
        Accounts payable   100
   d. Accounts payable   100
        Cash   100

3. The purpose of *posting* is to:
   a. Cross reference a company's journal and general ledger.
   b. Cross reference a company's journal and trial balance.
   c. Cross reference a company's income statement and journal.
   d. Cross reference a company's income statement and balance sheet.

4. Which financial analysis tests the equality of debit and credit account balances?
   a. Income statement.
   b. Trial balance.
   c. Balance sheet.
   d. Owner's equity account.

Answers

1. a

2. d

3. a

4. b

Chapter Summary

We have presented a detailed analysis of the first four steps in a company's accounting cycle. This is the process by which an organization accumulates monetary transactions within its accounting system. These four accounting cycle steps lead to the preparation of the two major financial statements, the income statement and the balance sheet. In the discussion of the first four steps of the accounting cycle, concepts such as debits, credits, journals, and general ledger accounts were introduced. In addition, the recording of monetary transactions in a journal and then the posting of this information to accounts within the general ledger were analyzed. The preparation of a *trial balance* to test the total monetary equality of accounts with *debit* balances and accounts with *credit* balances was also discussed and illustrated.

The sequence of performing the accounting cycle discussed in this chapter is

Step 1: Preparing original records.

Step 2: Recording monetary transactions in a journal.

Step 3: Posting monetary transactions from the journal to the general ledger and determining individual account balances.

Step 4: Preparing a trial balance.

We shall continue the detailed discussion of the accounting cycle by analyzing the remaining five steps in Chapter 3.

Chapter Problem

The solution to the problem is given in the appendix. However, the reader is urged first to attempt to work the problem on his own and then to check his work against the given solution.

Problem Situation

The balance sheet of the Harry Jungbluth Law Firm on September 30, 1983 is shown in Exhibit 2-17.

Exhibit 2-17

Harry Jungbluth Law Firm
Balance Sheet
September 30, 1983

ASSETS		*LIABILITIES & OWNER'S EQUITY*	
Cash	$500	Liabilities:	
Accounts receivable	200	Accounts payable	$100
Office supplies	100	Owner's equity:	
		Harry Jungbluth, capital,	
		September 30, 1983	700
		Total liabilities &	
Total assets	$800	owner's equity	$800

The law firm's types of accounts and the numbering system used for the accounts are indicated in Exhibit 2-18.

Exhibit 2-18

BALANCE SHEET ACCOUNTS		INCOME STATEMENT ACCOUNTS	
1. Assets		4. Revenues	
ACCOUNT NUMBER	*ACCOUNT TITLE*	*ACCOUNT NUMBER*	*ACCOUNT TITLE*
100	Cash	400	Revenue from
101	Accounts receivable		legal services
102	Office supplies		
103	Land	5. Expenses	
		500	Rent expense
2. Liabilities		501	Utilities expense
200	Accounts payable	502	Wages expense
201	Wages payable	503	Office supplies expense
3. Owner's Equity			
300	Harry Jungbluth, capital		

During the month of October 1983, the following monetary transactions occurred in the Harry Jungbluth Law Firm:

October 1   Paid $100 for the October rent on the law office.

October 5   Collected $50 from a client who had previously owed the law firm money as a result of legal services performed last month.

October 8   Performed legal services for a client and sent him a bill for $200.

October 12   Paid $25 of the accounts payable liability owed from last month.

October 20   Purchased a piece of land for $300. The payment for the land will be made next month.

October 25   Performed legal services for a client and received $300 cash.

October 28   Received a utilities bill for electricity and water. The entire amount of the bill, $50, was paid.

October 31   Paid the part-time secretary her monthly wages, $200.

October 31   Of the $100 worth of office supplies at the end of the previous month (see the law firm's balance sheet on September 30), it was determined that $50 of these supplies were *used* during October.

Problem Requirements

Using the above information for the Harry Jungbluth Law Firm during the month of October 1983, accumulate the accounting data in a *logical form* and prepare the law firm's financial statements on October 31, 1983.

Problem Objective and Solution Approach

Objective:

Utilization of the accounting cycle steps discussed in this chapter to accumulate the relevant data for the preparation of the law firm's financial statements. (The knowledge obtained from Chapter 1 should enable you to prepare the financial statements.)

Solution Approach:

1. Establish general ledger accounts for the financial items included on the law firm's September 30, 1983 balance sheet.

2. Record the October financial transactions in the law firm's journal (assume that page 5 of the journal is used).

3. Post the October journal entries to the proper general ledger accounts. Determine the monetary balance of each general ledger account.

4. Prepare a trial balance.

5. Using the information from the trial balance, prepare the law firm's monthly financial statements.

3

The
Accounting Cycle
Part II

A detailed analysis of steps 1 through 4 of the accounting cycle was presented in the previous chapter. The objective of Chapter 3 is to continue the analysis of the accounting cycle steps that are necessary to gather the monetary data for inclusion in a company's financial statements (i.e., the income statement and the balance sheet). After analyzing cycle steps 5 through 9, we will introduce the reader to an optional tool, called the *work sheet*, which may be used to help an organization perform its accounting cycle activities more efficiently.

Continuation of Accounting Cycle Steps

The last accounting cycle step discussed (step 4) in the previous chapter was the preparation of a company's *trial balance* after all the monetary transactions for an accounting period have been recorded in the journal and posted to the proper general ledger accounts.

Step 5. Recording Adjusting Entries in a Journal

Upon completion of step 4 of the accounting cycle, a company's general ledger accounts have dollar quantities, which represent the account

Accounting cycle after step 5:

Preparation of ⟶ Recording monetary ⟶ Posting   monetary   transactions
original records   transactions in a   from the journal to the general
                      journal   ledger and determining individ-
                                                 ual account balances
                                                          ↓
                                                 Preparing a trial balance
                                                          ↓
                                                 RECORDING ADJUSTING
                                                 ENTRIES IN A JOURNAL

balances at the end of a certain time period (a month, a year, etc.). However, before the company's financial statements are prepared, certain adjustments (called *adjusting entries*) may be necessary in the accounts. Before we discuss adjusting entries, the two accounting concepts known as the *periodicity concept* and the *matching concept*, will be analyzed. A knowledge of the periodicity and matching concepts should enable the reader to understand the logic behind adjusting entries.

Periodicity and Matching Concepts

The periodicity concept comes from the word "periodic," which means "occurring at regular intervals." In accounting, it is assumed that after a certain time period (a month, six months, a year, etc.), an organization can determine the monetary balances of its general ledger accounts and then prepare financial statements. This process is often called "adjusting and closing the books." (The *books* are a company's accounting records: the journal and the general ledger, for example. A special type of journal entry called *closing entries* will be discussed and illustrated in step 8 of the accounting cycle.) At the end of a month or year, when a business organization wants to prepare its financial statements, the *periodicity concept* assumes that the organization is at a certain "cutoff point" in its operating activities and can therefore provide relevant financial information to interested parties such as potential investors and creditors.

Even though the periodic adjusting and closing of an organization's books are accepted in accounting, it must be recognized that the organization continues to function from day to day without any actual closing of business activities. When, for example, an organization wants to prepare financial statements for the month of November, the accounting assumption is made that the organization can accurately compute its November net income (or net loss) and determine its individual balance sheet items as of November 30. However, various *uncertainties* may exist on November 30 concerning specific financial statement items, which will not be resolved until a later date. It is important to understand that the only time a company can determine its "real" income is when the company terminates business activities at the end of its life. Only then will various uncertainties about financial statement items be resolved. For example, the accounts receivable account on a balance sheet indicates how much cash is owed to an organization from business activities. But, at the end of a particular period, how does a company really know the dollar amount of receivables that will actually be collected? Some individuals who owe money may default and never pay. Accounting uncertainties will be discussed in later chapters, with an analysis of the manner in which accounting attempts to solve these uncertainties.

Management, investors, and creditors do not want to wait until the end of a business organization's life to obtain financial information. These parties want financial information at specific times throughout the organization's operating life. The *periodicity concept* enables a company to provide interested parties financial statements at specific time intervals prior to the termination of the company. Furthermore, an organization should attempt to present the most accurate financial statements possible at periodic intervals. The *matching concept* has as its objective the accurate computation of an organization's net income (or net loss) each time a financial statement is prepared. This will enable the financial statement users to have reliable information for financial decision-making activities relating to the organization. As discussed in Chapter 1, a company should recognize "revenues" when they have been *earned* by either selling a product or providing a service to someone, and "expenses" should be recognized upon receiving a *service* from someone (or something). The matching concept attempts to accurately relate a company's revenues earned to its expenses incurred in earning those revenues prior to the preparation of the financial statements. Because an accountant records revenues when they have been earned (regardless of whether cash has been received) and records expenses when services have been received (regardless of whether cash has been paid), the term "accrual accounting," rather than "cash accounting," is often used to describe the practice of accounting.

Having discussed the accounting concepts of periodicity and matching, we will now turn our attention specifically to step 5 of the accounting cycle, which is recording adjusting entries in a journal.

Adjusting Entries

At the end of an accounting period, when a company wants to prepare financial statements, it should make sure that all the accounts are updated so that the income statement and balance sheet can be prepared as accurately as possible. Various financial events, such as interest earned on a bank savings account, may have occurred during the period which have not been recognized in the company's accounting records. Therefore, before preparing periodic financial statements, *adjusting entries* are recorded by a company to update (i.e., adjust) its accounting records for any financial activities that have occurred but have not been recognized formally in the company's accounting system. As a result of recording adjusting entries, a better *matching* of revenues earned against expenses incurred during the period is achieved on the income statement, along with a more accurate presentation of monetary items on the balance sheet. If adjusting entries were not recorded prior to preparing periodic financial statements, the financial information disclosed within the income statement and the balance sheet would lack accuracy. Consequently, the information reported on the financial statements could be misleading to those parties (such as potential investors and creditors) who require financial information for their decision-making activities. For example, assume that a bank approved a $5,000 loan to a company on the basis of the company's balance sheet, which indicated a small monetary quantity of liabilities (debts) in relation to assets. If several unrecorded liabilities had actually existed at the end of the company's accounting period and the bank had been aware of these liabilities, it may have refused the $5,000 loan.

When adjusting entries are made at the end of an accounting period prior to preparing financial statements, they are recorded in the *journal*, the same format being used as that followed in recording a company's day-to-day business transactions (step 2 of the accounting cycle). For information purposes, the words "ADJUSTING ENTRIES" can be written on the page of the journal where the adjusting entries begin. Basically, there are four major types of adjusting entries:

1. Adjusting entries for accrued liabilities (commonly referred to as unrecorded expenses).

2. Adjusting entries for accrued assets (commonly referred to as unrecorded revenues).

3. Adjusting entries for prepaid assets (commonly referred to as deferred expenses or prepaid expenses).

4. Adjusting entries for advance payments by customers (commonly referred to as deferred revenues).

To help the reader understand the adjusting entry process, examples of each type of adjusting entry will now be presented. In the first three examples, it is assumed that the company involved, the Rotary Music Shop, prepares financial statements monthly and thus records monthly adjusting entries.

Example 1—adjusting entry for accrued liabilities (unrecorded expenses).

Assume that the Rotary Music Shop has ten employees who are paid every Friday for their week's work. Further assume that each employee earns $200 a week; therefore, the total weekly payroll is $2,000 ($200 × 10).

To simplify the example, ignore withholdings from the employees' paychecks for such things as union dues and social security taxes. The journal entry for the payment of the ten employees' wages would ordinarily be recorded each Friday, as follows:

Wages expense*	2000	
Cash		2000

*An account called "salaries expense" could have been used here rather than "wages expense." Some companies utilize the "wages expense" account to reflect the earnings of their employees who work on an hourly pay rate and utilize the "salaries expense" account to report the earnings of their employees who earn a specific weekly salary, regardless of the actual hours worked. Throughout this example, the "wages expense" account will be used to record all employees' earnings.

November 30, 1983 (the close of the monthly accounting period) falls on a Thursday, and the Rotary Music Shop thus wants to prepare its monthly financial statements on this date. The ten employees have already worked Monday, Tuesday, Wednesday, and Thursday and have therefore earned four days' wages by the end of November 30. (In accounting, we say that these four days of earnings have *accrued*, or *built up*, as of November 30.) However, since the employees do not get paid until Friday, the Rotary Music Shop has a *liability* to its employees on November 30 for four days' pay. Prior to preparing the company's financial statements for the month of November, the following *adjusting entry* would be recorded in the journal (it is assumed that there are five work days in a week):

Nov. 30	Wages expense	1600	
	(Accrued) wages payable		1600

Since the ten employees have already worked four of the week's five working days by the close of November 30, these employees have thus earned 4/5 of their $2,000 weekly total wages (4/5 × $2,000 = $1,600). The *debit* part of the November 30 adjusting entry has the effect of updating the Rotary Music Shop's November wages expense for the four days worked by its employees this month. If the above adjusting entry had not been recorded, the company's total expenses on its November income statement would have been *understated* (smaller than they should have been) by $1,600. This $1,600 understatement of expenses would have caused a $1,600 *overstatement* of the company's November net income, since a smaller dollar amount of expenses *subtracted* from revenues would result in a larger computed net income. Furthermore, because the company's computed net income is subsequently added to the owners' equity section of its balance sheet, the *overstated* net income would cause Rotary Music Shop's owners' equity also to be *overstated* by the same $1,600.

The *credit* part of the November 30 adjusting entry has the effect of reflecting the wages payable liability on the Rotary Music Shop's month-end balance sheet. By the end of November, the employees have worked four days for which they have not yet been paid. Thus, on November 30, the company has *incurred* a liability to its ten employees for four days' earned wages. If the adjusting entry for wages had not been recorded on November 30, the liabilities shown on the November balance sheet would have been *understated* by $1,600. When the wages payable liability account is credited on November 30, the word "accrued" (which is optional to use within the liability account title) indicates that something has increased (or built up) over time. Since the ten employees have earned four days' wages as of November 30, it can be said that the Rotary Music Shop has *accrued* a liability and *incurred* an expense for these wages at month's end.

Let us carry this example a step further by examining the Rotary Music Shop's journal entry recorded a day later (Friday, December 1) for the actual payment of the week's wages to its ten employees. Remember that the month of December represents a new accounting period; therefore, the following journal entry would be recorded on Friday, December 1 for the employees' wage payments:

Dec. 1	Wages expense	400	
	(Accrued) wages payable	1600	
	Cash		2000

The credit to the cash account reflects the $2,000 actually paid to the ten employees on Friday. The wages payable account is debited for $1,600 to eliminate the liability for four days' wages that was established in the Rotary Music Shop's November 30 adjusting entry. Since the company is now paying the wages owed its employees, a liability to them no longer exists. The debit to the wages expense account for $400 (1/5 × $2,000) recognizes the Rotary Music Shop's labor expense for the employees' work activities on Friday (the one work day in the new accounting period).

A relevant point to be emphasized, in analyzing the December 1 journal entry, is that you often must look back at adjusting entries of the previous accounting period before recording various journal entries in the new accounting period. Based upon the November 30 adjusting journal entry for the wages owed and the subsequent journal entry on December 1 for the payment of the ten employees' wages, the matching concept is accomplished in each accounting period (that is, November as well as December). Thus, the $1,600 of wages expense actually incurred by the Rotary Music Shop in November (see the November 30 adjusting entry) is matched against the November revenues on that month's income statement. In addition, the matching concept will also be achieved in the Rotary Music Shop's December income statement, since the December 1 payroll journal entry recognized only one of the five days' wages (which was $400) as a December expense. (This journal entry also eliminated the $1,600 payroll liability initially established in the November 30 adjusting entry.)

Example 2—adjusting entry for accrued assets (unrecorded revenues).

In this example, assume that the Rotary Music Shop owns a small office building, which it leases to the Jodie Jay Company for $3,000 a month. The rental lease stipulates that rent payments are due on the first of each month and cover the full month (assume the average length of a month to be 30 days). Thus, for example, Rotary Music Shop would receive $3,000 cash on October 1, 1983 and credit rent revenue for the whole month of October.

Assume next that on November 1 Jodie Jay is short of cash and only pays $2,000 (which covers 20 of the 30 days in the month), promising to pay the balance "soon." November 30 arrives (the close of the Rotary Music Shop's accounting period) and Jodie Jay is still delinquent because its rent check is in the mail. The Rotary Music Shop would record the following adjusting journal entry prior to preparing its November financial statements:

> Nov. 30   (Accrued) rent receivable   1000
>   Rent revenue (or Rent income*)   1000

* An alternative account title that can be used.

Revenues are earned by providing a service to someone. In this example, the Rotary Music Shop provides rental facilities (a service) to the Jodie Jay Company for operating its business. As of November 30, the Jodie Jay Company has utilized the rental facilities for 30 days and not paid for 10 days (1/3 of a month) rental services. However, since the Rotary Music Shop will prepare financial statements on November 30, the company must record the above November 30 adjusting entry for $1,000 (1/3 of a month × $3,000) to update its accounting records. The asset account "rent receivable" (the word "accrued" can be added to the account title) is debited for one-third of a month's rent, thereby recognizing the Rotary Music Shop's claim against the Jodie Jay Company for the lease rent that has *accrued* since the $2,000 rent payment on November 1, covering November 1 through November 20.

The account "rent revenue" is credited $1,000 in the November 30 adjusting entry, reflecting the additional one-third of a month's rent earned by the Rotary Music Shop as of November 30. The fact that the Rotary Music Shop provided rental facilities to the Jodie Jay Company from November 21 through November 30 justifies recognition of the $1,000 earned revenue.

If the Rotary Music Shop had not recorded the above adjusting entry for earned rent, its November 30 financial statements would be inaccurate. The rent receivable financial item is a balance sheet asset account. Failure to record the November 30 *debit* to rent receivable would cause the total assets shown on the company's balance sheet to be *understated* by $1,000.

Furthermore, if the $1,000 *credit* to the rent revenue account is not recognized, the total revenues on Rotary Music Shop's November income statement would be *understated* by $1,000. This $1,000 understatement of revenues would cause the company's net income (revenues *minus* expenses) to be *understated* by $1,000. Since net income increases the owners' asset interests, the owners' equity section of the Rotary Music Shop's balance sheet would also be *understated* by $1,000. Thus, as with Example 1, the purpose of recording adjusting journal entries is to update a company's accounting records before its financial statements are prepared so that more accurate financial information can be presented to interested parties.

Before leaving Example 2, we will now briefly discuss the Rotary Music Shop's journal entry on December 1 when it receives the Jodie Jay Company's $4,000 rent payment on this date for the lease rental period from November 21 through December 31. This journal entry would be:

Dec. 1	Cash	4000	
	(Accrued) rent receivable		1000
	Rent revenue		3000

The debit to the cash account reflects the $4,000 actually received for the 41 days of rent owed. The rent receivable account is credited for $1,000 to eliminate the asset claim for one-third of a month's rent that was recorded in the Rotary Music Shop's November 30 adjusting entry. Since Rotary Music Shop is now receiving this $1,000 (which is the amount due on the original $3,000 November rent), it no longer has an asset claim against the Jodie Jay Company. Finally, the credit to the rent revenue account for $3,000 recognizes the Rotary Music Shop's earned revenue from agreeing to provide rental facilities to the Jodie Jay Company (from December 1 through December 31) in the December accounting period.

Example 3–adjusting entry for prepaid assets (deferred or prepaid expenses).

Assume that the Rotary Music Shop purchased a one-year fire insurance policy on January 1, 1983 for $900 cash. As of the date this insurance policy is acquired (January 1), the premium payment represents a *prepaid asset*, since the Rotary Music Shop has the right to receive one year's benefits (which is the insurance coverage protection) from the insurance company. For each day that passes, the Rotary Music Shop obtains benefits from the insurance policy fire protection coverage. The insurance is an example of an asset that converts to an *expense* with the passage of time. As the insurance coverage benefits are received daily, the remaining insurance coverage protection under the policy declines. For example, after the passage of two months in 1983, the Rotary Music Shop has received two months' insurance coverage benefits (which   represents an *expense*) and has only ten months' coverage remaining (which represents an *asset*).

The insurance policy coverage paid on January 1, 1983 by the Rotary Music Shop sometimes is called a *deferred* (or *prepaid*) *expense*. It is important to understand that a deferred expense is an *asset* that becomes an expense as time passes and the resultant benefits are received from the asset. (Note that the word *deferred* means "delayed until a later date"; thus, the recognition of a *deferred* expense as an *actual expense* is delayed until the benefits are acquired from the deferred item.) Since the insurance policy premium was paid in advance of receiving the protection coverage, it can alternately be called a *prepaid expense*. For the Rotary Music Shop, as each day passes, 1/365 of a year's insurance coverage benefits are actually being received. It would be impractical, however, to have an accountant spend his valuable time recording a daily journal entry to recognize 1/365 of the insurance policy asset as a business expense. Rather, the usual procedure is to wait until an organization wants to prepare its end-of-period financial statements. At that particular time, the organization records an adjusting journal entry to recognize the portion of the insurance policy which has expired.

The journal entry recorded by the Rotary Music Shop on January 1, 1983 for the *purchase* of the one-year fire insurance policy is shown below:

Jan. 1	Prepaid insurance		
	(or Unexpired insurance*)	900	
	Cash		900

* An alternative account title that can be used.

The "prepaid insurance" account is an asset (a prepaid or deferred expense) representing benefits to be received by the Rotary Music Shop during the twelve-month insurance coverage period. Before preparing its financial statements at the end of January, the following adjusting entry would have been recorded in the Rotary Music Shop's journal:

Jan. 31	Insurance expense	75	
	Prepaid insurance		75

One month had passed since the insurance policy was purchased and the Rotary Music Shop had received one month's fire insurance coverage benefits worth $75 (1/12 × $900). Therefore, the "insurance expense" account was *debited* $75 for the January insurance.

The *credit* part of the January 31 adjusting entry reflects the reduction in the "prepaid insurance" asset account by 1/12 of the year's policy cost as a result of the company having received one month's insurance coverage benefits. The prepaid insurance account should also be reduced at the end of each remaining month in 1983 by 1/12 of the year's fire insurance policy cost to recognize the decline in the value of the insurance coverage. (In fact, the same adjusting journal entry as illustrated above on January 31 will be recorded on the last day of every remaining month during 1983.) Therefore, by the end of 1983, the prepaid insurance asset account will have a *zero* balance reflecting the fact that no additional 1983 insurance coverage benefits are due from the insurance company.

Example 4—adjusting entry for advance payments by customers (deferred revenues).

Our previous three examples dealt with the Rotary Music Shop and the preparation of monthly adjusting journal entries, since this company prepared monthly financial statements. In the current example we will assume that the business firm involved, the Honolulu Speedsters (a professional football team), prepares financial statements only once a year on December 31. Therefore, the Speedsters' adjusting entries to update its accounting records are recorded yearly (on December 31).

Prior to the September 1, 1983 start of the scheduled football games, the Speedsters sold a season ticket to Reggie Williamson on August 24, 1983 for $56 cash. This ticket allows Reggie to attend all seven home games played at Honolulu City Stadium during the 1983-84 football season. (Five of the seven home games will be played in 1983 and the remaining two will be played in 1984.) Shown below is the Speedsters' recorded journal entry on August 24 for the season ticket sale to Reggie Williamson:

Aug. 24	Cash	56	
	Advances by customers		
	(Unearned ticket revenues		
	or Deferred ticket revenues*)		56

* Alternative account titles that can be used.

Upon receiving the $56 advance payment (the "cash" account is thus *debited*), the Honolulu Speedsters football team business organization has a *liability* to Reggie Williamson for the performance of seven home games. Remember that revenues are earned only upon providing a service to someone. As of August 24, the organization has not provided any service to Reggie (since the first football game is not until September 1); therefore, it has not earned any of the $56 advance payment. The service that earns revenue for the football organization is the playing of the individual home games for the sports fans. The "advances by customers" account is a *liability* account indicating that the football team business firm has a liability to perform seven home games for its season ticket holder.

In the August 24 journal entry, the account title "deferred ticket revenues" could also be used for the $56 *credit*, since, as discussed in Example 3, the word *deferred* means to delay the recognition of something until a later date. In other words, the recognition of the earned revenue from the $56 season ticket advance payment is being delayed until the organization performs each of the seven football games for Reggie Williamson. It is assumed that the average price per football game is $8 ($56 season ticket price ÷ 7 home games). Therefore, as each football game is played, $8 of the original $56 unearned ticket revenues is *earned*. Since the organization prepares financial statements only on December 31, it can wait until year's end to record an adjusting journal entry for the ticket revenues that have been *earned*. The following adjusting entry is made on December 31, 1983, before the preparation of the Honolulu Speedsters' financial statements:

Dec. 31	Advances by customers	40	
	Earned ticket revenues		40

By the end of 1983, five of the seven home football games have been played, resulting in $40 (5 games × $8 average price per football game) of the $56 season ticket advance payment being earned. The debit to "advances by customers" reduces the organization's liability to Reggie Williamson by $40 since five games already have been performed. Note that after posting the $40 debit to the "advances by customers" account in the general ledger, this liability account will have a $16 *credit* balance ($56 credit on August 24 *minus* $40 debit on December 31). The $16 *credit* balance indicates that as of December 31, 1983, the organization still has a liability to Reggie Williamson for the performance of the remaining two home football games in 1984 (2 games remaining × $8 average price per football game). The credit part of the December 31 adjusting entry is to a *revenue* account, indicating that $40 of the August 24 season ticket selling price has now been earned. Since the two remaining home games relating to Reggie Williamson's season ticket purchase will be played in 1984, the football team organization would record the following adjusting journal entry at the close of its next accounting period (which is December 31, 1984):

Dec. 31	Advances by customers	16	
	Earned ticket revenues		16

The above adjusting entry at the end of 1984 will result in the elimination of the organization's liability to Reggie Williamson and the full recognition of the $56 season ticket advance payment as *earned revenue* ($40 earned revenue in 1983 and $16 earned revenue in 1984).

Summary of Adjusting Entries

The four examples of adjusting entries discussed in this chapter do not represent all the types of adjustments necessary by a business firm at the end of its accounting period. However, these examples do illustrate the adjusting entry concept. At the end of an accounting period when a company wants to prepare financial statements, it should strive for accuracy within the financial data. To achieve this accuracy, all the monetary activities during the accounting period should be examined and a determination made if anything has happened that is not presently recognized in the accounting records. If unrecorded economic events exist, adjusting entries are required. After all adjusting entries are recorded, an organization's financial data have been up-dated. The resultant financial statements reflect a more accurate picture of the organization's business activities for the accounting period, thereby pro-viding better decision-making information to the statements' users. Addi-tional types of adjusting journal entries are presented in subsequent chapters. However, the reader should be familiar with the general concept of adjusting entries based upon the analyses presented here.

Review Questions

At this point, answer the following multiple-choice questions to test your knowledge of the previous reading material. The solutions are given below.

1. The accounting concept that has as its objective the accurate presentation of a company's financial statements each accounting period is called:
   a. The periodicity concept.
   b. The monetary unit concept.
   c. The balance sheet equation concept.
   d. The matching concept.

2. Before the preparation of financial statements, no journal entry has been recorded for a company's $100 wages owed to its employees. What is the correct adjusting entry to reflect the wages?
   a. Wages expense   100
        Cash   100
   b. Cash   100
        Wages expense   100
   c. Wages expense   100
        Wages payable   100
   d. Wages payable   100
        Wages expense   100

3. A company paid $500 to a television station for future commercials. At the end of the current month, one-fourth of the commercials had been shown on television. What is the company's correct adjusting entry at month end?

   a. Advertising expense   500
        Cash   500
   b. Advertising expense   125
        Cash   125
   c. Advertising expense   125
        Prepaid advertising   125

   d. Prepaid advertising   125
        Advertising expense   125

4. The failure to record an adjusting entry for $100 sales revenue has what effect on a company's financial statements?
   a. Expenses *overstated* by $100.
   b. Expenses *understated* by $100.
   c. Net income *overstated* by $100.
   d. Net income *understated* by $100.

Answers

1. d

2. c

3. c (1/4 × $500 = $125)

4. d

Step 6. Posting Adjusting Journal Entries to the General Ledger, Determining Updated General Ledger Account Balances, and Preparing an Adjusted Trial Balance.

Accounting cycle after step 6:

Preparation of ⟶ Recording monetary ⟶ Posting monetary
original records   transactions in a journal   transactions from the
                                                  journal to the general
                                                  ledger and determining
                                                  individual account
                                                  balances
                                                        ↓
                                                  Preparing a trial balance
                                                        ↓
                                                  Recording adjusting
                                                  entries in a journal
                                                        ↙

POSTING ADJUSTING JOURNAL ENTRIES
TO THE GENERAL LEDGER, DETERMINING
UPDATED GENERAL LEDGER ACCOUNT
BALANCES, AND PREPARING AN ADJUSTED
TRIAL BALANCE

   After a company's adjusting entries are recorded in the journal, the debits and credits of these entries are then *posted* to the correct general ledger accounts in the same manner as the regular business transactions recorded during the accounting period. Upon finishing the posting work, the new updated monetary balances of those accounts affected by the adjusting journal entries are determined. The posting process for adjusting entries and the determination of the new account balances within the general ledger are performed the same way as previously illustrated in step 3 of our accounting cycle (see Chapter 2).

Once the updated general ledger account balances are determined, a company's financial data are then current for the preparation of its financial statements. Preceding the preparation of the company's income statement and balance sheet, however, is an *adjusted trial balance.* As discussed in step 4 of the accounting cycle (see Chapter 2), a trial balance discloses whether an organization's general ledger accounts with *debit* and *credit* balances are equal.

Since a trial balance is prepared after all business transactions during an accounting period are recorded and posted and each general ledger account balance is determined, the equality of total debits and total credits within the accounts is ascertained prior to recording and posting the adjusting journal entries. The purpose for preparing this second trial balance (called the "adjusted trial balance") is to determine if the equality of debit and credit account balances still exists upon the completion of the adjusting entry process. There is no change in format between a trial balance prepared before and one prepared after adjusting journal entries are recorded and posted. Therefore, an example of an adjusted trial balance is not presented at this point in the chapter.

Step 7. Preparation of Financial Statements From Adjusted Trial Balance

Accounting cycle after step 7:

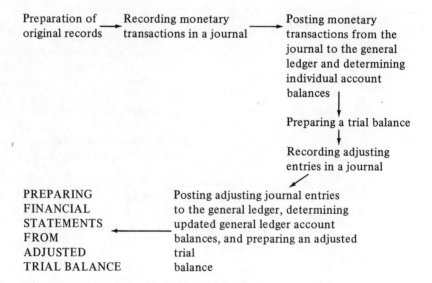

Preparation of original records → Recording monetary transactions in a journal → Posting monetary transactions from the journal to the general ledger and determining individual account balances ↓

Preparing a trial balance ↓

Recording adjusting entries in a journal

PREPARING FINANCIAL STATEMENTS FROM ADJUSTED TRIAL BALANCE ← Posting adjusting journal entries to the general ledger, determining updated general ledger account balances, and preparing an adjusted trial balance

When the adjusted trial balance is finished, the financial data of a company are updated and the financial statements can be prepared. The adjusted trial balance includes all information needed to prepare the financial statements. Exhibit 3-1 is the November 1983 adjusted trial balance of Radio House, whose business is repairing television sets, stereos, and other types of home appliances.

Exhibit 3-1

Radio House
Adjusted Trial Balance
November 30, 1983

	DEBIT	CREDIT
Cash	$1800	
Accounts receivable	800	
Repair tools	200	
Accounts payable		$ 500
John Barrack, capital*		2400
Revenue from appliance repairs		1000
Rent expense	300	
Wages expense	700	
Utilities expense	100	
	$3900	$3900

* The $2400 balance in the owner's equity account "John Barrack, capital" is actually the November 1, 1983 owner's equity account balance, since the *net income* or *net loss* for the month of November has not yet been transferred to the owner's equity account.

The balance sheet accounts and the income statement accounts are grouped together to make it easier to prepare the financial statements directly from the adjusted trial balance. Preceding the "revenue from appliance repairs" account are the balance sheet accounts. Starting with "revenue from appliance repairs," the income statement accounts are grouped together. As discussed in Chapter 1, the income statement is prepared before the balance sheet, since the net income or net loss computed on the income statement is *added* to (if a net income occurs) or *subtracted* from (if a net loss occurs) the owners' equity section of the balance sheet.

Exhibits 3-2 and 3-3 are the financial statements prepared by the Radio House directly from its adjusted trial balance:

Exhibit 3-2

Radio House
Income Statement
For the Month Ended November 30, 1983

Revenues
From appliance repairs $1000

Less: *Expenses*
    Rent expense $300
    Wages expense   700
    Utilities expense   100

      Total expenses   1100
    Net loss $ 100

Exhibit 3-3

Radio House
Balance Sheet
November 30, 1983

ASSETS		*LIABILITIES & OWNER'S EQUITY*		
Cash	$1800	Liabilities:		
Accounts receivable	800	Accounts payable		$ 500
Repair tools	200	Owner's equity:		
		John Barrack,		
		capital, Nov. 1,		
		1983	$2400	
		Less: Net loss		
		for the month		
		of November	100	
		John Barrack,		
		capital, Nov. 30, 1983		2300
		Total liabilities and		
Total assets	$2800	owner's equity		$2800

The Radio House's November *net loss* of $100 is *subtracted* from the owner's capital account on the balance sheet to reflect John Barrack's decreased interest in his company's assets. Thus, John Barrack's updated capital account balance on November 30 is $2300.

Step 8. Recording Closing Entries in a Journal, Posting Them to the General Ledger, and Determining New Balances of Those Accounts Affected by Closing Entries

Accounting cycle after step 8:

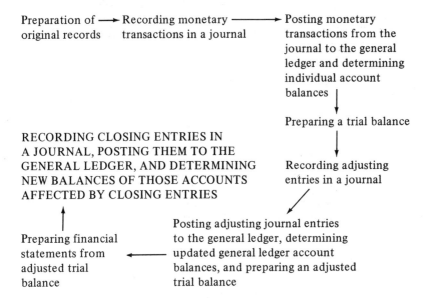

Preparation of → Recording monetary → Posting monetary
original records   transactions in a journal   transactions from the
journal to the general
ledger and determining
individual account
balances ↓

Preparing a trial balance

RECORDING CLOSING ENTRIES IN   ↓
A JOURNAL, POSTING THEM TO THE
GENERAL LEDGER, AND DETERMINING   Recording adjusting
NEW BALANCES OF THOSE ACCOUNTS   entries in a journal
AFFECTED BY CLOSING ENTRIES

↑   Posting adjusting journal entries
Preparing financial   to the general ledger, determining
statements from   ←——   updated general ledger account
adjusted trial   balances, and preparing an adjusted
balance   trial balance

As was emphasized during our discussion of general ledger accounts in Chapter 2, an organization's revenue and expense accounts are *subdivisions* of the owners' equity accounts. The major reason for utilizing separate revenue and expense accounts is to provide better information to management and other interested parties about a company's operating activities. Remember, however, that a company's net income or net loss belongs to its owner (or owners). Therefore, at the end of an accounting period, a company records *closing entries* (to *close* an account means to make its dollar balance become "zero") to eliminate its individual revenue and expense account balances and transfer the net income (or net loss) into the owner's (or owners') equity account (or accounts). Because revenue and expense accounts are subdivisions of the owners' equity accounts whose balances are closed at the end of an accounting period, revenue and expense accounts are often called *temporary accounts* or *nominal accounts* (since they are "temporarily" established each accounting period in order to accumulate the monetary information regarding the period's operating activities). On the other hand, balance sheet accounts (the asset, liability, and owners' equity accounts) are not subdivisions of any other business accounts whose balances are closed at period-end, and are thus often called *permanent accounts* or *real accounts*.

A company's closing entries are recorded in a journal (the words "CLOSING ENTRIES" can be written on the page of the journal where the closing entries begin) and then posted to general ledger accounts in the same manner as other accounting entries.

Assume that the revenue and expense accounts of the Bill Hunt Law Firm have the following balances on November 30, 1983. (Also assume that Bill Hunt's ownership interest in his law firm's assets was $3000 at the beginning of November.)

Revenue from law services	$2000
Wages expense	750
Rent expense	300
Utilities expense	100
Insurance expense	100

The law firm's closing entries at the end of November are as follows (the special account called "income summary" will be explained shortly):

Nov. 30	Revenue from law services	2000	
	Income summary		2000
	(To close the revenue account into the income summary account)		
30	Income summary	1250	
	Wages expense		750
	Rent expense		300
	Utilities expense		100
	Insurance expense		100
	(To close the expense accounts into the income summary account)		
30	Income summary	750	
	Bill Hunt, capital		750
	(To close the income summary account into the owner's equity account)		

If posting reference numbers and the specific dates on which the revenue and expense items occurred during November are ignored, the general ledger accounts and their balances appear as shown in Exhibit 3-4 after the closing entries are posted.

The "income summary" account is used only when closing entries are prepared. The function of the income summary account is to aid a company's closing entry process. It accumulates the revenue and expense items

Exhibit 3-4

Revenue From Law Services				Wages Expense		
1983		1983		1983	1983	
Nov. 30	Closing	Nov.	2000	Nov. 750	Nov. 30	Closing
	entry 2000					entry 750

Rent Expense				Utilities Expense		
1983	1983			1983	1983	
Nov. 300	Nov. 30	Closing		Nov. 100	Nov. 30	Closing
		entry	300			entry 100

Insurance Expense				Bill Hunt, Capital	
1983	1983				1983
Nov. 100	Nov. 30	Closing			Nov. 1 3000
		entry	100		30 Net income
					for Nov. 750
					3750

Income Summary					
1983				1983	
Nov. 30	Expenses			Nov. 30	Revenues
	closed	1250			closed 2000
30	Closed to				
	owner's				
	account	750			
		2000			2000

prior to the net effect of these items' [either a net income or a net loss depending on whether revenues exceed expenses (net income) or are less than expenses (net loss)] being transferred to the owner's equity account. The first closing entry transfers the *credit* balance of the revenue account to the *credit* side of the income summary account. Since a revenue account has a *credit* balance, it is closed by *debiting* the account for the same dollar amount. The second closing entry transfers the balances of the four expense accounts to the income summary account. (The "income summary" account is *debited* for the total of the four *credits* to the expense accounts.) Expense accounts have *debit* balances; thus, they are closed by *crediting* the accounts for the same dollar amounts.

At this point in the closing process, all the revenue and expense accounts have been closed to the income summary account. What has actually happened is a reclassification of accounts; that is, the credit balance in the revenue account is reclassified on the credit side of the income summary account, and the debit balances in the individual expense accounts are reclassified on the debit side of the income summary account. The income summary account can be thought of as an income statement in "T" account form, since the total of the credit column represents total revenues and the total of the debit column represents total expenses. Therefore, the monetary balance of the income summary account represents a company's net income (if a *credit* balance) or net loss (if a *debit* balance).

The final closing entry transfers the balance of the income summary account into the owner's equity account. The $750 credit balance in the income summary account represents the law firm's net income for November. This last closing entry achieves the end objective of the closing process by increasing the owner's account to reflect the $750 net income. The income summary account now has a zero balance and will not be used again until the law firm is ready to prepare closing entries at the end of its next accounting period.

The general ledger owner's equity account for "Bill Hunt, capital" indicates that at the beginning of November his ownership interest in the law firm's assets was $3000. As a result of the $750 November net income, Hunt's interest in the law firm's assets increased to $3750 by the end of the month. Upon the completion of the closing entries, each revenue and expense account has a zero balance (the debit and credit side of every revenue and expense account as well as the income summary account are double underlined to indicate that they are closed) and Bill Hunt's owner's equity account includes the November net income. The law firm is now ready to accumulate within its accounts the various revenue and expense items for the next accounting period.

Since the "income summary" account only facilitates the closing process (and is itself closed immediately), it really is completely unnecessary. Although many bookkeepers still use the income summary account, some modern accountants close the books simply by: debiting each revenue account for its balance (to close the account), crediting each expense account for its balance (to close the account), and crediting the resultant net income (or debiting if a net loss) to the owner's equity account. Of course, this simple closing entry is journalized and posted, as usual. Both methods of closing are still in use, but the advent of the computer enhances the simplicity of the latter method.

It is important for an organization to prepare financial statements as soon as possible after the close of its accounting period so that the information from the financial statements is available for analysis. The owner's equity account on a company's balance sheet reflects the net income (or net loss) for the particular period. However, prior to the recording and posting of closing entries, the owner's general ledger account does not reflect the net income (or net loss) for the accounting period. To update the owner's account and thereby have it agree with the owner's equity shown on the balance sheet, closing entries are recorded and posted upon completion of the financial statements. Most organizations record and post closing entries after finishing their financial statements in order to complete the statements promptly at the close of an accounting period.

Step 9. Preparing a Post-Closing Trial Balance

Accounting cycle after step 9:

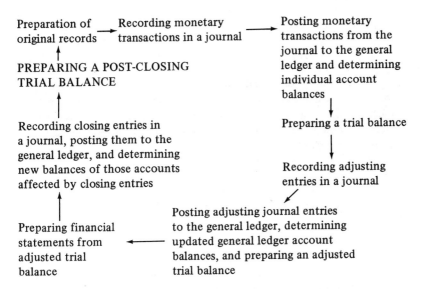

After closing entries are journalized and posted, all the revenue and expense accounts have a *zero* balance and the new monetary balance of the owner's equity account includes the period's net income (or net loss). A *post-closing trial balance* is then prepared to determine if the accounts with debit and credit balances are still equal.

Based upon the Bill Hunt Law Firm example, the post-closing trial balance in Exhibit 3-5 is prepared. (The monetary balances of the asset and liability accounts are assumed.)

It should be noted that revenue and expense accounts do not appear in the post-closing trial balance. All the revenue and expense accounts were previously closed into the owner's equity account. The $3750 balance of the "Bill Hunt, capital" account represents the $3000 on November 1 plus the $750 net income for the month of November.

Exhibit 3-5

Hunt Law Firm
Post-closing Trial Balance
November 30, 1983

	DEBIT	CREDIT
Cash	$ 900	
Accounts receivable	500	
Prepaid insurance	1100	
Office furniture	2000	
Accounts payable		$ 600
Wages payable		150
Bill Hunt, capital		3750
	$4500	$4500

The post-closing trial balance is the final accounting cycle step. The "equality" of debit and credit account balances gives the law firm some assurance that no errors were made in its accounting records during the period. The Hunt Law Firm is now ready to repeat the accounting cycle for its next accounting period.

Concluding Comments on the Accounting Cycle

Since the major objective in performing the nine accounting cycle steps is to enable a company to prepare its financial statements as well as update the dollar balances of its general ledger accounts, the length of the cycle is determined by how often these statements are prepared during the year. If monthly financial statements are desired, then the accounting cycle is repeated every month. On the other hand, if a firm prepares only annual financial statements, the accounting cycle is performed yearly. There are, however, exceptions to this rule, which specific companies incorporate into their accounting systems. For example, certain organizations may prepare monthly financial statements without going through the formal process of recording and posting their closing journal entries each month. Rather, the organizations wait until year-end to journalize and post the closing entries. The monthly performance of the accounting cycle would thus involve only steps 1 through 7 (step 7 being the preparation of the financial statements from the adjusted trial balance). Then, at the end of the year, accounting cycle steps 8 and 9 (involving the closing entry process and the post-closing trial balance) would also be performed along with steps 1 through 7.

Some business firms utilize what is called a *work sheet* to help them perform their periodic accounting cycle more efficiently. In this last section of the chapter, we will briefly examine the incorporation of the work sheet into an organization's accounting cycle activities.

Work Sheet Approach for Preparing Financial Statements

A work sheet is an optional device used by an organization to accumulate and organize monetary data. The information on the work sheet is necessary for the subsequent preparation of the company's formal financial statements that are read by investors, etc. In effect, the work sheet is simply a sheet of paper, divided into columns, which enables accountants to *informally* prepare organizations' adjusting entries, adjusted trial balance, and the resultant financial statements. Using a work sheet is analogous to working a homework problem on scratch paper before transferring the final solution to a clean piece of paper.

Let us assume that the Shiny Disk Company (which sells stereo albums, etc.) elects to use a work sheet within its accounting cycle to aid the process involved in preparing its November 1983 financial statements. Exhibit 3-6 on page 72 illustrates the company's work sheet (the dollar amounts are assumed) for the month of November (explanations will immediately follow).

The work sheet's first two columns reflect the Shiny Disk Company's *trial balance*, which tests the equality of debit and credit account balances from the general ledger. Thus, these two work sheet columns represent the performance of accounting cycle step 4 (preparing a trial balance). As discussed in the chapter, the next accounting cycle activity (step 5) would involve the recording of adjusting entries in the company's journal. Rather than formally journalizing the adjusting entries at this point, however, the required adjustments are entered directly in the two columns provided within the work sheet. The Shiny Disk Company recorded two adjusting journal entries at the end of November. These two adjustments are numbered, and a brief explanation of each one is provided at the bottom of the work sheet. The debit and credit columns of the adjustments are totaled to check their equality. If an adjusting entry requires an account not previously reflected on the trial balance, it is inserted below the other trial balance financial items. Since the expense account "office supplies expense" and the liability account "wages payable" are needed for the company's adjustments, these two accounts are added below the existing accounts on the trial balance.

Exhibit 3-6

Shiny Disk Company
Work Sheet
For the Month Ended November 30, 1983

	TRIAL BALANCE		ADJUSTMENTS		ADJUSTED TRIAL BALANCE		INCOME STATEMENT		BALANCE SHEET	
	DEBIT	CREDIT	DEBIT	CREDIT	DEBIT	CREDIT	DEBIT	CREDIT	DEBIT	CREDIT
Cash	$ 3,000				$ 3,000				$ 3,000	
Accounts receivable	500				500				500	
Merchandise inventory	8,000				8,000				8,000	
Office supplies	400			(1) $100	300				300	
Office equipment	9,000				9,000				9,000	
Accounts payable		$ 6,000				$ 6,000				$ 6,000
Carl Platter, capital		12,450				12,450				12,450
Revenue from stereo album sales		15,000				15,000		$15,000		
Cost of stereo albums sold	7,000				7,000		$ 7,000			
Wages expense	5,000		(2) $800		5,800		5,800			
Rent expense	400				400		400			
Utilities expense	100				100		100			
Insurance expense	50				50		50			
	$33,450	$33,450								
Office supplies expense			(1) 100		100		100			
Wages payable				(2) 800		800				800
			$900	$900	$34,250	$34,250	$13,450	$15,000	$20,800	$19,250
Net income							1,550			1,550
							$15,000	$15,000	$20,800	$20,800

(1) Adjusting entry for office supplies used.
(2) Adjusting entry for accrued employee wages.

The end objective of accounting cycle step 6 is to report a company's updated account balances in an *adjusted trial balance.* To accomplish this objective, the adjusting journal entries recorded in cycle step 5 must be posted to general ledger accounts, followed by a determination of the updated general ledger account balances. The use of a work sheet enables a company to prepare its adjusted trial balance without having to immediately journalize and post its adjusting entries. As shown in Exhibit 3-6, the Shiny Disk Company's adjusted trial balance is prepared on the two work sheet columns following the two columns for adjustments. The updated balances of those accounts affected by adjustments are thus reported in this trial balance (for example, the "office supplies" asset account has an updated balance of $300—$400 debit balance prior to an adjustment *minus* $100 credit in the work sheet adjustments section). The financial items appearing in the adjusted trial balance columns are then transferred to the work sheet columns representing the company's financial statements. Those accounts that appear on the income statement (revenues and expenses) are transferred to the income statement work sheet columns, and those accounts that appear on the balance sheet (assets, liabilities, and owner's equity) are transferred to the balance sheet columns.

Directing your attention to the income statement columns, it can be seen that the *debit* column reflects expenses and the *credit* column reflects revenues. The $15,000 credit column total exceeds the $13,450 debit column total by $1,550 (which is the Shiny Disk Company's November net income). To complete the income statement columns of the work sheet, the $1,550 is then added to the debit column so that both columns are equal. (This process is simply called "balancing-down the columns" since the debit and credit column balances are made equal to one another.)

The *debit* column of the balance sheet portion of the work sheet is for listing the company's assets, which total $20,800. The balance sheet *credit* column is for reporting the interests in these assets, the liabilities and the owner's equity (which total $19,250). However, Carl Platter's $12,450 ownership equity in the company's assets does not include his $1,550 increased interest resulting from the November net income. This $1,550 net income (computed in the income statement columns of the work sheet) is then added to the balance sheet credit column to reflect Platter's increased ownership equity in his company's assets. After adding the net income to the credit column, the debit and credit columns equal one another and these two balance sheet columns are thus "in balance."

Upon completing the Shiny Disk Company's work sheet, its formal income statement and balance sheet can then be prepared (step 7 of the accounting cycle) directly from the income statement and balance sheet columns. The work sheet's principal advantage is that it enables a business firm to accumulate and organize the financial data required for its income statement and balance sheet reports in a shorter amount of time at the end of an accounting period than if a work sheet were not utilized. As a result, the firm can provide more timely financial statement decision-making information to its management, creditors, potential investors, etc. What allows a company who uses a work sheet approach to prepare these timelier financial statements is the fact that the formal performance of accounting cycle steps 5 (recording adjusting entries in a journal) and 6 (posting adjusting journal entries to general ledger accounts and determining the updated account balances that appear on the adjusted trial balance) is temporarily delayed (except for the adjusted trial balance preparation phase of cycle step 6) until after the financial statements are prepared. The company's adjusting journal entries are recorded directly on the work sheet along with the adjusted trial balance data needed to prepare the end-of-period financial statements.

After the financial statements are prepared from the work sheet information, the company's accountant can then formally record and post the adjusting journal entries (and also compute within the general ledger the updated balances of those accounts affected by the adjusting entries) directly from the adjustments section of the work sheet. Upon completing this accounting work relating to adjusting entries, accounting cycle steps 8 (recording and posting the closing journal entries as well as determining the new balances of those accounts affected by the closing entries) and 9 (preparing a post-closing trial balance) would be performed in their usual manner in order to finish the period's accounting cycle activities.

Some accountants take a further shortcut when using a work sheet. They omit the "Adjusted Trial Balance" on the work sheet entirely (the middle two columns). Instead, they extend accounts (after *adjustments*) directly across either to the income statement or to the balance sheet columns of the work sheet. This is merely another example of simplification by accountants for efficiency and timesaving.

Review Questions

At this point, answer the following multiple-choice questions to test your knowledge of the previous reading material. The solutions are given below.

1. A $500 net income has what effect on a company's balance sheet?
   a. *Increases* the owner's equity by $500.
   b. *Decreases* the assets by $500.
   c. *Increases* the liabilities by $500.
   d. *Increases* the expenses by $500.

2. What is the correct closing entry for a company's $800 "rent expense" account balance?
   a. Cash   800
         Rent expense   800

b. Rent expense		800	
	Owner's equity account		800
c. Rent expense		800	
	Income summary		800
d. Income summary		800	
	Rent expense		800

3. What type of account does not appear in a post-closing trial balance?
   a. Asset account.
   b. Liability account.
   c. Revenue account.
   d. Owner's equity account.

4. The end objective of the accounting cycle is:
   a. To enable a company to prepare its financial statements.
   b. To enable a company to prepare closing entries each accounting period.
   c. To establish the equality of total debits and credits within a company's general ledger accounts.
   d. To transfer the debits and credits of journal entries to correct general ledger accounts.

5. A work sheet is:
   a. An optional device which may be used within a company's accounting cycle activities.
   b. Required in the performance of a company's accounting cycle activities.
   c. An important financial statement prepared by a company for external parties.
   d. A substitute for a company's general ledger.

Answers

1. a

2. d

3. c

4. a

5. a

Chapter Summary

We have now completed the step-by-step analysis of the accounting cycle. In the discussion of steps 5 through 9, the concept of *adjusting entries* was analyzed thoroughly. The need for adjusting entries is based upon two important accounting concepts: *periodicity* and *matching*. To transfer revenues and expenses to the owner's equity account at the end of an accounting period, closing entries are recorded and posted.

The sequence in performing the last five accounting cycle steps is:

Step 5. Recording adjusting entries in a journal.

Step 6. Posting adjusting journal entries to the general ledger, determining updated general ledger account balances, and preparing an adjusted trial balance.

Step 7. Preparing financial statements from adjusted trial balance.

Step 8. Recording closing entries in a journal, posting them to the general ledger, and determining new balances of those accounts affected by closing entries.

Step 9. Preparing a post-closing trial balance.

This chapter also introduced the reader to an optional device, called the *work sheet*, that may be utilized within a business firm's accounting cycle to help prepare its end-of-period financial statements. The work sheet helps a company accumulate and organize the monetary data that will be reported on its financial statements. Since adjusting entries are reflected directly on the work sheet rather than initially recording them in the journal and then posting each adjustment to the correct general ledger accounts (and determining the updated general ledger account balances), the company is able to prepare its financial statements much faster at the end of an accounting period by incorporating a work sheet approach into the accounting cycle. The shorter time span required at period-end to prepare the financial statements will enable an organization to provide more timely financial information for decision-making to interested parties such as management and creditors.

Chapter Problem

The solution to the following problem is given in the appendix. However, the reader is urged first to attempt to work the problem on his own and then to check his work against the given solution.

Problem Situation

The Kool Playhouse is a theatrical production company presenting dramatic plays throughout the year. Within the company's accounting system, financial statements are prepared monthly. Assume that the current date is October 31, 1983, and that the Kool Playhouse wants to prepare its October financial statements.

Problem Requirements

Complete the requirements specified in parts a and b of each financial activity.

1. The employees of the Kool Playhouse earn total weekly salaries of $5000, which are paid to the employees each Friday afternoon. The employees' salaries are based upon a five-day work week from Monday through Friday. The salaries expense of the Kool Playhouse is ordinarily recorded in the company's journal every Friday afternoon when the salaries are actually paid to the employees. October 31, 1983 falls on a Thursday.
   a. Prepare the *adjusting entry* required in the Kool Playhouse's journal on October 31, 1983 (the close of the accounting period) for the salaries owed to its employees.
   b. Prepare the *entry* in the Kool Playhouse's journal for the actual payment of the week's salaries to the employees on Friday, November 1, 1983 (the first day of the new accounting period).

2. The Kool Playhouse leases the building where its theatrical plays are performed. On October 1, 1983, the Kool Playhouse paid one year's rent of $2400 to its landlord. This $2400 payment covers the period from October 1, 1983 to October 1, 1984.
   a. Prepare the *entry* in the Kool Playhouse's journal on October 1, 1983 for the $2400 rent payment to its landlord.
   b. Prepare the *adjusting entry* required in the Kool Playhouse's journal on October 31, 1983 (the close of the accounting period) as a result of utilizing the rented building during the month of October.

3. The Kool Playhouse offers its theater patrons (customers) a ticket package plan whereby a customer can purchase at one time tickets to several future plays at a reduced cost compared to the regular price per ticket. On October 7, 1983 the Kool Playhouse received $6000 cash from the sale of theater tickets for its drama series consisting of five different plays. The five plays included in this series will be presented on the following dates (assume that the $6000 is apportioned equally among the five plays):

Play A	October	10–17
Play B	October	20–27
Play C	November	4–10
Play D	November	14–20
Play E	November	24–30

   a. Prepare the *entry* in the Kool Playhouse's journal on October 7, 1983 for the $6,000 cash received from the drama series ticket sales.
   b. Prepare the *adjusting entry* required in the Kool Playhouse's journal on October 31, 1983 (the close of the accounting period) as a result of the drama series plays that were actually performed during the month of October.

4. The Kool Playhouse owns a small office building across town which is rented to the Plymouth Company at $450 a month. The Plymouth Company ordinarily pays the rent on the first day of each month. However, on October 1, 1983 the Plymouth Company is having some financial problems and received permission from the Kool Playhouse to pay the October rent one month late. Both the October and November rent will be paid by the Plymouth Company on November 1, 1983.

   a. Prepare the *adjusting entry* required in the Kool Playhouse's journal on October 31, 1983 (the close of the accounting period) for the October rent due from the Plymouth Company.

   b. Prepare the *entry* in the Kool Playhouse's journal on November 1, 1983 (the first day of the new accounting period) for the collection of both the October and November rent from the Plymouth Company.

5. On October 1, 1983 the Kool Playhouse had $300 worth of office supplies on hand from the previous month. Additional office supplies were purchased for $500 cash on October 9, 1983. As of October 31, 1983 the Kool Playhouse determined that $200 worth of its office supplies were used during October.

   a. Prepare the *entry* in the Kool Playhouse's journal on October 9, 1983 for the $500 cash purchase of office supplies.

   b. Prepare the *adjusting entry* required in the Kool Playhouse's journal on October 31, 1983 (the close of the accounting period) for the $200 worth of office supplies used in October.

Problem Objective and Solution Approach

Objective:

Based upon the periodicity and matching concepts, develop an understanding of the interrelationship between regular journal entries during an accounting period and adjusting journal entries at the end of an accounting period so that a company's period-end financial statements will be more accurate.

Solution Approach:

1. Analyze each financial activity and make the necessary mathematical computations to correctly reflect the activity.

2. Recognize the financial effects of each activity in the company's accounting system by recording the correct journal entries during October and November as well as the correct adjusting entries at the end of October.

4

Financial Statement Analysis

Cash and Accounts Receivable

Before proceeding, the reader should have a general understanding of financial statements (Chapter 1) and the accounting cycle, which accumulates relevant information for the preparation of financial statements (Chapters 2 and 3). Beginning with this chapter and concluding with Chapter 8, individual balance sheet and income statement items are analyzed in considerable depth. This will give the reader a good understanding of financial statement components. The approach used is first to analyze the current asset section of the balance sheet in Chapters 4, 5, and 6 (including a discussion of current and long-term liabilities in Chapter 6) followed by a discussion of long-term assets in Chapters 7 and 8. (Current and long-term financial items are defined in the next section of this chapter.) In addition, various revenue and expense items that appear on an income statement and are closely associated with the specific assets and liabilities discussed in Chapters 4 through 8 are analyzed.

Classified Balance Sheet

The balance sheets illustrated previously were oversimplified to illustrate the basic concept of this financial statement. A *classified* balance sheet (the form in which a balance sheet is often prepared) is a more sophisticated presentation method and provides better information. Exhibit 4-1 illustrates the classified balance sheet of the John Lyle Company on December 31, 1983.

Exhibit 4-1

John Lyle Company
Balance Sheet
December 31, 1983

	ASSETS			*LIABILITIES & OWNER'S EQUITY*		
Current assets:			Current liabilities:			
Cash	$ 8,000		Accounts payable	$ 7,000		
Accounts receivable	7,000		Notes payable	4,000		
Merchandise			Wages payable	2,750		
inventory	12,000		Total current liabilities		$ 13,750	
Prepaid insurance	500					
Total current assets		$ 27,500	Long-term liabilities:			
			Mortgage payable	$40,000		
Long-term assets:			Long-term note			
Land	$15,000		payable	3,000		
Building	70,000		Total long-term liabilities		43,000	
Total long-term assets		85,000	Total liabilities		$ 56,750	
			Owner's equity:			
			Lyle, capital,			
			Jan. 1, 1983	$40,000		
			Plus: Net income			
			for 1983	15,750		
			Lyle, capital,			
			Dec. 31, 1983		55,750	
			Total liabilities and			
Total assets		$112,500	owner's equity		$112,500	

The asset side includes *current assets* and *long-term assets* (also called "fixed assets" or "plant and equipment assets"). *Current assets* are already in the form of cash or are expected to be converted into cash or consumed within approximately a one-year period. Prepaid expenses are current assets, since they have been paid in advance and will be consumed (thereby becoming expenses) within approximately one year.

The current assets are listed on the balance sheet in their order of *liquidity*. Liquidity means how quickly the assets can be converted into cash. Since a prepaid expense is not converted into cash, the Lyle Company's prepaid insurance item is therefore the last item in the balance sheet's current asset section.

Long-term assets are permanent-type assets that are not expected to be converted into cash within a one-year time period. For example, a building is a long-term asset, since a company may estimate that its building can be used for at least fifty years.

The liability side of the balance sheet is classified into current and long-term liabilities. *Current liabilities* are expected to be paid within approximately a one-year period, whereas *long-term liabilities* are due for payment beyond one year. If a company borrows money from the bank on January 30, 1983, and signs a three-year note (a note payable) due January 30, 1986, the "note payable" is classified as a long-term liability on the 1983 and 1984 year-end balance sheets. However, on the 1985 year-end balance sheet, the note payable would be reclassified as a current liability, since payment is now due within a one-year period.

The reason for classifying assets and liabilities as either current or long-term is to provide financial statement readers more useful information about a company's financial condition. Many significant analyses can be made from a classified balance sheet. Financial statement analysis is discussed in advanced accounting books. However, a short example is presented at this point.

When a company needs cash and applies to a bank for a short-term loan (for example, a 90-day loan), one of the major concerns of the bank in approving the loan is the ability of the company to pay back the borrowed cash *plus* interest. A well-run business organization is expected to pay its current debts (liabilities) with its current assets. If a company has insufficient current assets to pay current liabilities as they become due, the company may be forced to quickly sell some of its long-term assets to raise cash. This would be a very unfortunate situation, since long-term assets are not originally purchased with the intent of quickly converting them into cash to pay off maturing current liabilities.

Before a bank grants a short-term loan, it normally examines a company's *current ratio.* This figure is computed by dividing *current assets* by *current liabilities.* The current ratio gives the bank an indication of the company's ability to pay its current liabilities as they mature. The Lyle Company's current ratio is 2 to 1 (See Exhibit 4-1. Current assets *divided by* current liabilities = $27,500 *divided by* $13,750 = 2 to 1.) This means that for every $1 of current liabilities, the company has $2 of current assets to cover the eventual payments. A 2-to-1 current ratio is adequate for most companies. However, it is difficult to generalize about the strength or weakness of a particular ratio. It depends largely upon the specific operating characteristics of each company as to whether a certain ratio is good or bad. The important point of this example is that the presentation of assets and liabilities into current and long-term categories enables a better analysis of a company's financial activities.

Management has a responsibility to maintain a stable financial condition in its organization. If management is incurring too many short-term liabilities without sufficient current assets to cover the debts, the company's financial future may be in danger. Before a business operating decision is made, management should consider the effects of the decision on its company's current ratio. For example, if a potential transaction involving the incurrence of a large current liability to purchase equipment would cause a weakened current ratio, management should examine other possible alternatives to finance the equipment purchase.

Internal Control

This concept is concerned with various methods and procedures developed within a business organization (1) to safeguard its assets against improper use and theft, (2) to enable accuracy in accounting data, and (3) to insure efficient and effective business operations that contribute toward achieving the goals and objectives established by management.

The concept of an accounting system was briefly discussed in Chapter 1. It was emphasized that a business system must be established that provides relevant information concerning a company's operating activities. A system includes the designing of forms (sales invoices, purchase orders, inventory records, etc.) to accumulate relevant data about business activities. It also assigns employees to perform various organizational functions (the inventory purchase function, the selling function, the accounting function, etc.). Finally, a system controls the flow of data through an organization so that relevant information is provided to internal and external parties.

Included within a company's system design should be internal controls that contribute to operating efficiency and effectiveness. An important internal control is competent, highly trained employees. Since people must operate a system, it is very important that employees be adequately trained and able to perform efficiently in the established business system. The best planned system "on paper" is not effective in actual practice unless the employees are capable of efficiently performing their assigned duties and responsibilities.

A good internal control system safeguards a company's assets against *misuse* and *theft*. Misuse of a company's machinery, for example, can probably be prevented by training the employees to correctly operate the machines and by a regular maintenance program on the machinery. Internal control to prevent the theft of assets requires separation of duties between the employee who maintains physical custody of the assets and the employee who performs the record-keeping function. For example, an employee handling a company's cash should not also have access to the accounting records. Through this *separation of duties*, one employee acts as a check on the work of the other. If a cashier attempts an embezzlement, he will not be able to manipulate the accounting records to cover up his theft. Also, the employee performing the record-keeping function is unable to embezzle cash, since he does not have access to the actual cash. Thus, it is hoped that the separation-of-duty aspect of internal control prevents the theft of cash and, as a result, contributes toward overall operating efficiency in an organization. A cashier and bookkeeper could devise a collusive method to embezzle cash. However, the risk of theft is less with separation of duties in the cash-handling and record-keeping functions.

This brief discussion emphasizes the importance of controls within a company. Additional internal control aspects of a business organization are analyzed later.

Current Asset—Cash

Cash is the most liquid of a company's assets. It includes coins and currency, money in a savings account, and money in a checking account.

A Checking Account: An Important Internal Control

We have emphasized that it is important to have separation of employee duties with regard to the custody of assets and the record keeping. The separation-of-duty concept is especially important for cash because of its high liquidity. Cash is easily transferable from one person to another, and unless a company has good internal control over cash transactions, an embezzlement can occur.

A business organization ordinarily establishes a bank checking account to handle the majority of its cash transactions. The proper use of a checking account contributes to good internal control over cash activities. As cash receipts are collected, they should be deposited intact each day. This results in less opportunity for embezzlement by dishonest employees, since the cash is not allowed to accumulate in the company's office, where it could be misappropriated. Another positive internal control aspect of daily bank deposits is that a company has outside verification of its cash receipts. By comparing the cash receipts shown in the accounting records with the cash deposits indicated on the monthly bank statement, the company can ascertain that all cash receipts are correctly deposited. An additional element of good internal control over cash transactions is that cash disbursements be made by *check*. A check is a written instrument ordering the bank to pay a designated quantity of money to someone. For stronger internal control, some companies require two individuals to sign cash disbursement checks. An advantage of using checks rather than coins and currency is that the former provide written proof of cash disbursement dollar amounts. All checks should be prenumbered to enable a company to maintain a record of both its issued and unissued checks.

Before a check is signed for the payment of a bill, all supporting documents relating to the cash disbursement should be examined by the check signer (or signers) to establish the authenticity of the dollar amount owed. The supporting documents for a cash disbursement are called *vouchers*. For example, the treasurer of the Wayne Kelley Sporting Goods Company is asked to sign a $300 check to the Arvin Company for merchandise purchased. Before signing the check, the treasurer should examine the following supporting documents to establish that the $300 is for a legitimate purchase of merchandise:

1. A copy of the *purchase order* prepared by the Kelley Company's purchasing department when the merchandise was originally ordered from the Arvin Company. The purchase order indicates the company's intent to buy the merchandise at a specified cost.

2. A copy of the *receiving report* prepared by the shipping and receiving department when the merchandise was delivered. Upon arrival of the merchandise, the receiving department would have unpacked the goods and listed the types and quantities on the receiving report.

3. A copy of the *purchase invoice* from the Arvin Company indicating the dollar amount owed. The purchase invoice should be compared to the purchase order and the receiving report before the treasurer signs the $300 check.

The Bank Reconciliation Statement

An organization's checking account balance represents an asset claim against the bank. The bank increases the checking account balance each time a deposit is made and decreases the balance when an organization issues a check to pay a debt.

The bank typically mails a depositor a monthly statement indicating the increases and decreases to the depositor's account. In addition, the bank statement shows the depositor's end-of-month checking account balance. Enclosed with the monthly bank statement are all the checks written by an organization that have *cleared* the bank during the month, duplicate copies of deposit slips, and any other supporting documents indicating increases or decreases to the account. Checks paid by the bank for its depositor and therefore considered to have cleared the bank are called *cancelled checks*, since those checks cannot be reissued again.

When a depositor receives his monthly bank statement, the information on the statement should be compared to the depositor's own checking account records. Ideally, the bank's records (represented by the monthly bank statement) and the depositor's records should agree.

There are two major causes for a difference in the bank's and the depositor's records regarding the latter's month-end checking account balance:

1. A *timing* difference between when the depositor records a checking account activity and when the bank records the activity.

2. *Errors* by either the depositor or the bank in recording checking account activities.

Whenever the month-end bank statement balance differs from a company's checking account records, the company should determine the causes by preparing a *bank reconciliation statement*. For good internal control, the statement should be prepared by a company employee who does not record cash transactions. If the employee responsible for the cash accounting records also prepares the monthly bank reconciliation statement, this employee could attempt to conceal cash shortages by falsifying the reconciliation statement.

Illustration of a Bank Reconciliation Statement

The Wayne Kelley Sporting Goods Company began business on January 1, 1983, and opened a checking account on this same date at the Hawaiian Municipal Bank.

When the Kelley Company received its January 31, 1983 bank statement, the bank reconciliation statement in Exhibit 4-2 was prepared. (Explanations of the various reconciling items are presented immediately after the reconciliation statement.)

The first step when one is preparing the bank reconciliation statement is to match financial items recorded in the company's records against those on the bank statement. The financial items that are different on the company's records compared to the bank statement appear in the reconciliation.

The left column of the bank reconciliation statement begins with the final balance on the January 31 bank statement (which was $128). Next, the deposits in the company's accounting records are matched against the deposits shown on the bank statement. The Kelley Company's records indicate a $200 deposit on January 30, which does not appear on the January bank statement. This $200 deposit is a reconciling item caused by a *timing* difference in recording the transaction. The company mailed the deposit to the bank on January 30. However, the time delay until the bank actually received the $200 caused the deposit to be unrecorded by the bank in

Exhibit 4-2

Wayne Kelley Sporting Goods Company
Bank Reconciliation Statement
January 31, 1983

Balance per bank statement, Jan. 31.	$128	Balance per Kelley Company's records, Jan. 31.	$233

Add:		Deduct:	
Deposit of Jan. 30, not recorded by bank in January (deposit in transit).	200	Check received by Kelley Company on Jan. 15 for a prior sale and shown on bank statement as a	
	$328	Jan. 17 deposit. The maker of the check, the Bird	
Deduct:		Company, did not have	
Checks written by Kelley Company in January, but not clearing the bank by the end of January (outstanding checks).		sufficient funds in its account to cover the check. The check was therefore charged back to the Kelley Company on Jan. 29.	$50
Check no. 5 $ 50			
Check no. 6 100	150	Bank service charge on Jan. 31.	2
		Error by Kelley Company in recording check no. 1. This check was recorded in the company's accounting records at $27, whereas the correct amount of the check that cleared the bank on Jan. 10 was $30 ($30 minus $27 = $3 error in Kelley Company's records). 3	55
Adjusted balance per bank statement, Jan. 31.	$178	Adjusted balance per Kelley Company's records, Jan. 31.	$178

January. Therefore, since the company's records indicate a $200 *increase* in its checking account balance but the bank's records do not reflect this increase, the $200 deposit is *added* to the bank balance to reconcile the item. When Kelley Company receives the February bank statement, it should find the $200 appearing as a deposit within the first few days of February. As a result, the $200 deposit will not be a reconciling item when the February bank reconcilation statement is prepared. This is true because both the company and the bank have now recorded the deposit.

The checks written during January are now *matched* against the checks that cleared the bank. Check numbers 5 and 6 recorded by the company do not appear on the bank statement. Therefore, to reconcile the bank and company records, these two checks are *subtracted* from the bank balance. Cash disbursement checks 5 and 6 are called "outstanding checks," because they have not yet reached the Hawaiian Municipal Bank for payment. Consequently, the January 31 "balance per bank statement" does not include a reduction for these two checks. When the February bank statement is received, the company can determine if check numbers 5 and 6 cleared the bank. If the checks have cleared, they are no longer reconciling items, since both the company and the bank have now recorded the cash disbursement checks. However, if either or both of these checks are still outstanding by the end of February, they would again appear on the February bank reconciliation statement. If a check remains outstanding for a long time period (six months, for example), the company should ask the check recipient why the check has not been cashed. After the $178 adjusted bank balance has been determined, the right column of the bank reconciliation statement is then prepared. This column starts with the Kelley Company's unadjusted checking account balance on January 31 (which was $233).

On January 15, the Kelley Sporting Goods Company received a $50 check from a customer and recorded the $50 as a deposit. This deposit appears as an *increase* in the company's checking account balance on the January bank statement. At this point, both the company and the bank records agree with regard to the $50 deposit. However, the bank is notified on January 29 that the individual who wrote the $50 check to the Kelley Company does not have enough cash in his account to cover the check (called an NSF check, meaning "not sufficient funds"). Since the bank previously increased the Kelley Company's balance on January 17 for the $50 check, the bank decreases the company's account on January 29. The Kelley Company is unaware of this $50 bank deduction until it receives the January bank statement. Therefore, to reconcile its records to the bank's, the company *deducts* $50 from its January 31 checking account balance. It is the Kelley Company's responsibility to attempt to collect the money from the individual who wrote the bad check.

The $2 bank service charge is another item appearing in the bank reconciliation statement. This $2 was *deducted* by the bank on January 31 but not by the company during January. As a result, the $2 service charge is *subtracted* from the company's January 31 unadjusted account balance.

On January 5, the Kelley Company recorded check number 1 for $27, whereas the correct amount of the check was $30. This check cleared the bank on January 10. Because the Kelley Company *understated* its cash disbursement check by $3, the bank reconciliation statement reflects a $3 reduction from the company's unadjusted January 31 balance.

After all adjustments have been made, the company's checking account balance is $178 (which equals the adjusted bank balance). The bank reconciliation is now finished, since the Kelley Company has explained the difference between its accounting records and the bank statement.

Required Journal Entries Based Upon the Bank Reconciliation Statement:

Presented below are the Kelley Company's journal entries on January 31 for the items in the bank reconciliation statement (explanations will follow):

January 31	Accounts receivable	50	
	Cash		50
	(To establish an account receivable against the customer whose check failed to clear the bank)		
31	Bank service charge expense (or Miscellaneous expense)	2	
	Cash		2
	(To recognize expense for January bank service charge)		
31	Accounts payable	3	
	Cash		3
	(To correct the error in recording check #1)		

Journal entries are required for only the items affecting the "Balance per Kelley Company's records, January 31" in the bank reconciliation statement (see Exhibit 4-2). The bank will eventually make entries for those financial items listed under the "Balance per bank statement, January 31" section of the reconciliation statement. For example, the $200 "deposit in transit" has already been recorded in the company's accounting records. When the bank receives this deposit during February, it will record the *increase* in the company's checking account balance. The same logic applies to the "outstanding checks" *subtracted* from the bank statement balance. The Kelley Company recorded checks 5 and 6 (the outstanding checks) as January cash disbursements. Thus, no further journal entries are required in the company's accounting records. The bank will reduce the company's account balance when these two checks are presented for payment by the check recipients.

The first journal entry establishes an account receivable asset claim against the customer whose check did not clear the bank because of insufficient funds. The bank has already reduced the Kelley Company's checking account balance for the $50 NSF check. Therefore, the *credit* side of this journal entry reflects the reduction in the company's cash balance.

The second journal entry recognizes the company's January *expense* from receiving bank checking account privileges.

Cash disbursement check 1 (for an account payable liability) was originally recorded at $27 rather than the $30 actual amount. The third journal entry corrects the company's accounting records for this $3 error. The accounts payable account is *debited* for $3, since it was previously debited for only $27 instead of $30. The $3 *credit* to "cash" reduces this account to the correct balance based upon the $30 check actually issued.

Petty Cash Fund

Good internal control necessitates that cash disbursements be made by check. However, a company may have various *small* cash expenditures to make during an accounting period. It is more efficient to issue *cash* for these expenditures rather than to follow the formal company procedure to have a check approved. For example, an executive may want the company car washed. This expenditure is so small (perhaps $2) that the time required to have a cash disbursement check prepared and signed would not be justified.

For such small expenditures, a company may use a *petty cash fund*. To achieve good internal control, one employee, called the petty cash custodian, is given the responsibility for handling the petty cash fund. The cash should be kept under the custodian's control (perhaps in a locked box), and he should be the only individual having access to the fund. The journal entry to establish a company's $50 petty cash fund is

Petty cash fund	50	
Cash		50

As needs arise for small expenditures, the individual requesting the cash goes to the petty cash custodian. The custodian then prepares a receipt (called a *petty cash voucher*), which is signed by the person obtaining the cash. For example, assume that John Peterson is the petty cash custodian for the Wayne Kelley Sporting Goods Company and that the petty cash fund was initially established for $50. A messenger boy delivers a telegram for which $3 is due. Rather than having a $3 check approved, it is more efficient to pay the $3 from the petty cash fund. Exhibit 4-3 is the petty cash receipt voucher prepared by John Peterson and signed by the messenger boy for the payment of the $3.

No accounting entry is recorded for the $3 payment. Rather, the custodian places the petty cash receipt in his petty cash box to represent evidence of the $3 telegram payment. The same procedure is followed for other disbursements from the petty cash fund. Thus, at any point in time, the custodian will have so many dollars of actual cash in the petty cash box *plus* receipts for cash issued from the fund. The Kelley Company's petty cash custodian should always have cash *plus* voucher receipts totaling $50.

Exhibit 4-3

```
┌─────────────────────────────────────────────────────────────────┐
│                        Petty Cash Receipt                         │
│                                                                   │
│   Receipt Number ___4___              Date __February 26, 1983__  │
│                                                                   │
│   Paid to _____Honolulu Telegraph Company_____                   │
│                                                                   │
│   For ____Telegram from the Ennis Supply Company___   Amount __$3.00__  │
│                                                                   │
│   DEBIT TO ____Telephone and Telegraph Expense___                 │
│                                                                   │
│                              Payment Approved By:                 │
│                                                                   │
│   Sam Moore   (Messenger Boy)      John Peterson                  │
└─────────────────────────────────────────────────────────────────┘
```

When the cash in the fund runs low, the petty cash custodian requests a reimbursement. This means to replace the accumulated petty cash receipts with cash. The custodian accumulates all the receipts and gives them to the treasurer. The treasurer examines the receipts and cancels each one by stamping it "PAID." Cash is then issued to the custodian for the total of all the cancelled receipts. Following reimbursement, the petty cash custodian again has $50 cash in the fund and is ready to continue issuing receipts for small cash disbursements. At the time the fund is reimbursed, a journal entry is recorded for the expenses paid from the petty cash box. If, for example, reimbursement to John Peterson totaled $40 for three categories of expenses, the following journal entry is made (The expense dollar amounts are assumed.):

Miscellaneous office expense	15	
Telephone and telegraph expense	20	
Entertainment expense	5	
Cash		40

At the end of an accounting period when a company updates its financial records by preparing adjusting entries, the petty cash fund is reimbursed regardless of the actual cash within the fund. This is necessary in order that the various expenses paid from the fund since the last reimbursement are included in the company's financial statements.

In the reimbursing entry, no debit or credit is made to the petty cash fund account. This account was initially established for $50 by debiting the petty cash fund account and crediting the cash account. As long as the company continues to maintain the fund at the same $50 level, the petty cash account is not debited or credited. The reimbursing entry has no effect on the petty cash account, since the various expense accounts are debited for the payments made from the fund and the cash account is credited to reestablish the fund at $50. However, if the Kelley Company decides to increase its petty cash fund from $50 to $75 (an increase of $25), the following journal entry is then recorded:

Petty cash fund	25	
Cash		25

The petty cash account balance is normally *small* compared to a company's other cash items. As a result, it is common business practice to combine the petty cash account with the other cash accounts on a company's balance sheet. In fact, most business organizations include all their cash items (coins and currency on hand, savings accounts, checking accounts, etc.) under the single account called "cash" on their balance sheets.

A concept in accounting called *materiality* justifies adding the petty cash account balance to the other cash items on a company's balance sheet. Since a material financial item is large in relation to other financial items, its monetary balance could influence decisions by financial statement readers. Therefore, all material monetary accounts should be fully disclosed on a company's financial statements. An immaterial item (the petty cash account, for example) is considered so small that its dollar balance will not affect financial decisions. Consequently, immaterial financial accounts do not require separate disclosure on financial statements.

Cash Planning by Management

Budgeting was briefly discussed in Chapter 1 as an important management planning and controlling mechanism. Through cash budgeting, a company attempts to project its future cash balance for each month of the coming year. Management will then be aware when the cash balance is either too large or too small. For example, a company does not earn an adequate return on its cash if too large a checking account balance is maintained at the bank. A cash budget informs management of those months when the checking account balance will be larger than needed to operate its business. Management can then make advance plans to invest this excess cash. A decision may be reached to purchase some United States government bonds (often referred to as "marketable securities"—a current asset) with the extra cash.

On the other hand, a cash budget will also disclose to management those months when its company's cash balance will be insufficient to handle business operating activities. Awareness of future cash shortages permits management to make advance arrangements to borrow cash.

Review Questions

At this point, answer the following multiple-choice questions to test your knowledge of the previous reading material. The solutions are given below.

1. Where on a company's balance sheet is a note payable due in 90 days classified?
   a. A current asset.
   b. A long-term asset.
   c. A long-term liability.
   d. A current liability.

2. For good internal control, the cashier of a company should not:
   a. Be responsible for the cash accounting records.
   b. Be an employee of the company.
   c. Be responsible for making change from the cash register.
   d. Be adequately trained to perform his function.

3. On a bank reconciliation statement, outstanding checks are
   a. *Added* to the bank statement balance.
   b. *Subtracted* from the bank statement balance.
   c. *Added* to the checking account balance in the company's records.
   d. *Subtracted* from the checking account balance in the company's records.

4. When are petty cash fund expenditures recognized in a company's accounting records?
   a. A cash expenditure is made from the fund.
   b. A petty cash voucher receipt is prepared.
   c. The petty cash custodian places a voucher receipt in his locked box.
   d. The petty cash fund is reimbursed.

Answers

1. d

2. a

3. b

4. d

Current Asset—Accounts Receivable

Accounts receivable typically result from a company's sales of merchandise for which the purchaser agrees to pay within so many days following the sale. A very popular buying method today is through the use of a credit card. The consumer goes into a store and purchases some merchandise. Rather than paying cash immediately, the purchaser charges the merchandise on his credit card. He usually pays the amount owed within 30 to 60 days after the purchase. From the seller's point of view, this sale is called a "sale on account" (meaning that an *account receivable* is established against the buyer) or a "credit sale."

Assume that Howard Hawk purchases $100 of merchandise from the Seth Company and charges this purchase on his credit card. The Seth Company's journal entry for the sale is

Accounts receivable	100	
Sales		100

The "accounts receivable" represents a current asset that the company expects to collect in the near future (30 to 60 days). The *credit* to the sales account shows the revenue earned from the sale to Howard Hawk. When Mr. Hawk eventually mails his payment for the merchandise purchased, the Seth Company's journal entry would be

Cash	100	
Accounts receivable		100

The $100 *credit* to accounts receivable eliminates the asset claim against Howard Hawk, since he no longer owes the money to Seth Company.

For efficiency within a company, a "credit and collection department" is ordinarily established. Its responsibility is to investigate the financial background of individuals applying for credit cards. The company thereby has reasonable assurance that people who buy on credit will later pay their bills. The credit department establishes dollar limits for each customer so that the balance that he owes the company does not become excessive.

An organization with a large number of credit customers should maintain detailed records showing each customer's balance so that monthly bills can be mailed. The accounts receivable account does not disclose information concerning individual customer account balances. Rather, it shows the total monetary amount of all receivables. The purpose of an accounts receivable *subsidiary ledger* is to provide a record of each customer's balance. Exhibit 4-4 illustrates the Seth Company's accounts receivable general ledger account along with the subsidiary ledger of individual customer accounts.

It should be noted that the $400 balance of the accounts receivable general ledger account is equal to the total of the customer account balances within the subsidiary ledger. This equality is always true, since the subsidiary ledger information represents a detailed breakdown of the general ledger accounts receivable account. In fact, the general ledger accounts receivable account is often called a *control* account because it controls the details of the subsidiary ledger.

For good internal control, there should be a separation of duties in the accounts receivable record-keeping function. If one individual maintains the subsidiary ledger and another the accounts receivable general ledger

Exhibit 4-4

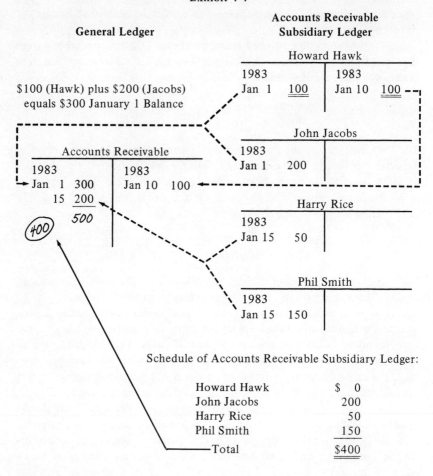

General Ledger

Accounts Receivable
Subsidiary Ledger

$100 (Hawk) plus $200 (Jacobs)
equals $300 January 1 Balance

Howard Hawk

1983		1983	
Jan 1	100	Jan 10	100

John Jacobs

1983	
Jan 1	200

Accounts Receivable

1983			1983	
Jan 1	300		Jan 10	100
15	200			
(400)	500			

Harry Rice

1983	
Jan 15	50

Phil Smith

1983	
Jan 15	150

Schedule of Accounts Receivable Subsidiary Ledger:

Howard Hawk	$ 0
John Jacobs	200
Harry Rice	50
Phil Smith	150
Total	$400

account, each person acts as a check on the other's work. The employee in charge of the subsidiary ledger can prepare a list of customer account balances and compare this total to the accounts receivable control account maintained by a different employee. If the two separately computed balances agree, there is strong evidence that the accounts receivable records are accurate.

Adjusting Entry Process for Estimated Uncollectible Accounts Receivable

As discussed in Chapter 3, adjusting entries are prepared at the close of an accounting period to update a company's financial records for unrecorded events that have occurred. Adjusting entries achieve a better matching of revenues earned against expenses incurred on an income statement.

Ideally, when a company makes credit sales, it expects to eventually collect the receivables. Before a customer is granted credit, the credit and collection department should investigate the customer's financial status and approve credit purchases only if it appears that he will pay on time. However, even with credit checks, it is a realistic fact of business life that some people will default on their accounts. The failure of credit customers to pay their account balances is one of the risks involved in operating a business organization.

Assume that the Wayne Kelley Sporting Goods Company closes its accounting records on December 31 to prepare yearly financial statements. The company had $6000 worth of credit sales during 1983. These sales will be recognized as earned revenue on the 1983 income statement. According to the matching concept, all the expenses incurred during 1983 to earn the $6000 revenue should be shown on the income statement in order that the net income (or net loss) can be determined. The company realizes that a portion of its $6000 credit sales will not be collected in the following year because of default by specific customers. The dollar quantity of uncollectible receivables represents an expense associated with earning the $6000 revenue. However, at the end of 1983 when the Kelley Company wants to prepare financial statements, it does not know all the specific customers who will eventually fail to pay their accounts. Therefore, the company should attempt to estimate the uncollectible portion of its 1983 credit sales in order that an "uncollectible accounts expense" can be matched against the $6000 revenue on the 1983 income statement. Since the $6000 worth of credit sales is recognized as earned revenue in 1983, the expense of eventually not collecting a portion of that earned revenue should also be recognized in 1983.

There are a few methods available for estimating a company's uncollectible accounts expense at the end of an accounting period. A popular one is called the "percentage of sales method."

Percentage of Sales Method (An Income Statement Approach)

When the percentage of sales method is used, the estimation of uncollectible accounts is based upon the sales account (an income statement account). To illustrate this method, we use the information concerning the Kelley Company's $6000 credit sales in 1983.

Organizations use various techniques when attempting to estimate their uncollectible accounts expense on the basis of credit sales. A common procedure is to review a company's credit and collection record over the past few years. With this knowledge, the company attempts to estimate the percentage of uncollectible accounts in the current year. Assume that on December 31, 1983, the Kelley Company estimates that 3 percent of its

1983 credit sales will probably be uncollectible. The following adjusting entry is then recorded on December 31:

Uncollectible accounts expense   180
Allowance for uncollectibles   180

The $180 (3 percent $\times$ $6000) uncollectible accounts expense appears on the 1983 income statement as an operating expense in order that a better matching of revenues earned against expenses incurred may be achieved. The allowance for uncollectibles is a *contra* account to the accounts receivable account, and its balance is *subtracted* from the latter. A contra account is directly related to another account, and the two accounts are shown together on the financial statements. At first glance you might think that the credit in the above entry should have been recorded directly to the accounts receivable account. However, since the company is only estimating its uncollectible accounts at year's end and does not know all the specific customers who will default on their accounts in the following year, the special contra account called "allowance for uncollectibles" is *credited*.

Illustrated below is the method used to disclose a company's accounts receivable information in the current asset section of its balance sheet (the dollar amounts are assumed):

Current assets:		
Cash		$ 1000
Accounts receivable	$3000	
Less: Allowance for uncollectibles	100	2900 ←
Merchandise inventory		8000
Prepaid expenses		500
Total current assets		$12,400

The $2900 appearing by the *arrow* is called the "net realizable value" of the accounts receivables. The net realizable value is what a company *realistically* expects to collect from its receivables. Remember, the allowance for uncollectibles account represents a company's estimation of its uncollectible receivables. Therefore, if the $100 balance of the allowance account is subtracted from the $3000 total receivables available for collection, the $2900 difference indicates the organization's receivables that it expects to eventually collect.

Journal Entry To Write Off a Specific Customer's Account

After all efforts have been made to collect a particular past-due account, a company records a journal entry to write off the customer's account. Continuing our example of the Wayne Kelley Sporting Goods Company, assume that the $50 account balance of Jack Billington is determined uncollectible in Feburary 1983. The journal entry to write off Billington's account is:

Allowance for uncollectibles	50	
Accounts receivable		50
(To write off the uncollectible		
account of Jack Billington)		

The reader should clearly understand that the above journal entry does not cause an expense for the Kelley Company. The expense for uncollectible accounts was already recognized in the adjusting entry at the end of 1983 to achieve a matching of revenues earned against expenses incurred on the 1983 income statement. Writing off a specific customer's uncollectible account causes two things to happen. First, the write off specifically confirms a portion of a company's original estimate of uncollectible accounts. Consequently, this causes the remaining balance of estimated uncollectible receivables to be smaller. Further, to reduce the allowance for uncollectibles account (which normally has a credit balance as a result of the end of period adjusting entry), it is *debited* in the journal entry.

Second, since the customer who defaulted in paying his account is known, the accounts receivable account can now be *credited* to indicate a reduction in the monetary balance of receivables still owed the company. In addition to crediting the general ledger accounts receivable control account, Billington's account within the company's accounts receivable subsidiary ledger should also be reduced for the uncollectible amount.

Subsequent Collection of a Written-off Account Receivable

Occasionally a customer pays his account balance after it has been written off as uncollectible. This could happen for a number of reasons. For example, a company's credit department may have acted prematurely in writing off a customer's account rather than giving him additional time to make payment. Or, a customer may have left town for several months and forgotten to pay his bill. If the company was unable to locate this customer after a reasonable time, his account was written off as uncollectible. However, at a later date, the customer remembers his debt to the company and mails the payment.

Assume that the written-off account of Jack Billington is subsequently paid. The following two journal entries are recorded by the Kelley Company upon collecting Billington's account:

Accounts receivable	50	
Allowance for uncollectibles		50
(To reestablish Jack Billington's		
previous written-off account		
receivable)		

Cash	50	
Accounts receivable		50

(To collect the amount owed from
Jack Billington on his account
receivable)

The first journal entry reverses the previous entry recorded when Billington's account was written off as uncollectible. The effect of this entry is to restore Jack Billington's good credit rating with the Kelley Company. The second journal entry reflects the $50 cash payment by Billington.

Effect on Financial Statements From Estimating Uncollectible Accounts

As discussed previously, the uncollectible accounts expense is an estimated figure. Inclusion of this estimated expense on an income statement causes a company's computed net income (or net loss) also to be an estimate. When the estimated net income is transferred (through the closing entry process) to the owner's equity account on the balance sheet, this account balance also represents an estimate. In addition, the *net realizable value* of the accounts receivables on the balance sheet is not an exact dollar figure, since the estimated allowance for uncollectibles is included in the computation. It is quite proper to use estimates in certain accounting computations. Additional examples of accounting estimations will be presented in later chapters.

Accounting Estimates for Management Decision Making

The management of a business often requires immediate accounting reports in order to make effective decisions. Expedient reports allow feedback about financial activities soon after they occur. Corrective action can then be taken to eliminate inefficient operating activities. Preparing relevant managerial reports frequently requires accountants to estimate certain financial items. For example, management may request a report analyzing the probable uncollectible accounts receivables. This information enables management to evaluate the credit-granting policies of its credit and collection department. Assume that a company's receivables from credit sales total $4000. The accountant prepares an accounts receivable aging analysis for management (see Exhibit 4-5).

This analysis indicates the time period that customers' account balances have been outstanding. In general, the longer a customer's account is outstanding, the less likelihood there is of collecting the account. The accountant provides management a monetary estimate, based upon the dollar amounts within each age category, of the receivables that he believes are uncollectible in the future. If management feels that the estimated uncol-

Exhibit 4-5

ACCOUNTS RECEIVABLE BALANCE	PORTION OF BALANCE THAT IS NOT PAST DUE	PORTION OF BALANCE THAT IS PAST DUE			
		1-30 Days	31-60 Days	61-90 Days	Over 90 Days
$4000	$3000	$500	$300	$175	$25

lectible receivables are too large, it can institute changes in the company's credit-granting policies.

An accounts receivable aging analysis along with the probable uncollectibles is a good example of the usefulness to management of including estimates in accounting reports. If management is unaware of uncollectible receivables until they are finally written off, it may be too late for significant operating policy changes. Even though the dollar amount of uncollectibles computed from the aging analysis is an estimate, it is better to provide management with this estimate rather than delaying a report until the specific uncollectibles amount is known.

As an alternative to the percentage of sales method, some companies prefer to compute their end-of-period uncollectible accounts expense on the basis of an accounts receivable aging analysis. This is done by estimating the dollar portion of uncollectible receivables within each age category of the aging analysis. The estimates for the separate age categories are then added together to determine the end-of-period adjusting entry dollar amount for uncollectable accounts expense.

Specialized Journals

Up to this point, all accounting transactions that we have examined have been recorded in a general journal. However, if a company has a large volume of repetitive accounting transactions, considerable posting time can be saved by utilizing specialized journals. The number of specialized journals in a company is dependent upon the company's particular needs. One of the many that could be used is briefly discussed below.

Specialized Sales Journal

A business organization with a large volume of credit sales may decide to use a specialized sales journal rather than the general journal for recording its sales. Assume that the Wayne Kelley Sporting Goods Company records its high volume of credit sales in a specialized sales journal. Exhibit 4-6 is the Kelley Company's sales journal for February 1983 (the number of transactions has been kept to a minimum in order to illustrate the specialized journal concept).

Exhibit 4-6

Wayne Kelley Sporting Goods Company
Sales Journal
February, 1983

Page _10_

DATE	*CUSTOMER'S NAME (ACCOUNT DEBITED)*	*ACCOUNTS RECEIVABLE SUBSIDIARY LEDGER POSTING REFERENCE*	*DOLLAR AMOUNT OF ACCOUNTS RECEIVABLE DEBIT AND SALES CREDIT*
February 1	Jack Harmon	✓	100
10	Bill Bicksley	✓	200
15	Edward Moore	✓	50
24	Mike Williams	✓	100
			450
			(12) (50)

Since the only items appearing in the sales journal are credit sales, the $450 total represents a debit to the accounts receivable account and a credit to the sales account. The number 12 below the $450 is the account number of accounts receivable in the general ledger. This number indicates the posting of the $450 as a debit to the accounts receivable account. [To complete the posting process, the reference number S10 (meaning "Sales Journal, page 10") would be placed in the posting reference column of the accounts receivable account in the general ledger.] The number 50 (the sales account number) shows that the $450 was also posted to the credit side of the sales account.

If this specialized journal had not been utilized, each of the four sales transactions would require a separate entry in the general journal and separate posting to the general ledger accounts. The specialized sales journal saves time by requiring only one set of postings (a debit to accounts receivable and a credit to sales) to the general ledger for the total monthly credit sales.

A company having a large number of credit customers will usually establish a subsidiary ledger with a separate account for each customer. This subsidiary ledger gives a detailed breakdown of the monetary items comprising the general ledger accounts receivable control account. The individual accounts within an organization's accounts receivable subsidiary ledger are ordinarily maintained alphabetically. When a monetary item is posted to the subsidiary ledger, a check mark is placed in the posting reference column of the sales journal. The check marks appearing in the sales journal posting reference column indicate that each customer's account in the subsidiary ledger has been updated for the credit sales.

Specialized journals are also popular for cash receipts, cash disbursements, and inventory purchases. With a system of specialized journals, the general journal is used only for transactions (such as adjusting entries and closing entries) not recorded in one of the specialized journals.

Voucher System for Cash Disbursements

To maintain better control over cash disbursements, some organizations use a *voucher system*. A voucher was previously defined as a supporting document relating to a cash disbursement. For example, before a company issues a check for merchandise purchased, one of the vouchers examined is the *receiving report*, which indicates that the merchandise was actually delivered.

In a voucher system, the term "voucher" has a somewhat different meaning. The voucher is a document authorizing a cash disbursement by a company. All supporting documents relating to a particular cash disbursement are attached to the voucher. After a review of these documents by the person responsible for approving cash disbursements, the voucher can then be paid.

To illustrate a voucher system, assume that the Wayne Kelley Sporting Goods Company purchased $100 of office supplies from the Tuttle Company. Before payment is approved, the following supporting documents are accumulated and attached to a voucher: the *purchase order* indicating the original intent of the Kelley Company to buy the office supplies, the *receiving report* showing that the office supplies have been delivered to the Kelley Company, and the *purchase invoice* from the Tuttle Company indicating the dollar amount owed. Exhibit 4-7 is the voucher prepared by the Kelley Company's bookkeeper on March 13, 1983 for the $100 purchase of office supplies.

The accounts debited and credited are also entered on the voucher. The account called "vouchers payable" (which means the same thing as an "accounts payable" in a nonvoucher system) is credited for the liability to the Tuttle Company. The voucher and the supporting documents are reviewed by the treasurer to ascertain the authenticity of the $100 liability to the Tuttle Company. After the treasurer has reviewed these documents, he approves the voucher for payment. Since the cash disbursement to the Tuttle

Exhibit 4-7

Wayne Kelley Sporting Goods Company

VOUCHER

Cash Disbursement To Be Made To:	Tuttle Company	Voucher No. 107
	7510 South King Street	
	Honolulu, Hawaii 96813	Date March 13, 1983

Accounts	Debit	Credit	
Office supplies	100		
Vouchers payable		100	

Explanation: Purchase of office supplies from the Tuttle Company on purchase order number 85.

Voucher Prepared By:	Voucher Approved By:	Date Voucher Paid:	Check Number:
Jim Jensen	Harold Snow	March 20, 1983	198
(Bookkeeper)	(Treasurer)		

Company is not immediately required, the approved voucher is placed in an unpaid vouchers file. On the payment date, the voucher is pulled from the unpaid vouchers file and a check is prepared, signed, and mailed to the Tuttle Company. The voucher is then marked "paid" and placed in a paid vouchers file for future reference. Also, after a voucher has been paid, all the supporting documents should be cancelled by marking them "paid." This prevents the documents from being presented to the treasurer at a later date for a second payment. The vouchers payable account is debited and the cash account is credited upon payment of the liability.

The preceding example gives the reader a general idea of how a voucher system operates. Individual companies would undoubtedly vary the specific procedures employed in their voucher system. However, the important point for the reader to understand is the increased *control* over cash disbursements that results from a voucher system. Since a voucher cannot be approved for payment until the supporting documents are reviewed, the possibility of irregular (fraudulent) cash payments is greatly reduced. A voucher system forces a thorough review of all supporting documents relating to a cash disbursement and thus contributes toward good internal control.

Review Questions

At this point, answer the following multiple-choice questions to test your knowledge of the previous reading material. The solutions are given below.

1. On December 31, a company estimates that $300 of its credit sales will be uncollectible in the following accounting period. The adjusting entry to reflect this estimate is
   a. Uncollectible accounts expense   300
           Accounts receivable   300
   b. Uncollectible accounts expense   300
           Allowance for uncollectibles   300
   c. Sales   300
           Allowance for uncollectibles   300
   d. Sales   300
           Accounts receivable   300

2. A $50 account receivable from John Justin is determined uncollectible. The journal entry to write off Mr. Justin's account is
   a. Uncollectible accounts expense   50
           Accounts receivable   50
   b. Allowance for uncollectibles   50
           Uncollectible accounts expense   50
   c. Allowance for uncollectibles   50
           Accounts receivable   50
   d. Sales   50
           Allowance for uncollectibles   50

3. A major advantage of specialized journals is
   a. To decrease the quantity of posting work.
   b. To increase the quantity of posting work.
   c. To eliminate the need for a general ledger.
   d. To eliminate the need for a trial balance.

4. Under a voucher system, a cash disbursement should not be made until
   a. Supporting documents are correctly filed.
   b. A voucher is prepared and approved.
   c. The end of the month.
   d. Management is provided an estimate of the dollar expenditure.

Answers

1. b

2. c

3. a

4. b

Chapter Summary

A balance sheet that classifies assets and liabilities into current and long-term categories provides better information with which to analyze a company's financial position.

A good internal control system contributes toward efficient business operating activities. Because of the high liquidity of cash, it is very important to have effective controls over cash activities. As part of cash control, most disbursements in a company should be made by check. A bank sends a monthly statement to a company indicating deposits, cleared checks, and any other increases or decreases. The month-end cash balance shown in a company's accounting records may be different from the bank statement balance. When it is, a bank reconciliation statement is prepared to determine the causes of the discrepancy. Most organizations maintain a petty cash fund to make small cash disbursements rather than writing checks for these minor expenditures.

To achieve a better matching of revenues earned against expenses incurred on the income statement, a company estimates the dollar portion of its receivable from credit sales that will be uncollectible in the following accounting period. An adjusting entry is then recorded for the estimated uncollectible receivables. The percentage of sales method for estimating an organization's uncollectible accounts expense is often used.

A company with a large volume of repetitious transactions can save posting time by utilizing specialized journals. A voucher system gives better control over cash disbursements, since the supporting documents relating to a disbursement are attached to a voucher and then reviewed before payment is approved.

Chapter Problem

The solution to the problem is given in the appendix. However, the reader is urged to first attempt to work the problem on his own and then to check his work against the given solution.

Problem Situation

The Elmwood Company has a checking account at the Central National Bank. Upon receiving its monthly bank statement, the company prepares a bank reconciliation statement in order to determine the causes of any discrepancies between its accounting records and the bank statement.

Exhibit 4-8 is the Elmwood Company's bank reconciliation statement for March 1983.

Exhibit 4-8

The Elmwood Company
Bank Reconciliation Statement
March 31, 1983

Balance per bank statement, March 31	$450	Balance per Elmwood Company's records, March 31	$403
Add: Deposit in Transit— Deposit of March 31, not recorded by the bank in March.	50	Deduct: Bank service charge on March 31.	3
	$500		
Deduct: Outstanding checks Check 131 $25 Check 133 75	100		
Adjusted balance per bank statement, March 31	$400	Adjusted balance per Elmwood Company's records, March 31	$400

The Elmwood Company's checking account records during April were as follows:

Checking account balance, April 1, 1983 $400

Plus: Deposits to checking account

April 6	$300	
April 29	200	500
		$900

Less: Cash disbursements from checking account

April 4: Check 134	$100	
April 15: Check 135	150	
April 23: Check 136	125	
April 30: Check 137	25	400

Checking account balance, April 30, 1983 $500

When the Elmwood Company received its April bank statement, the following information was extracted.

    1. Deposits of the Elmwood Company recorded by the bank in April:

$ 50 (the Elmwood Company's March 31 deposit)
$300 (the Elmwood Company's April 6 deposit)

2. Cash disbursement checks written by the Elmwood Company and clearing the bank in April:

Check 131 $ 25
Check 134 $100
Check 135 $150

3. The April bank service charge was $2. (The Elmwood Company did not record this service charge in its accounting records during April.)

4. Included in the Elmwood Company's April 6 deposit was a $50 check from the Aztec Company. This check represented an account receivable payment to the Elmwood Company. The Aztec Company had insufficient cash in its account. The check was, therefore, charged back to the Elmwood Company's account on April 28. (The Elmwood Company did not record this NSF check in its accounting records during April.)

5. The bank statement indicated that the Elmwood Company's April 30, 1983 checking account balance was $473.

Problem Requirements

The Elmwood Company wants to determine the causes of the discrepancy between its accounting records and the bank statement with regard to the April 30 checking account balance. To help the Elmwood Company, perform the following functions:

1. Prepare a bank reconciliation statement for the Elmwood Company on April 30, 1983.

2. Prepare the Elmwood Company's required journal entries on April 30, 1983 to update its accounting records for the financial transactions recognized by the bank but not the company.

Problem Objectives and Solution Approach

Objectives:

1. Utilizing a bank reconciliation statement to explain why a company's checking account records differ from the bank's records.

2. Using the results from a bank reconciliation statement to prepare journal entries that update a company's accounting records.

Solution Approach:

1. Look for any discrepancies between company records and bank records regarding April checking account activities.

2. On the basis of these discrepancies, prepare the Elmwood Company's April bank reconciliation statement.

3. Using the bank reconciliation statement information, prepare the company's April 30 journal entries.

5

Financial Statement Analysis

Merchandise Inventory

Inventory Systems

A company that sells a physical product to customers must maintain an inventory of merchandise. Without an adequate level of inventory, the company will continually run short of its sales products and be unable to satisfy customers' demands. As a result, customers may look to other companies for the merchandise.

Every organization should determine its optimal inventory quantity. There are inherent dangers of having either too large or too small a physical inventory balance. The negative aspects of the former are

1. A large storage area is needed. A company may have to rent some additional storage space or find space within its own premises. Using its own facilities for storage may result in the company's not being able to use that space for another, more important activity. For example, space currently devoted to inventory storage might be used to develop and manufacture a new product line.

2. There is the need for additional insurance coverage. Most organizations have insurance coverage on their inventories to protect them against a fire or other catastrophe. A larger than necessary physical inventory balance throughout the year requires more insurance coverage.

3. Additional dollars to be invested in inventory is required. As a result, a company loses the opportunity to invest these dollars in more profitable business activities. Money spent on excessive amounts of inventory does not usually earn the company a profitable return.

4. The company runs the risk of inventory obsolescence. Our economy is characterized by rapid technological development, with new products continually appearing on the market. A company may find itself "stuck" with large quantities of unsalable inventory if new products become available that cause its inventory items to be obsolete.

One negative aspect of having too small a physical inventory balance is the risk of inventory shortage. Also, a company purchasing in small quantities may lose the opportunity to receive *trade discounts* from its supplier. A trade discount is a percentage reduction off the inventory cost, which is typically offered to companies buying large quantities.

With negative implications of either too large or too small a physical inventory balance, the obvious conclusion is that an inventory quantity between these two extremes should be maintained. Each organization must attempt to determine its own optimal inventory level based upon such things as customer demand and lead time (length of time required to receive inventory items ordered from a supplier). Many organizations use highly sophisticated mathematical techniques to determine their optimal inventory levels.

Revenue and Expense Recognition From the Sale of Inventory

The cost of merchandise inventory is a current asset. When inventory is sold to customers, the inventory cost becomes an expense (called "cost of merchandise sold"), while the retail selling price represents earned revenue. (Remember, revenue is earned by selling a product or providing a service to someone.) A company earns revenue from its merchandise inventory when a *sales transaction* occurs.

When merchandise from a sale is shipped to a customer, either the seller or the buyer is responsible for paying the freight cost. To illustrate the recognition of freight charges in the accounting records, assume that the Wayne Kelley Sporting Goods Company sells merchandise to George Cantrell and is required to pay the $25 freight bill. The following journal entry is recorded by the Kelley Company for the freight payment:

Transportation out	25	
(or Freight out)		
Cash		25
(To pay freight on merchandise		
sold to George Cantrell)		

The "transportation-out" account is an expense account indicating one of the company's operating expenses associated with the sales transaction. This account discloses the freight expense on merchandise going *out of* a company from a sale.

A company purchasing merchandise inventory may be responsible for the freight payment on the delivered goods. Assume that the Wayne Kelley Sporting Goods Company purchases merchandise from the Morell Company and is required to pay the $30 freight charge. The Kelley Company's journal entry is:

Transportation in	30	
(or Freight in)		
Cash		30
(To pay freight on the		
merchandise purchased		
from the Morell Company)		

The "transportation-in" account indicates the freight cost on merchandise coming *into* a company from a purchase. When an organization is required to pay the freight on merchandise purchased, this increases the *total cost* of the merchandise. For example, if a company purchases $100 of merchandise inventory and pays $5 freight (called "transportation in"), the total cost of the acquired inventory is actually $105. Basically, the cost of merchandise inventory includes *all* costs incurred in getting the inventory ready to sell. In addition to freight, the costs incurred to unpack and place the merchandise on store shelves increase the actual inventory cost.

Because the freight paid on inventory purchases causes an increase in a company's inventory cost, the reader may ask the following question: Why not directly debit the inventory account rather than the transportation-in account for freight payments? This would not be a valid procedure. If the inventory account is debited, a company's management may lose sight of the total freight cost, since it would be lumped together with the inventory purchase cost. By establishing a special transportation-in account, management is provided valuable information concerning the dollar amount of freight charges on merchandise purchased. When the freight costs appear too large in relation to the quantity of merchandise purchased, management can investigate alternate shipping methods.

Perpetual Versus Periodic Inventory Systems

There are two major inventory systems available for use by a business organization: the *perpetual* inventory system and the *periodic* inventory system.

The term *perpetual* means "continuous." Under a perpetual system, an organization updates inventory records each time a transaction occurs affecting its inventory. When a company buys inventory, the merchandise inventory asset account is debited for the cost of the merchandise purchased. The sale of inventory causes a credit to this account for the cost of the merchandise. Thus, a continuous updated dollar balance exists in the merchandise inventory account. A perpetual inventory system is typically used by a company whose inventory items have a large unit cost. Immediately updating the merchandise inventory account for every transaction allows a company to maintain better control. Management always has current information about the unsold quantity of merchandise and can better plan future purchases. For example, a company selling automobiles would probably maintain a perpetual inventory system for its cars, since each one has a significant dollar cost.

An organization with inventory items of small unit cost would probably utilize a periodic inventory system. With a periodic system, the merchandise inventory account is not updated at the time an inventory purchase or sale occurs. For example, a large discount store selling hundreds of different small-cost inventory items ordinarily uses a periodic inventory system. The cost of maintaining the discount store's inventory accounting records would be too expensive if its merchandise inventory account were immediately updated for every sale (as, for example, a 5¢ pencil). In most cases, a company with a periodic inventory system updates its inventory records only when financial statements are prepared at the end of an accounting period. As discussed in Chapter 3, *adjusting entries* are recorded before financial statements are prepared. Thus, period-end adjustments to update the inventory records are required by a company utilizing a periodic inventory system.

A company's management must decide whether to use a periodic or perpetual system for its inventory. From the point of view of providing current day-to-day inventory information, a perpetual system is definitely superior. However, the costs of operating a perpetual inventory system are significantly more than for a periodic system. The accountant should provide management a cost-benefit analysis of operating a perpetual versus a periodic system. This analysis includes an estimate of the expected future costs and benefits from utilizing the two inventory systems. The benefits are the valuable decision-making information provided to management from each system. Quantifying the value of management decision-making information may be rather difficult but is not impossible. After the cost-benefit analysis is prepared, management has a basis for selecting an inventory system for its organization. Ideally, the inventory system with the greater amount of benefits in relation to costs would be chosen.

Perpetual and periodic inventory systems may be used together in the same organization. For example, many discount stores have some inventory items with a large unit cost (television sets, stereos, furniture, etc.) and other inventory items with a small unit cost (pencils, notebook paper, toothpaste, etc.). In this type of company, a perpetual system could be used for the inventory items having a large unit cost and a periodic system for the items of small unit cost.

Effective internal control procedures for maintaining inventory records are important regardless of whether a periodic or perpetual system is utilized. An employee whose job is to receive and subsequently issue inventory items from the storeroom should not be responsible for recording these inventory transactions in the accounting records. This function should be performed by another individual. With a separation of duties between inventory handling and record keeping, the misappropriation of inventory items is difficult to accomplish. For example, if the same employee is in charge of both the physical inventory items and the record-keeping function, he could possibly steal inventory and conceal his theft by falsifying the records. However, if this employee has no access to the records, his dishonesty would likely be discovered when a reconciliation of the physical inventory to the inventory records is performed.

To illustrate the required accounting entries with perpetual and periodic inventory systems, assume that the Wayne Kelley Sporting Goods Company utilizes a perpetual system for its large unit cost inventory items and a periodic system for the small unit cost inventory items. Presented in Exhibit 5-1 are transactions and journal entries for the purchase and sale of the Kelley Company's inventory items. (The use of the purchases account in a periodic inventory system is discussed on the following pages.)

Under the perpetual system, the merchandise inventory asset account is updated each time a transaction affects inventory. The $500 purchase of fishing boats increases the company's inventory and causes a debit to the merchandise inventory account. When a sale is made, two journal entries are recorded. The first entry recognizes the sale of the merchandise at retail price. The debit in the second entry reflects the company's expense for the wholesale cost of the sold merchandise. The credit part of this entry reduces the inventory account balance for the merchandise that was sold. Thus, at any time during the accounting period, the company knows its expense for cost of merchandise sold and also the dollar balance of its merchandise inventory asset account.

With a periodic system, the merchandise inventory account is updated only when the company prepares financial statements at the end of an accounting period. Inventory transactions during the period are not

Exhibit 5-1

PERPETUAL SYSTEM			*PERIODIC SYSTEM*		
Purchased 5 fishing boats at a cost of $100 per boat. Bill to be paid in 30 days (5 boats at $100 per boat = $500).			Purchased 50 baseballs at a total cost of $90. Bill to be paid in 30 days.		
Merchandise inventory	500		Purchases	90	
Accounts payable		500	Accounts payable		90
Paid $40 freight on fishing boats purchased.			Paid $3 freight on baseballs purchased.		
Transportation in	40		Transportation in	3	
Cash		40	Cash		3
Sold one of the boats at a $175 retail price to a customer who will pay in 20 days. The Kelley Company's wholesale cost for the fishing boat was $100.			Sold a baseball to a customer for $2.50 cash.		
			Cash	2.50	
			Sales		2.50
Accounts receivable	175		*No journal entry recorded on the sale date to update merchandise inventory account and recognize cost of merchandise sold.*		
Sales		175			
Cost of merchandise sold	100				
Merchandise inventory		100			

recorded in this account. Rather, a special account called "purchases" is debited each time that inventory is acquired. When a sale occurs, only the entry for the retail selling price is recorded. There is no recognition of the cost of merchandise sold and the inventory reduction at the time of a sale. The entry for the freight payment is the same under both inventory systems; that is, a debit to the transportation-in account.

At the end of an accounting period when a company wants to prepare financial statements, updated dollar cost figures are needed for the merchandise inventory and cost of merchandise sold accounts. Under the perpetual inventory system, this information is already available in the company's accounting records, since the merchandise inventory asset account was continually updated for each inventory purchase or sale and the cost of merchandise sold expense was determined for every sale. With a periodic system, however, updated inventory and cost of merchandise sold account balances have not been maintained.

Assume that the Potter Company uses a periodic system for its inventory. On December 31, 1983, the company wants to prepare yearly financial statements. The following information concerning inventory is available from the company's general ledger accounts on December 31:

Merchandise inventory, January 1, 1983	$ 5,000
Purchases	15,000
Transportation in	1,000
Cost of merchandise sold	0

Since the Potter Company closes its books annually to prepare financial statements, the merchandise inventory account is updated only once a year—on December 31. Therefore, the general ledger merchandise inventory account (with a cost of $5000) represents the inventory balance of a year ago. Throughout 1983, the purchases account was debited each time that inventory was purchased and the merchandise inventory account was untouched. Also, the cost of merchandise sold account has a zero balance, since no computation of this expense was made for each sale during the year.

The Potter Company must make *two adjustments* to update its accounting records prior to preparing financial statements:

1. Since the merchandise inventory account balance is actually 12 months old (the January 1, 1983 balance of $5,000) on December 31, 1983, the company must determine the quantity and dollar cost of its *inventory on hand* at the end of the year. This is achieved by having employees physically count the inventory items on hand at year's end. Every organization has its own system for counting its end-of-period inventory. Many companies have their employees work in teams of two. Upon assigning teams to specific areas of the inventory, one member counts the inventory items and the other team member records the count on inventory sheets. After the count has been completed, the inventory items are then multiplied by their unit costs to determine the total dollar cost of the year-end inventory.

2. Since the cost of merchandise sold has not been previously determined, a computation of this expense is necessary. The cost of merchandise sold is one of the expenses that must appear on the income statement in order that a proper matching of revenues earned against expenses incurred can be achieved.

On December 31, 1983 the Potter Company counted the year-end inventory and determined its cost to be $4000. On the basis of this count and the other inventory information, the company's *cost of merchandise sold* expense is computed as shown in Exhibit 5-2.

Exhibit 5-2

Merchandise inventory, January 1, 1983		$ 5,000
Plus: Purchases of merchandise during the year	$15,000	
+ Freight charges on merchandise purchased during the year	1,000	
Total cost of merchandise purchased during the year		16,000
Cost of merchandise available for sale during the year		$21,000
Less: Merchandise inventory, December 31, 1983		4,000
Cost of merchandise sold for the year		$17,000

The January 1 inventory represents the dollar cost of the company's merchandise inventory *available for sale* at the beginning of the accounting period. To this is added the merchandise purchased during the accounting period (which is reflected in the purchases account). Since freight charges increase the actual inventory cost, the $1000 freight is *added* to the $15,000 worth of purchases to obtain the $16,000 total inventory purchase cost. The summation of this $16,000 inventory cost and the $5000 January 1 cost, $21,000, represents the company's *cost of merchandise available for sale* during the accounting period. You can think of the $21,000 as representing the maximum dollar cost of merchandise that could have been sold in 1983. If, for example, the company has no December 31 inventory, then the merchandise available for sale is completely sold, and $21,000 represents the *cost of merchandise sold expense.* This naturally assumes the absence of theft or an undiscovered shortage of the inventory available for sale during the accounting period. The Potter Company's December 31 inventory is $4000. Therefore, $4000 is *subtracted* from the merchandise available for sale to determine the 1983 cost of merchandise sold expense.

The cost of merchandise sold computation must be reflected in the general ledger accounts. You can think of the purchases and transportation-in accounts as subdivisions of the merchandise inventory account. At the end of a period, a series of journal entries must be recorded so that the cost of merchandise sold expense and the updated merchandise inventory balance are included in the general ledger accounts. This is achieved by the Potter Company through the adjusting and closing entries on December 31, 1983 given in Exhibit 5-3.

Exhibit 5-3

Dec. 31	Cost of merchandise sold	5000	
	Merchandise inventory		5000
	(To close Jan. 1 inventory balance into cost of merchandise sold)		

31	Cost of merchandise sold	16,000	
	Purchases		15,000
	Transportation in		1000
	(To close the purchases and transportation-in accounts to cost of merchandise sold)		

31	Merchandise inventory	4000	
	Cost of merchandise sold		4000
	(To establish dollar cost of merchandise inventory at year's end based upon physical count)		

31	Income summary	17,000	
	Cost of merchandise sold		17,000
	(To close balance of cost of merchandise sold expense account into the income summary account)		

The adjusting and closing entries in Exhibit 5-3 result from several assumptions. The first journal entry assumes that the January 1 inventory was sold and is therefore closed to the cost of merchandise sold account. The second journal entry further assumes that the merchandise purchased during the accounting period was also sold. As a result, the purchases and transportation-in accounts are closed to the cost of merchandise sold account. At this point, the cost of merchandise sold account has a $21,000 balance ($5,000 + $16,000). The $21,000 represents the cost of merchandise available for sale and would be the correct expense for merchandise sold only if the company has no December 31 inventory. Since the December 31 inventory is $4000, the third entry (an adjusting entry) establishes this year-end inventory (which appears as a current asset on the balance sheet) and reduces the cost of merchandise sold expense. The $4000 December 31 inventory is included in the cost of merchandise sold account prior to this adjusting entry, since the two previous closing entries assumed that the inventory available for sale was completely sold. Therefore, to reduce the cost of merchandise sold expense account for the unsold end of year inventory, $4000 is *credited* to this account. The final journal entry transfers the cost of merchandise sold account balance into the income summary account. After the above entries are recorded and posted, the general ledger accounts will properly reflect the company's inventory activity for 1983.

Classified Income Statement

In previous chapters, expenses were listed together under one income statement category called "operating expenses." However, a business organization may prepare a classified income statement, grouping the operating expenses into functional categories. (A classified income statement is illustrated at the end of this chapter.) Two major categories commonly used are *administrative expenses* and *selling expenses.*

The *administrative* category (also called the *general* operating expenses) includes salaries of clerical workers and administrative executives, the rent expense on the administrative offices, office supplies expense, etc. Within the *selling* category are those expenses incurred by a company in selling its merchandise inventory. The transportation-out expense and the uncollectible accounts expense are selling expenses resulting from a company's sales activities. Other examples are advertising expense to promote a company's products, and salaries and commissions paid to salesmen.

Classifying operating expenses into administrative and selling categories provides financial statement readers better information about the composition of the expenses incurred to earn revenues. On a classified income statement, the computation of cost of merchandise sold expense (under the periodic inventory system) is typically presented. The cost of merchandise sold is then subtracted from the sales revenue in order to compute the gross profit. A partial income statement is shown in Exhibit 5-4 to illustrate the *gross profit* calculation (the dollar figures are assumed).

Exhibit 5-4

Revenue from sale of product			$40,000
Less: Cost of merchandise sold			
Beginning inventory, Jan 1		$ 8,000	
Plus: Purchases during accounting			
period	$26,000		
+ Freight on purchases	2,000		
Total cost of merchandise purchases		$28,000	
Cost of merchandise available for sale		$36,000	
Less: Ending inventory, Dec. 31		11,000	
Cost of merchandise sold			25,000
Gross profit (or gross margin) on sales			$15,000

The *gross profit* (also called *gross margin*) is a very useful income statement figure. It indicates the dollar excess of the retail price of merchandise sold over the company's cost for the merchandise. Also, the gross profit discloses the number of dollars available to cover the administrative and selling operating expenses. If the gross profit exceeds these operating expenses, a net income is earned. Many companies compute a gross profit ratio to analyze this important relationship between sales revenue and cost of merchandise sold. The gross profit ratio in the above example is 37½ percent $\left(\frac{\text{gross profit on sales}}{\text{sales revenue}} = \frac{\$15,000}{\$40,000} = 37\frac{1}{2} \text{ percent} \right)$. A company's management compares the current year gross profit ratio to previous years' ratios in order to ascertain if the gross profit trend is up or down. In addition, management may compare other companies' gross profit ratios to its own as an indication of efficient operating performance.

With a perpetual inventory system, the cost of merchandise sold computation is not made on the income statement, because it is already reflected in a general ledger account. However, the dollar balance of the transportation-in account must be added to the cost of merchandise sold before the gross profit on sales is computed. (Under the perpetual system, the transportation-in account balance is closed at period-end to the income summary account.)

Review Questions

At this point, answer the following multiple-choice questions to test your knowledge of the previous reading material. The solutions are given below.

1. A positive aspect of having a larger than necessary inventory balance throughout the year is
   a. The extra inventory storage space required.
   b. The extra dollars invested in the inventory.
   c. The obsolescence of inventory items.
   d. The reduced risk of inventory shortages.

2. A company paid $50 freight on merchandise inventory purchased from a supplier. The correct journal entry is

   a. Transportation in   50
        Cash   50

   b. Transportation out   50
        Cash   50

   c. Cost of merchandise sold   50
        Cash   50

   d. Purchases   50
        Cash   50

3. Under a periodic system, which journal entry is recorded for a $500 purchase of merchandise inventory (payment will be made in 30 days)?
   a. Merchandise inventory   500
      Accounts payable   500
   b. Cost of merchandise sold   500
      Accounts payable   500
   c. Cost of merchandise sold   500
      Purchases   500
   d. Purchases   500
      Accounts payable   500

4. A company's cost of merchandise available for sale is $700 on December 31, 1983. On this date, the merchandise inventory balance is $100 and the total administrative and selling operating expenses are $300. What is the company's cost of merchandise sold?
   a. $300.
   b. $400.
   c. $600.
   d. $700.

Answers

1. d

2. a

3. d

4. c ($700 – $100 = $600)

Inventory Costing Methods

Prior discussion has emphasized the need for a company to compute the dollar cost of its inventory at the end of an accounting period. With a periodic inventory system the dollar cost of the ending inventory is necessary in order to compute the cost of merchandise sold expense.

Before year-end financial statements are prepared, an organization counts the quantity of unsold inventory items. This quantity must then be converted into a dollar cost figure for the financial statements. If the various inventory items were originally purchased at the same unit costs, it would be quite easy to compute the inventory dollar cost. You could *multiply* the quantity of each type of inventory item by its constant unit cost to determine the total inventory cost. However, this situation would be quite unusual. Ordinarily, a company purchases inventory items throughout the year at different unit costs. The inflation in our economy typically causes unit inventory costs to increase. For example, an inventory item costing $3 per unit in February 1983 may cost $3.50 per unit six months later.

A company's year-end physical inventory quantity normally includes items of different unit costs. The problem faced by a company is to attach a total dollar cost to these inventory items at the end of its accounting period. Four major methods for determining a company's inventory cost are now discussed.

Specific Identification

Under this costing method, a company is able to "specifically identify" its inventory items purchased and sold with their actual unit costs. It is typically used by a company having a perpetual inventory system with large unit cost inventory items.

Assume that the Rand Motors Company has a perpetual system for its inventory of new cars. On June 10, the total cost of the company's inventory is $80,000. Since the cost of each automobile is significant, a specific identification inventory costing method is used. An automobile is sold for $3000 cash on June 11. The inventory records indicate a $2000 cost for this car. The following two journal entries are recorded on June 11:

Cash	3000	
Revenue from automobile sales		3000
(To recognize the revenue from an		
automobile sale)		
Cost of merchandise sold	2000	
Merchandise inventory		2000
(To recognize the cost of the		
automobile sold and the		
inventory reduction)		

After the merchandise inventory has been reduced by $2000 for the cost of the sold automobile, the updated inventory is $78,000 ($80,000 on June 10 minus $2000). A perpetual inventory system with a specific identification costing method gives an organization good control over its inventory activities, since the actual cost of sold and unsold inventory items is known at all times. Therefore, accurate and current cost information is available to management concerning its company's inventory.

A specific identification costing method is impractical for a company having a large volume of small unit cost inventory items purchased at different costs throughout the year. For example, if a discount store selling hundreds of different small-cost items attempted to specifically identify the actual per unit cost of every inventory item sold daily, the costs of maintaining these inventory records would be extremely high. Therefore, as an alternative to a specific identification costing method, the accounting profession permits the use of three other methods that do not attempt to specifically identify inventory items sold with their actual unit costs. These three methods are based upon assumptions concerning the relationship between sold inventory items and their unit costs.

To illustrate the three costing methods, the data in Exhibit 5-5 are presented for one of the Kelley Company's inventory items during 1983 under its periodic inventory system.

On the basis of the schedule in Exhibit 5-5, the inventory quantity on December 31, 1983 is determined in the following manner:

Total units of inventory available for sale during the year	210 units
Less: Total units of inventory sold during the year	140 units
Ending inventory, Dec. 31 (units available for sale that are unsold)	70 units

The Kelley Company's employees counted the inventory on December 31 and determined that the actual physical quantity was also 70 units. The question to be answered now is: What is the *dollar cost* of the 70 inventory items?

The inventory at the beginning of the year and the additional items purchased during the year have four different per unit costs ($2 for the January 1 beginning inventory, $3 for the March 10 purchase, $4 for the September 30 purchase, and $5 for the December 15 purchase). For every sale during the year, the actual unit cost of the item sold was not determined. Therefore, the Kelley Company must make an assumption on December 31 concerning the physical flow of the inventory items sold in order to determine the dollar cost of the 70 units. Each of the three inventory flow assumptions is now discussed and illustrated.

First In, First Out (FIFO)

This inventory costing method assumes that the inventory items purchased earliest (the *first in*) are sold (the *first out*) before the items purchased later. Therefore, a company's period-end inventory consists of the most recently purchased merchandise.

Based upon the inventory data in Exhibit 5-5 and the computation above, the Kelley Company's December 31 computation of its merchandise inventory dollar cost and cost of merchandise sold expense under FIFO is shown in Exhibit 5-6.

FIFO assumes that the inventory items purchased earliest are sold first. Thus, to cost the 70 inventory units on December 31, you start with the most recently purchased inventory units from December 15. Then, the next most recent purchase on September 30 is included in the inventory calcula-

Exhibit 5-5

	INVENTORY PURCHASED			INVENTORY SOLD		
DATE	*QUANTITY*	*UNIT COST*	*TOTAL COST**	*QUANTITY*	*UNIT SELLING PRICE*	*TOTAL SELLING PRICE†*
Jan. 1 (inventory on hand at beginning of the year)	100	$2	$200			
Jan. 15				50	$5	$250
March 10	50	$3	$150	60	$6	$360
June 5	40	$4	$160			
Sept. 30				30	$7	$210
Nov. 11	20	$5	$100			
Dec. 15						
TOTALS	210 units		$610	140 units		$820
	Total units available for sale during the year		Total cost of units available for sale during the year	Total units sold during the year		Total retail price of units sold during the year

*Total cost = quantity purchased × unit cost
† Total selling price = quantity sold × unit selling price

123

Exhibit 5-6

Computation of inventory dollar cost at December 31:
        Total units in December 31 inventory
        (computed on page 122)   70 units

        From Dec. 15 purchase   20 units at $5 per unit = $100
        From Sept. 30 purchase   40 units at $4 per unit = 160
        From March 10 purchase   10 units at $3 per unit =   30
                                   70 units $290

                        Total units   Total dollar cost of
                        accounted for in   70 units in Dec. 31
                        Dec. 31 inventory   inventory

Computation of cost of merchandise sold at December 31:

        Total cost of units available for sale
        during the year (from inventory schedule
        in Exhibit 5-5) $610
Less: Inventory, Dec. 31 (computed above)   290
                Cost of merchandise sold for 1983 $320

tion. At this point, 60 units of inventory (20 units from Dec. 15 + 40 units from Sept. 30) are accounted for in the year-end inventory. Since the December 31 inventory is 70 units, 10 additional units must still be included. Therefore, from the next most recent purchase (50 units at $3 per unit on March 10), the cost of only 10 units belongs in the December 31 inventory. The $290 inventory cost will appear on the Kelley Company's year-end balance sheet under current assets.

Once the December 31 inventory cost has been computed, it is deducted from the cost of units available for sale so that the 1983 cost of merchandise sold expense may be determined. This $320 expense is subtracted from the company's sales revenue on its year-end income statement to compute the gross profit.

Last In, First Out (LIFO)

Compared to FIFO, this inventory costing method makes the *opposite* assumption. The LIFO method assumes that the most recent inventory items purchased (the *last in*) are sold first (the *first out*). Therefore, the period-end inventory consists of the merchandise purchased earliest.

On the basis of the inventory data in Exhibit 5-5, the LIFO computation of the Kelley Company's December 31 merchandise inventory dollar cost and cost of merchandise sold expense is shown in Exhibit 5-7.

Exhibit 5-7

Computation of inventory dollar cost at December 31:

Total units in December 31 inventory
(computed on page 122)   70 units

From Jan. 1 beginning inventory   70 units at $2 per unit = $140

Total dollar cost
of 70 units in
Dec. 31 inventory

Computation of cost of merchandise sold at December 31:

Total cost of units available for sale during the year (from inventory schedule in Exhibit 5-5)	$610
Less: Inventory, Dec. 31 (computed above)	140
Cost of merchandise sold for 1983	$470

With the LIFO assumption of the most recently purchased merchandise being sold first, the December 31 inventory consists of the earliest
inventory items acquired. For the Kelley Company, the earliest inventory
acquisitions are from the January 1 inventory (100 items at a $2 per unit
cost). Only 70 of these 100 items are included in the December 31 inventory
calculation, since the year-end inventory quantity is 70 units. Thus, the entire
December 31 inventory is costed at $2 per unit. This $140 inventory figure
will appear on the December 31, 1983 balance sheet under current assets.
Assume for a moment that the Kelley Company's December 31 inventory
was 130 items rather than 70. The LIFO cost of the inventory would have
been $290 (all 100 units in the January 1 inventory at $2 per unit + 30 units
at $3 per unit from the next earliest purchase on March 10).

The 1983 cost of merchandise sold expense is determined by *subtracting* the $140 December 31 inventory from the cost of units available for
sale during 1983.

Average Cost

The "average cost" method assumes that each unit of sold and
unsold inventory should absorb an equal share of the total inventory cost.
Thus, each inventory item is assigned an *average cost* based upon the total
merchandise purchase transactions.

Under a periodic system, the average unit inventory cost is called
a *weighted average cost*. Since an organization's cost of merchandise sold expense and its updated inventory is determined only at the end of an accounting period, one average cost figure is computed for the entire accounting

period. This average cost figure is based upon the inventory data at the beginning of the period plus all inventory purchases during the accounting period. Thus, you can think of the computed average cost as a *weighted* figure affected by all the purchase costs incurred in acquiring inventory.

On the basis of the inventory cost data in Exhibit 5-5, the Kelley Company's weighted average cost per unit of inventory for 1983 is

Weighted average cost per unit of inventory = $\dfrac{\text{Total cost of units available for sale during the accounting period}}{\text{Total units available for sale during the accounting period}} = \dfrac{\$610}{210 \text{ units}} = $ $2.90 per unit (rounded-off figure)

Computation of inventory dollar cost at December 31:

Total units in December 31 inventory (computed on page 122) <u>70 units</u>

70 units X $2.90 (weighted average cost per inventory item) = $203

Computation of cost of merchandise sold at December 31:

Total cost of units available for sale during the year (from inventory schedule in Exhibit 5-5)	$610
Less: Inventory, Dec. 31 (computed above)	203
Cost of merchandise sold for 1983	$407

After the $2.90 weighted average cost has been computed, each of the 70 units in the December 31 inventory is assigned this cost. The $203 year-end inventory cost is then subtracted from the cost of units available for sale to determine the 1983 cost of merchandise sold expense.

Net Income Effect From Using FIFO, LIFO, or Average Cost

Presented in Exhibit 5-8 is the Kelley Company's gross profit calculation under the three inventory costing methods based upon physical flow assumptions. The specific identification cost method is excluded from this discussion, since it is not based upon an assumption concerning the physical flow of inventory items.

The LIFO computation results in the largest cost of merchandise sold expense and the smallest gross profit. When the administrative and selling operating expenses are subtracted from this gross profit computed under LIFO, the net income will be less than with FIFO or average cost.

In an inflationary period when inventory purchase costs are rising throughout the year, the use of LIFO always causes a company's accounting computation of net income to be the smallest. LIFO assumes that the most recently purchased inventory items are sold prior to the earlier inventory

Exhibit 5-8

	FIFO	LIFO	AVERAGE COST
Revenue from sales*	$820	$820	$820
Less: Cost of merchandise sold	320	470	407
Gross profit from sales	$500	$350	$413

* Revenue from sales is computed by adding the "total selling price" column under Inventory Sold on the inventory schedule (Exhibit 5-5). The total sales revenue is the same regardless of the inventory costing method used by the company.

purchases. Inflation causes the more current inventory acquisitions to have a larger unit cost. Therefore, with the use of LIFO (compared to FIFO or average cost), the cost of merchandise sold is larger as a result of including higher unit inventory costs in this expense. The effect of a larger period-end cost of merchandise sold expense is smaller gross profit and net income amounts.

Our economy has been in a state of gradually rising costs for a number of years. For this reason, many business organizations find LIFO an attractive inventory costing method in order to reduce their tax liability to the government. Since a business pays taxes based upon its net income, a smaller net income calculation causes a lower tax liability. Naturally, this tax advantage from LIFO exists only in a period of rising inventory costs. When unit inventory costs are declining (a deflationary environment), FIFO gives the smallest net income calculation. In a period of declining costs, the earliest inventory items purchased have a larger unit cost than the later inventory acquisitions. Under FIFO, these larger unit costs from the earlier inventory purchases are included in the cost of merchandise sold calculation, causing a larger expense for merchandise sold. This larger expense results in smaller gross profit and net income amounts. The consequence of the smaller net income is a reduced tax liability at year's end.

When per unit inventory purchase costs are changing throughout an accounting period, a company's net income will vary according to the inventory costing method used. The reader may ask the following question: What prevents a company from switching inventory costing methods from year to year in order to achieve a desired level of net income each year? An accounting principle called *consistency* prevents this from happening. A company can use any one of the inventory costing methods discussed in this chapter. However, after a particular inventory costing method has been selected, the consistency principle requires a company to utilize the same method each accounting period. The company violates generally accepted accounting principles if it changes the inventory costing method in a subsequent period. To provide financial statement readers information, the balance sheet should disclose the inventory costing method used. This disclosure is normally made by a parenthetical note next to the merchandise inventory current asset.

Returns and Allowances on Purchases and Sales of Merchandise Inventory

Assume that the Wayne Kelley Sporting Goods Company has a periodic inventory system and makes a $100 credit sale to the Golding Appliance Company (which also uses a periodic inventory system). Presented below are the journal entries by the seller and buyer.

KELLEY SPORTING GOODS COMPANY (SELLER)		*GOLDING APPLIANCE COMPANY (BUYER)*	
Accounts receivable	100	Purchases	100
Sales	100	Accounts payable	100
(To recognize sale of merchandise to the Golding Appliance Company)		(To recognize purchase of merchandise from the Kelley Sporting Goods Company)	

The Golding Appliance Company was dissatisfied with $30 worth of the merchandise received from the Kelley Company. After discussion, both parties agreed that this merchandise could be returned. Since the Golding Appliance Company has not paid any of its liability on the $100 purchase, the following journal entries are recorded by the two companies for the merchandise returned:

KELLEY SPORTING GOODS COMPANY (SELLER)		*GOLDING APPLIANCE COMPANY (BUYER)*	
Sales returns and allowances	30	Accounts payable	30
Accounts receivable	30	Purchase returns and allowances	30
(To recognize the return of merchandise from the Golding Appliance Company)		(To recognize the return of merchandise to the Kelley Sporting Goods Company)	

Upon returning the merchandise, the Golding Appliance Company issues a $30 *debit memorandum* to the Kelley Company. The debit memorandum is a document indicating Golding's reduced liability. The debit to accounts payable in Golding's journal entry reflects this $30 reduction.

The Golding Appliance Company must also reduce its purchases account $30. However, instead of a direct credit to this account, a special contra account to the purchases account called "purchase returns and allowances" is credited for the $30 returned merchandise.

When a company's cost of merchandise sold expense on its income statement is computed, the purchase returns and allowances account (having a credit balance) is subtracted from the purchases account (having a debit balance) in order that the *net* merchandise purchased may be determined. Also, when period-end closing entries are prepared, the former account is closed along with the latter account into the cost of merchandise sold expense account.

The purchase returns and allowances account provides valuable information to a company's management concerning the dollar amount of purchased merchandise subsequently returned to suppliers. If the purchases account is directly credited for returned merchandise, the total dollar returns are "buried" in the balance of this account. Utilization of a special purchase returns and allowances account enables management to know the dollar amount of returns at any time. For example, if the purchase returns are too large in relation to the total dollar amount of purchased merchandise, management may decide to look for a different supplier for merchandise. A large purchase returns and allowances balance could indicate that the current supplier is careless and inefficient. This inefficiency may cause acquired merchandise to be continually returned because of poor quality.

When the Kelley Company receives the returned merchandise, it issues a $30 *credit memorandum* to Golding Appliance Company. The credit memorandum is a document indicating Kelley Company's reduced asset claim against Golding Appliance Company. The credit to accounts receivable in Kelley Company's journal entry reflects this $30 asset reduction. If merchandise from a previous recognized sale is later returned, the actual net sales are reduced. Instead of a debit to the sales account for returned merchandise, a special contra account to the sales account called sales returns and allowances is debited (see the Kelley Company's journal entry). On an income statement, the sales returns and allowances account is subtracted from the sales account to determine the *net* sales. Also, in the period-end closing entries, the former account is closed along with the latter account into the income summary account.

The same reasoning applies for having a sales returns and allowances account as was previously discussed for the purchase returns and allowances account. A company's management wants to know the dollar amount of its sales returns, since a large amount of returns may indicate inefficiencies in the company's selling activities. These inefficiencies can then be investigated and, it is hoped, corrected. If the sales account is directly debited for returned merchandise, the total dollar returns are "buried" in the balance of this account. Utilization of a special sales returns and allowances account helps management evaluate the efficiency of its company's sales activity.

Discounts on Purchases and Sales of Merchandise Inventory

Two types of discounts are discussed in this section of the chapter: *trade discounts* and *cash discounts*. A trade discount is a reduction off the list price of a company's sales merchandise. This discount is given for the following reasons:

1. A company may want to reduce the list price of a certain merchandise item in its sales catalog. Rather than printing a new catalog to reflect the reduced selling price, it offers the customer a trade discount.

2. A company often gives trade discounts to customers that purchase large quantities of its merchandise. The trade discount represents a price cut for big-volume purchasers.

One of the products offered for sale by the Kelley Company has a $100 list price. A customer purchases ten of these product items with a trade discount of 10/5. This means that the customer receives *two* trade discounts. The first discount is 10 percent and the second is 5 percent. Presented below is the computation of the after-discount selling price along with the sales entry by the Kelley Company:

Total list price: $100 per unit list price X 10 items sold = $1000

First trade discount:	$1000 list price X 10% = $100.
Second trade discount:	$1000 list price – $100 first trade discount = $900 (basis for the second trade discount). $900 X 5% = $45 (second trade discount).
Actual selling price:	$900 (selling price after first trade discount) – $45 (second trade discount) = $855.

Journal entry for the sale:

Accounts receivable	855	
Sales		855

When a company gives a trade discount, the actual selling price of its product is the dollar amount after the discount is deducted from the product's list price. Thus, $855 is recorded in the Kelley Company's sales entry. The merchandise purchaser also records this transaction at $855 in his accounting records.

In addition to giving customers trade discounts, a company may also offer *cash discounts*. The purpose of cash discounts is to encourage customers to pay their bills promptly. If an individual purchases merchandise with cash discount terms of 2/10, n/30 (n means net), he receives a 2 percent reduction off the invoice price if payment is made within ten days from the purchase date. Failure to pay by the tenth day causes the discount to be lost. The customer must then pay the full invoice price within days 11 through 30. His account is delinquent if the invoice is still unpaid after the thirtieth day.

As another example, an organization's cash discount terms might read 1/10, e.o.m. (e.o.m. means "end of month"). Under these terms, the customer is allowed a 1 percent cash discount if he pays within ten days after the month of purchase. A customer purchasing merchandise on January 18 has until February 10 to pay his bill and still receive a 1 percent cash discount. Even though the final payment date is not specified, the usual assumption is that the customer has 30 days from the purchase date to pay his bill before it is considered past due.

To illustrate the accounting aspects of cash discounts, assume that the Wayne Kelley Sporting Goods Company purchases $100 of merchandise from the Covin Supply Company with terms of 2/10, n/30. Exhibit 5-9 presents journal entries by the purchaser and the seller relating to this transaction. (Both companies utilize a periodic inventory system.)

Exhibit 5-9

TRANSACTION	KELLEY SPORTING GOODS COMPANY (PURCHASER'S RECORDS)		COVIN SUPPLY COMPANY (SELLER'S RECORDS)	

Kelley Company purchased $100 of merchandise from Covin Supply Company with cash discount terms of 2/10, n/30.	Purchases
	    Accounts payable
		100
		    100
			Accounts receivable 100
			Sales
				
				    100

Assume that Kelley Company paid Covin Supply Company within the 10-day discount period.	Accounts payable
	    Cash
	    Purchase discounts
		100
		    98*
		    2*
			Cash
			Sales discounts
			    Accounts receivable
				98
				2
				    100

Assume that Kelley Company paid Covin Supply Company after the 10-day discount period.	Accounts payable
	    Cash
		100
		    100†
			Cash
			    Accounts receivable
				100
				    100

* $100 minus $2 cash discount ($100 × 2 percent) = $98 cash paid.

† The full $100 purchase price is paid.

The journal entries of the Covin Supply Company are analyzed first. When the sale is made, a $100 accounts receivable against the Kelley Company is recognized along with a credit to the sales account for the earned revenue. When payment is received within the discount period, the cash account is debited for $98 [$100 minus $2 discount ($100 × 2 percent)]. However, since a $100 accounts receivable was originally established on the sale date, this account is now credited for $100 to eliminate the asset claim against the Kelley Company. The $2 difference represents the cash discount given the Kelley Company for paying within ten days. From the seller's point of view, this cash discount is called a *sales discount*. When a customer pays his bill within the specified discount period, the amount of the discount represents a reduction in the selling company's total dollar sales. A contra account to the sales account called "sales discounts" is debited for cash discounts taken by customers. If the sales account is debited for customer cash discounts, a company's management will not have specific information about the total dollar discounts. Using a sales discounts account enables management to have the cash discount information immediately. This account is handled in the same manner as the sales returns and allowances account on an income statement. The sales discount balance is subtracted from the sales account to determine the net sales. When period-end closing entries are recorded, the sales discounts account (as well as the sales returns and allowances and sales accounts) is closed into the income summary account. Presented below (with *assumed* dollar figures) is a partial income statement illustrating the computation of net sales:

Revenues:			
	Sales		$1000
Less:	Sales returns and allowances	$30	
	Sales discounts	20	50
	Net sales		$ 950

A sales discount is not allowed if payment is received after the cash discount period. Thus, the Covin Supply Company's third journal entry (see Exhibit 5-9) reflects the full $100 sales price being collected from the Kelley Company.

The journal entries recorded by the Kelley Company are now briefly analyzed. The first entry recognizes the company's $100 merchandise purchase and its liability to the Covin Supply Company. When payment is made within the ten-day discount period, the cash account is credited for $98 ($100 minus $2 discount). However, since a $100 accounts payable was originally established on the purchase date, this account is now debited for $100 to eliminate the liability to the Covin Supply Company. The $2 difference representing the cash discount is credited to a special contra account to the purchases account called "purchase discounts." The balance of this account is subtracted from total purchases when cost of merchandise sold expense is computed on the income statement. Also, the purchase discounts account is closed (in the same entry that closes the purchases account) to the cost of merchandise sold account at the end of an accounting period. Exhibit 5-10 presents a partial income statement illustrating the effect of purchase discounts as well as purchase returns and allowances on the cost of merchandise sold computation (the dollar figures are *assumed*):

Exhibit 5-10

Cost of merchandise sold:

Merchandise inventory, January 1		$10,000
Plus: Purchases	$12,000	
Transportation in	800	
	$12,800	
Less: Purchase returns and		
allowances	$200	
Purchase discounts	225	425
Net purchases		12,375
Cost of merchandise available for sale		$22,375
Less: Merchandise inventory, December 31		12,000
Cost of merchandise sold for the year		$10,375

The Kelley Company's third journal entry (see Exhibit 5-9) assumes payment after the ten-day discount period. Thus, the cash discount is lost and the full $100 purchase price must be paid.

Inventory Valuation at "Lower of Cost or Market"

A *cost basis* for valuing a company's merchandise inventory has been emphasized throughout this chapter. Another valuation technique is to compare the actual cost of the inventory to its current replacement cost in the market (the cost today to buy the items). The *lower* of these two figures is utilized as the period-end merchandise inventory balance.

Some accountants oppose the "lower of cost or market" inventory valuation method because of its conservatism and inconsistency. A current replacement cost is recognized when the market price is less than the actual inventory cost but ignored when the market price is greater than the cost. Therefore, only a decline in a company's merchandise inventory asset is recorded.

Review Questions

At this point, answer the following multiple-choice questions to test your knowledge of the previous reading material. The solutions are given below.

1. The Seth Company has a perpetual inventory system. A $500 cash sale is made on January 10. The sold merchandise has a wholesale cost of $300. The correct journal entry (or entries) for this sale is
   a. Cash   500
       Sales   500
   b. Cash   500
       Sales   500
       Cost of merchandise sold   300
       Merchandise inventory   300
   c. Cash   500
       Sales   500
       Cost of merchandise sold   300
       Purchases   300
   d. Cash   500
       Sales   500
       Merchandise inventory   300
       Cost of merchandise sold   300

2. In a period of *declining* inventory purchase costs, which inventory costing method causes the smallest net income?
   a. Average cost
   b. LIFO
   c. FIFO

3. The Aloha Company has a periodic inventory system. A $400 sale with cash discount terms of 1/10, n/30 is made on February 26. The sold merchandise has a wholesale cost of $200. The correct journal entry (or entries) on February 26 is
   a. Accounts receivable   400
       Sales   400
       Cost of merchandise sold   200
       Merchandise inventory   200
   b. Accounts receivable   400
       Sales   400
       Cost of merchandise sold   200
       Purchases   200
   c. Sales   400
       Accounts receivable   400
   d. Accounts receivable   400
       Sales   400

4. Referring to question 3, assume that the Aloha Company received payment from the $400 sale within the cash discount period. The correct journal entry for the cash collection is

a. Cash	396	
Sales discounts	4	
Accounts receivable		400
b. Cash	400	
Accounts receivable		400
c. Cash	400	
Accounts receivable		396
Purchase discounts		4
d. Cash	396	
Purchase discounts	4	
Accounts receivable		400

Answers

1. b

2. c

3. d

4. a (cash discount: $400 × 1 percent = $4; cash received: $400 – $4 discount = $396)

Chapter Summary

All organizations selling a physical product must maintain an inventory of merchandise. The two major inventory systems are the *perpetual* and the *periodic*. A perpetual system is typically used for inventory items having a large unit cost, whereas a periodic system is common for an inventory of smaller unit cost items.

In addition to the specific identification inventory costing methods, there are three methods based upon assumptions concerning the physical flow of inventory. First in, first out (FIFO) assumes that the earliest purchased inventory items are sold first, whereas the last in, first out (LIFO) assumption is that the most recent inventory acquisitions are the first to be sold. The average cost method assumes that each sold and unsold inventory item equally shares the total inventory cost. In an inflationary period, the LIFO cost method causes the smallest net income computation and less income taxes paid to the government. After selecting an inventory costing method, an organization must consistently use that method every accounting period. An additional inventory valuation method called the "lower of cost or market" was also briefly discussed in this chapter.

To illustrate the financial statement location of the major accounts discussed in this chapter, the 1983 classified income statement and classified balance sheet of the Spencer Appliance Company (which uses a periodic inventory system) are presented in Exhibits 5-11 and 5-12. The new items from this chapter are designated by *arrows* (the dollar figures are assumed).

Exhibit 5-11

Spencer Appliance Company
Income Statement
For the Year Ended December 31, 1983

Sales			$10,000
Less: Sales returns and allowances ◄———		$300	
Sales discounts ◄———		200	500
Net sales ◄———			$9,500
Cost of merchandise sold: ◄———			
Merchandise inventory, January 1 ◄———			$ 5,000
Plus: Purchases ◄———	$8,000		
Transportation in ◄———	500		
	$8,500		
Less: Purchase returns and			
allowances ◄——— $400			
Purchase discounts ◄—— 150	550		
Net purchases ◄———		7,950	
Cost of merchandise available for sale ◄———		$12,950	
Less: Merchandise inventory, ◄———			
December 31		7,250	
Cost of merchandise sold ◄———			5,700
Gross profit on sales ◄———			$ 3,800
Operating expenses			
Administrative expenses: ◄———			
Wages expense	$1,500		
Rent expense	1,000		
Utilities expense	100	$2,600	
Selling expenses: ◄———			
Transportation out ◄——$ 400			
Uncollectible accounts			
Expense	100	500	
Total operating expenses			3,100
Net income			$ 700

Chapter Problem

The solution to the following problem is given in the appendix. However, the reader is urged first to attempt to work the problem on his own and then to check his work against the given solution.

Exhibit 5-12

Spencer Appliance Company
Balance Sheet
December 31, 1983

ASSETS				*LIABILITIES & OWNER'S EQUITY*		
Current assets:				Current liabilities:		
Cash (includes				Accounts payable	$ 6,000	
petty cash				Notes payable	2,000	
fund of $50)		$5,000		Total current liabilities		$8,000
Accounts						
receivable	$ 3,000			Long-term liabilities:		
Less: Allow-				Mortgage payable	$20,000	
ance for un-				Long-term notes		
collectibles	150	2,850		payable	3,000	
Merchandise				Total long-term liabilities		23,000
inventory ◄———				Total liabilities		$31,000
(on a LIFO						
cost basis)		7,250		Owner's equity:		
Prepaid insurance		900		Spencer, capital,		
Total current assets			$16,000	Jan. 1, 1983	$44,300	
				Plus: Net income		
Long-term assets:				for 1983	700	
Land	$10,000			Spencer, capital,		
Building	50,000			Dec. 31, 1983		45,000
Total long-term assets			60,000	Total liabilities and		
Total assets			$76,000	owner's equity		$76,000

Problem Situation

The Sunshine Dress Shop started business on January 1, 1983. The company sells all types of clothing for women (for example, dresses, shorts, blouses, etc.). The dress shop plans to close its accounting books monthly in order to prepare financial statements. Also, because of the small wholesale cost of each item in its merchandise inventory, the company utilizes a *periodic inventory system.*

Presented below are the January, 1983 merchandise inventory purchase and sales transactions relating to a specific style of blouses offered for sale by the Sunshine Dress Shop (this is only one of the many types of inventory items sold by the dress shop):

January 1   Purchased six blouses at a wholesale cost of $2 per blouse.

January 20   Sold three blouses at a retail price of $4 per blouse.

January 23   Purchased four blouses at a wholesale cost of $2.25 per blouse.

January 28   Sold one blouse at a retail price of $4.30.

Problem Requirements

Since 1983 is the first year of business operations, the owners of the dress shop are very much concerned about selecting the inventory costing method (either LIFO, FIFO, or average cost) that will result in the *smallest* payment of income taxes to the federal government at the end of 1983. Because of the current inflation, the dress shop owners believe that the per unit wholesale costs for purchasing its various merchandise inventory items will continue to *increase* throughout 1983.

Part A

On January 31, 1983, the Sunshine Dress Shop wants to prepare its January financial statements and therefore needs to determine the dollar cost of its month-end merchandise inventory asset and the dollar amount of its cost of merchandise sold expense. Bearing in mind the dress shop's objective of paying the smallest possible income taxes in 1983, determine which inventory costing method should be used for its periodic system. Then compute the monetary balance of the dress shop's January 31 merchandise inventory and the January cost of merchandise sold expense for blouses.

Part B

For demonstration purposes only, compute the Sunshine Dress Shop's January 31 merchandise inventory dollar balance and the January cost of merchandise sold expense for blouses under the two inventory costing methods not selected in Part A. In other words, if FIFO was chosen in Part A, then LIFO and average cost should be used in Part B.

Problem Objectives and Solution Approach

Objectives:

1. To utilize knowledge regarding the inventory costing methods in order that the proper method can be selected for the Sunshine Dress Shop.

2. To understand the computational aspects of FIFO, LIFO, and average cost under a periodic inventory system by determining the dress shop's month-end inventory dollar balance and cost of merchandise sold expense.

Solution Approach:

1. Select the inventory costing method that will minimize the dress shop's 1983 income tax payment.

2. Using this inventory method, compute the dress shop's January 31 monetary balance of blouses.

3. On the basis of the January 31 blouse inventory balance determined in 2 above, compute the January cost of merchandise sold expense for the blouses.

4. Repeat the same procedures as in 2 and 3 above for the two inventory costing methods not selected in Part A of the problem.

6

Financial Statement Analysis

Additional Current Assets; Liabilities

This chapter has two major objectives: to complete the discussion of current assets and to present some important aspects of liabilities not discussed in prior chapters. The current asset areas covered are *Notes Receivable* and *Prepaid Expenses.* An analysis of the *Notes Payable* liability is included in the discussion of notes receivable. The subject of payroll accounting is introduced along with the expense and current liability accounts associated with a company's payroll procedures. Finally, the topic of *Long-Term Liabilities* is briefly examined.

Promissory Notes

A "note receivable" is similar to an account receivable, since both indicate that someone owes a company money. The major differences between these types of receivables are

1. A note receivable is more *legal* type of claim against someone than an account receivable. A formal legal document called a *promissory note* is prepared for a note receivable. It represents a written promise to pay a specified amount of money on

demand or at the end of a certain time period indicated on the note.

2. A promissory note states the amount of money borrowed (called the *principal* or *face value*) and the interest charged on the note. Most notes require the payment of interest in addition to the face amount. Interest is not typically charged on an account receivable.

3. A note is usually issued for a longer time period compared to an account receivable. The latter is normally collected within 30 to 60 days after its recognition, whereas the payment date for a note may be considerably later than 60 days.

4. A note receivable is easier to transfer than an account receivable. By endorsing the note (in the same manner as a check), one can sell it to another party.

A company may require a customer who is delinquent in paying his account receivable to sign a note to replace the receivable. The note gives the company more legal assurance of collecting the amount owed. For example, assume that the Wayne Kelley Sporting Goods Company makes a $600 credit sale to the Cantrell Company on September 1, 1983 with cash discount terms of 2/10, n/30. The following journal entries are recorded by both companies for this sale:

KELLEY COMPANY			CANTRELL COMPANY		
			Sporting goods		
Accounts receivable	600		equipment	600	
Sales		600	Accounts payable		600

The Cantrell Company debited the account "sporting goods equipment." This account is classified as a *long-term asset* on its balance sheet, since the company plans to use the equipment for longer than a year. As of December 1, 1983 (three months later), the $600 due to the Kelley Company from the Cantrell Company is still unpaid. Consequently, the Kelley Company requests the Cantrell Company to sign a 90-day note at 12 percent interest to replace the delinquent account receivable. The Cantrell Company agrees, and the following journal entries are recorded on December 1 by the two companies:

KELLEY COMPANY			CANTRELL COMPANY		
Notes receivable	600		Accounts payable	600	
Accounts receivable		600	Notes payable		600

A copy of the interest-bearing note is presented in Exhibit 6-1.

Exhibit 6-1

```
  $600.00                         Honolulu, Hawaii  December 1, 19 83

    Ninety Days      After Date    We       Promise to Pay to
  The Order of         Wayne Kelley Sporting Goods Company

      Six Hundred 00/100 .....................................  Dollars

  Payable at      Hawaiian Central Bank

  Value Received with Interest at    12%

  No.   28    Due   March 1, 1984

                                            CANTRELL COMPANY

                                              Jim Cantrell
                                                  Treasurer
```

The company making the promise to pay (the Cantrell Company) is called the *maker* of the note. The one to whom the note is payable (the Kelley Company) is called the *payee*.

      The promissory note is a current asset to the Kelley Company (recorded at its $600 face value in the "notes receivable" account) and a current liability to the Cantrell Company (recorded at $600 in the "notes payable" account). The Kelley Company's accounts receivable *credit* eliminates its previous asset claim, since a note against the Cantrell Company now exists. Cantrell's debit to accounts payable eliminates this liability, and the $600 notes payable credit recognizes its promissory note liability.

      The interest on a note is ordinarily due on the note's maturity date. On this date, both the principal amount ($600 in our example) and the interest are paid to the note holder. From the payee's (the Kelley Company) point of view, a note's interest represents revenue. The interest *accrues* (builds up) each day during the note's life. However, it is unnecessary to record a daily journal entry for interest. Rather, an organization usually waits until the note's maturity date and then records one journal entry for the collection of principal and interest.

      A note's interest is an *expense* to the maker (the Cantrell Company). This expense accrues during the note's life and represents a benefit received by the maker from being allowed a designated time period to pay his liability to the note holder. Rather than preparing a daily entry for the accrued interest expense, the maker usually waits until the note matures and then records a single journal entry for the payment of principal and interest.

      If the accounting periods of the maker and the payee end prior to the note's maturity date, *adjusting entries* must be recorded for the accrued interest (*interest expense* to the maker and *interest revenue* to the payee) at the close of the period. Using the previous example of the 90-day, 12 percent note issued December 1 to the Kelley Company from the Cantrell Company, assume that both companies close their books and prepare their annual financial statements on December 31. The following December 31 adjusting entries are recorded by the companies:

KELLEY COMPANY		*CANTRELL COMPANY*	
Accrued interest receivable	6	Interest expense	6
Interest earned	6	Accrued interest payable	6

Computation of accrued interest on December 31:

Principal of note	$600
multiplied by interest rate	X 0.12 (12%)
	$ 72 per year interest

Since the note's life is only 90 days (3 months), the total interest is 90/360 X $72 = $18. As of December 31, one of the note's three months has passed. Therefore, one month's interest has accrued: 1/3 X $18 = $6.

Several factors require emphasis when interest is computed on a note. First, the note's interest rate is usually expressed in terms of a full year even though the life of the note may be less than a year. Second, the stated interest rate is *multiplied by* the principal of the note to determine the yearly interest. Third, for purposes of computing a fractional year's interest, 360 days is typically considered a business year with each month having 30 days.

In the Kelley Company's adjusting entry, the $6 debit to accrued interest receivable establishes an asset claim against the Cantrell Company for the earned interest as of December 31. The accrued interest receivable account is a current asset on the Kelley Company's December 31 balance sheet. The interest earned account discloses the interest revenue earned by the Kelley Company as of December 31, 1983 on the 90-day note and appears on the income statement.

The $6 accrued interest is an expense of the Cantrell Company; thus, the debit in its adjusting entry is to the interest expense account. Since one month's note interest has accrued, the Cantrell Company also has a liability to the Kelley Company for this interest. The account "accrued interest payable" is credited for $6 to reflect the current liability that appears on the Cantrell Company's December 31 balance sheet.

The adjusting entries for accrued interest achieve a better *matching* of revenues against expenses on both companies' year-end income statements. One month's interest from the note receivable is recognized as *earned revenue* on the Kelley Company's 1983 income statement. The Cantrell Company's *interest expense* for one month on the note payable is included on its 1983 income statement.

The note matures on March 1, 1984 (the end of the 90-day period). The following journal entries are recorded by the two companies on this date:

KELLEY COMPANY			CANTRELL COMPANY		
Cash	618		Notes payable	600	
Notes receivable		600	Accrued interest payable	6	
Accrued interest receivable		6	Interest expense	12	
Interest earned		12	Cash		618

In the Kelley Company's journal entry, the $618 debit to "cash" includes the $600 note principal *plus* the three months' interest of $18. As a result of the note's having been collected, two asset accounts previously established are now eliminated. First, the notes receivable account is credited for $600 (the dollar amount of the original debit). Second, the $6 accrued interest receivable recognized in the Kelley Company's adjusting entry on December 31, 1983, is eliminated, since this interest is now collected as part of the $618. The $12 credit to "interest earned"represents the interest revenue for January and February (60 days) of 1984. Remember, $6 accrued interest for December was recognized in the December 31, 1983 adjusting entry. When the note is collected on March 1, 1984, $18 interest is actually received. However, only $12 of this interest

$$\left(\frac{60 \text{ days in } 1984}{90\text{-day life of note}} \times \$18 \text{ total interest} = \$12 \right)$$

is earned revenue in 1984.

The Cantrell Company credits its cash account $618 for the payment of the $600 note principal *plus* the $18 interest. This March 1 cash disbursement eliminates two liability accounts. The "notes payable" debit is necessary to eliminate the note liability recognized on December 1, 1983. The $6 debit to "accrued interest payable" eliminates the liability from the December 31, 1983 adjusting entry. The accrued interest liability no longer exists, since it is now being paid as part of the March 1 cash disbursement for the note's principal and interest. The $12 debit to "interest expense" reflects the interest for January and February (60 days) of 1984. The Cantrell Company actually pays $18 interest on March 1. However, $6 of this interest was already recognized as a December expense in the December 31, 1983 adjusting entry. Therefore, the interest expense in

1984 is only $12 $\left(\dfrac{60 \text{ days in } 1984}{90\text{-day life of note}} \times \$18 \text{ total interest} = \$12 \right).$

The interest earned on notes as well as on bank savings accounts is not the major revenue source for most organizations. Rather, a company's major revenue source comes from its principal operating activity. For example, the principal operating activity of the Wayne Kelley Sporting Goods Company is earning revenue from its retail sales of sporting goods. The Kelley

Company's sporting goods sales therefore represent *operating revenue*. Since note transactions are not a major operating function of the Kelley Company, its earned interest on notes is called *nonoperating revenue*.

A company's *operating expenses* such as rent and salaries are caused by the daily operating activities and contribute to the principal revenue earning function. This is not true for interest expense on a note payable liability. The interest charge results from borrowing money or some other type of financing transaction and is called a *nonoperating expense*.

To provide financial statement readers better information about a company's income-producing activities, the nonoperating revenues and expenses appear below the "Income from Operations" on the income statement. The operating income is computed by subtracting the operating expenses from the operating revenues. Then, by adding any nonoperating revenues and subtracting any nonoperating expenses from the income from operations, the final net income is determined. An income statement with nonoperating items is illustrated later in this chapter.

Discounting a Note Receivable

When an organization obtains a note from someone, the principal and interest will hopefully be collected on the note's maturity date. However, should a situation arise causing the organization to need cash immediately, a decision might be made to sell the note to a bank (or another type of company) before it matures. This process is called *discounting* a note. The bank, in effect, buys the note, and for this service, charges the note seller an interest fee (called the *discount rate*). When the note becomes due on its maturity date, the maker then pays the entire principal and interest to the new owner, the bank.

To illustrate the computations involved for a discounted note, assume that on June 1, 1983 the Joe Doakes Company received a $3000, 60-day note at 10% annual interest from Jack Jackson. The note's maturity date is thus July 31. However, on July 17, the Joe Doakes Company is short of cash and decides to discount Jack Jackson's note at the Happy Day Bank. The bank's annual discount rate for buying this note is 8%. The following computation would be made July 17 to ascertain the amount of cash received by the Joe Doakes Company on its discounted note:

Principal value	$3000.00
Plus: Interest on note ($3000 × 10% interest rate × 60/360)	50.00
Maturity value	$3050.00
Less: Bank discount charge ($3050 × 8% discount rate × 15/360)	10.17
Cash Proceeds	$3039.83

The first step is to determine the note's value at the end of its 60-day life. Since $50 interest accrues by the end of this 60-day period, the note's maturity value will be the $3000 principal plus the $50 accrued interest. If the Joe Doakes Company held this note until the maturity date, it would receive $3050 from the maker, Jack Jackson. However, since the company elects to sell the note prior to its maturity date, a lesser amount of cash will be received on the discounting date.

The bank charges the discount fee based upon the number of days it owns the note. In our example, this would be 15 days (from the July 17 discount date through the July 31 maturity date). Therefore, the Happy Day Bank's discount charge is 8% (the annual discount rate) of the note's $3050 maturity value for 15/360 of a year. After subtracting the $10.17 (rounded-off amount) discount charge, the Joe Doakes Company receives $3039.83 cash from the bank on July 17.

The Happy Day Bank now owns Jack Jackson's note, and Mr. Jackson will be immediately informed of this ownership change. On the note's July 31 maturity date, Mr. Jackson should pay the $3050 maturity value to Happy Day Bank.

To protect a bank from the possibility of the note maker defaulting on his payment at maturity date, it is common business practice for banks to acquire discounted notes *with recourse*. This means that if the maker fails to pay on his note's maturity date, the bank can then collect the full maturity value from the individual or company that originally sold the note to the bank. In our example, the Happy Day Bank can legally collect the $3050 note maturity value from the Joe Doakes Company if Jack Jackson defaults on July 31. Assuming this should occur and the Joe Doakes Company pays the note's maturity value to the bank, the company is then responsible for initiating legal action to collect the $3050 from Jack Jackson.

When a note is sold to a bank with recourse, the note seller has a *contingent liability* to the bank from the date the note is discounted until the note is paid at its maturity date by the maker. (If a note is sold "without recourse," the note seller would not have a contingent liability.) A contingent liability is not an *actual* liability. Rather, it reflects a situation where an actual liability could result at some future date from some future event. In our example above, the Joe Doakes Company has a contingent liability to the Happy Day Bank from July 17 (the day the note was sold to the bank) until Jack Jackson pays the note's maturity value to the bank on July 31. When Mr. Jackson pays the $3050 maturity value to the bank, the Joe Doakes Company's contingent liability disappears. However, should Jack Jackson fail to pay the bank on the note's maturity date, the Joe Doakes Company's contingent liability becomes an actual liability to the bank. For information purposes to financial statement readers, a company's contingent liabilities that exist at the end of an accounting period are shown in a footnote to the company's balance sheet.

Prepaid Expenses

The common characteristic of prepaid expenses is that they are current assets at the time of purchase that become expenses as the benefits are received from using the assets. The benefits from most prepaid expenses occur during the specific year they are acquired. Current assets have previously been defined as assets that are already in the form of cash or are expected to be converted into cash or consumed within approximately a one-year time period. Since a prepaid expense is paid in advance and will be consumed within approximately a one-year time period, a company's prepaid expense items are classified as current assets on its balance sheet.

Example of Prepaid Expense

Office Supplies

Some organizations classify office supplies as a separate current asset on their balance sheets rather than including them under prepaid expenses. However, the concept underlying office supplies fits closely that of prepaid items, and they are therefore treated as a type of prepaid expense.

Office supplies encompass various types of miscellaneous items such as typing paper, pencils, filing folders, etc. Assume that on January 1, 1983, the Wayne Kelley Sporting Goods Company has $300 worth of office supplies on hand from last year. Additional supplies costing $100 are purchased January 15, 1983. The following journal entry is recorded for this purchase:

Office supplies	100	
Cash		100

The office supplies account is a current asset representing a prepaid expense. The supplies become an *expense* as they are used by the Kelley Company in its daily operations. Rather than maintaining detailed records of each day's office supply utilization, a company typically waits until period end to determine its office supplies expense.

The Kelley Company's only acquisition of office supplies during 1983 was on January 15. At the close of its accounting period (December 31), a physical count revealed that $150 worth of supplies were still unused. The office supplies expense for the year is determined as follows:

January 1, 1983 inventory of office supplies (given above)	$300
Plus: Office supplies purchased during 1983 (the January 15 purchase was the only acquisition during the year)	100
Office supplies available for use during the year	$400
Less: December 31, 1983 inventory of office supplies	150
Office supplies used during 1983	$250

The $150 year-end inventory (the unused supplies) is subtracted from the office supplies available during 1983 to determine the expense for supplies used.

The following *adjusting entry* is recorded by the Kelley Company on December 31 to reflect the office supplies activity for the year:

Office supplies expense	250	
Office supplies		250

The debit in the adjusting entry recognizes the company's expense for the supplies used during the year. This expense appears on the income statement as an administrative operating expense. The credit reflects the reduction in the office supplies asset account caused by using $250 of supplies during 1983. The $150 year-end balance of office supplies is classified under current assets on the Kelley Company's December 31, 1983 balance sheet.

Financial Statement Presentation of Prepaid Expenses

Prepaid expenses are current assets. Compared to an organization's other assets, the individual prepaid expenses are usually small in dollar amount. Therefore, it is common practice to combine the prepaid items into one monetary figure on the balance sheet rather than listing them separately.

For example, the Jax Company has two prepaid items prior to preparing its December 31, 1983 balance sheet: prepaid rent of $150 and prepaid insurance of $200. If the individual dollar balances of these two prepaid items are small in relation to the company's other assets, they would be added together (totaling $350) on the balance sheet. Presented below is a partial balance sheet illustrating the disclosure of the Jax Company's prepaid expenses (the dollar figures for the other current assets are assumed):

Current assets	
Cash	$10,000
Accounts receivable	13,000
Merchandise inventory	10,000
Prepaid expenses	350
Total current assets	$33,350

Introduction to Payroll Accounting

In an organization having many employees, its labor costs and related payroll taxes are a major expense. Due to the large number of payroll frauds and embezzlements that have occurred in organizations (for example, keeping an employee's name on the payroll after he has terminated employment, and future paychecks with his name printed on them being divided among the organization's employees who are committing this fraud), good internal control procedures are important. A few of these effective internal controls are as follows:

1. Employees should be paid by check rather than cash, since the former is easier to trace if an irregularity occurs.

2. The timekeeping function (maintaining records of hours worked by employees), the payroll preparation function, and the paycheck distribution function should be performed by different people within an organization. If, for example, the same person performed all three of these functions, he could conceivably falsify the hours worked for a nonexistent employee, prepare a paycheck for this employee, and then keep the paycheck.

Many organizations with a large employee work force have their payroll preparation function performed by the computer. The payroll data regarding hours worked, etc. are input into the computer, and this electronic machine actually prints out each employee's paycheck.

A simplified payroll accounting example is now presented. Explanations will follow this example. Assume that the Paste Company has two administrative employees, Mr. Shoe and Miss Foote. Every Friday afternoon, these two employees receive their weekly paychecks. The company prepares its payroll each Thursday and records the payroll journal entries on this day. Then, on Friday, the checks are distributed. Today is the last Thursday in the month of November. Prior to this week, the *gross earnings* (that is, employees' salaries before taxes and other deductions are subtracted from their salaries) of Shoe and Foote are $2400 (Shoe was hired only two months ago) and $18,800, respectively. After it is determined that Shoe's gross pay for this week is $300 and Foote's is $400, the following two journal entries are recorded (explanations will follow):

Administrative Salaries expense	700.00	
FICA tax payable		15.00
Employees federal income tax payable		105.00
Salaries payable		580.00
Administrative Payroll taxes expense	24.00	
FICA tax payable		15.00
State unemployment compensation tax payable		7.50
Federal unemployment compensation tax payable		1.50

Examining the first journal entry, the debit to "administrative salaries expense" is for the total gross earnings ($300 + $400) of the two employees. (For salaries earned by salesmen and other employees associated with a company's selling activities, the account "selling salaries expense" would be debited.) The three credits are to current liability accounts of the Paste Company. The "FICA tax payable" account reflects social security taxes (under the Federal Insurance Contributions Act) withheld from the employees' paychecks. The federal government requires social security tax deductions based upon a specified dollar amount of each employee's gross earnings during the year at a specified percentage rate. Since the specific gross earnings subject to social security tax and the rate have been changing over the years, it is assumed in this example that the employees are charged the tax on their first $16,000 of gross earnings during the year at a 10% rate. Thus, on any dollars earned over $16,000, no social security tax payment is required. Of the specified FICA tax rate, the employee is charged half (5% in our example) and the employer the other half (5% in our example). Since Foote's gross earnings exceed $16,000 as of this pay period, none of her earnings are subject to the FICA tax. Mr. Shoe has not earned $16,000 during the current year. Therefore, the $15 credit to "FICA tax payable" represents the 5% withheld from Shoe's weekly earnings (5% × $300).

Under our "pay as you go" tax system, federal income taxes are withheld from the employees every pay period. The specific amount withheld is determined by an employee's gross earnings, his marital status, and the number of exemptions claimed. A schedule indicating the amount of taxes to withhold from an employee's pay is provided by the federal government. In our example, $105 federal income tax was withheld from the two employees' salaries, and the liability account "employees federal income tax payable" credited for this amount. The $580 credit to "salaries payable" indicates the actual cash (the *net pay*) that the employees will receive on Friday. It represents the difference between the gross earnings ($700) and the total taxes withheld ($120). On Friday when the employees are paid, the Paste Company's accountant will debit "salaries payable" and credit "cash" for $580.

The second journal entry reflects the company's expense for payroll taxes. The $15 credit to the current liability account "FICA tax payable" is for the Paste Company's share of the social security tax (5% × $300). Every state requires the payment of unemployment compensation taxes, both federal and state taxes. In most states, these unemployment compensation taxes are paid entirely by the employer for his employees. It is assumed here that the state unemployment tax rate is 2.5% on each employee's first $4200 of gross earnings, and the federal unemployment tax rate is .5% on each employee's first $4200 of gross earnings. Since Miss Foote has already earned over $4200 this year, the Paste Company's expense for state and federal unemployment compensation tax is only on Mr. Shoe's $300 gross pay. Thus, the current liability account "state unemployment compensation tax payable" is credited $7.50 (2.5% × $300), and the current liability account "federal unemployment compensation tax payable" is credited $1.50 (.5% × $300). The Paste Company's total payroll taxes expense is the summation of its FICA tax, and its state and federal unemployment compensation tax, totaling $24. This $24 is debited to the account "administrative payroll taxes expense." (The account "selling payroll taxes expense" would be debited for the payroll taxes expense associated with those employees involved in a company's selling activities.)

The Paste Company must maintain detailed payroll records for each employee, indicating his (or her) gross earnings and all payroll deductions. Accurate data supporting the dollar balances of the liability accounts for FICA taxes, federal income taxes withheld, state unemployment compensation taxes, and federal unemployment compensation taxes must also be maintained. At specified times during the year, the amounts accumulated in these four current liability accounts are paid to the federal and state governments, thereby eliminating the company's liabilities for the payroll taxes of its employees.

Long-Term Liabilities

Long-term liabilities are debts of a company due for payment beyond a one-year time period. These are in contrast to current liabilities, which must be paid within a one-year time period. If, for example, an organization borrows $5000 from a bank on June 15, 1983 and signs a two-year note (due June 15, 1985), this "note payable" liability is classified as a long-term liability on the December 31, 1983 balance sheet. However, on the December 31, 1984 balance sheet, the note is *reclassified* as a current liability, since it is now due for payment within a one-year time period (the note's maturity date, June 15, 1985, is only 5½ months away).

Corporations may obtain cash by selling bonds. If a corporation issues bonds for $100,000 cash, the journal entry is

Cash	100,000	
Bonds payable		100,000

A corporation issuing bonds to raise cash must pay its bondholders a specified amount of interest each year. The interest rate is stated on the bond certificates along with the maturity date of the bonds. On the maturity date, the corporation is required to pay the bondholders the *face value* of the bonds. The face value represents the dollar amount stated on the bond certificates when they were originally issued. When the $100,000 face value bonds mature, the following journal entry is recorded:

Bonds payable	100,000	
Cash		100,000

It is quite common for bonds to be issued with a maturity date of 25 years or longer from the date of sale. Consequently, the "bonds payable" account is classified as a long-term liability on the balance sheet.

The above discussion of bonds was simplified in order to illustrate the basic concept of long-term liabilities. Bond transactions can become quite complex if a corporation issues its bonds at a *premium* (the selling price is *greater than* face value) or a *discount* (the selling price is *less than* face value). A detailed analysis of bonds can be found in advanced accounting books.

Review Questions

At this point, answer the following multiple-choice questions to test your knowledge of the previous reading material. The solutions are given below.

1. The Jefferson Company receives a 60-day, $500 note from a customer at a 6 percent annual interest rate. The interest earned over the life of the note is
   a. $5.
   b. $10.
   c. $20.
   d. $30.

2. An individual incurring a liability for the issuance of a note is called the
   a. payee.
   b. endorser.
   c. maker.
   d. receiver.

3. As of December 31, 1983, the Bayview Company had $500 worth of office supplies that were available for use during the year. The year-end office supplies inventory was determined to be $300. The company's December 31 adjusting entry relating to office supplies is
   a. Office supplies expense   200
          Office supplies   200
   b. Office supplies expense   300
          Office supplies   300
   c. Office supplies   300
          Office supplies expense   300
   d. Office supplies   500
          Office supplies expense   500

4. The Proctor Company sold $50,000 of bonds on January 15, 1983. These bonds mature in 25 years. Under what classification category should this bond debt appear on the company's December 31, 1986 financial statements?
   a. Long-term assets.
   b. Current liabilities.
   c. Long-term liabilities.
   d. Owner's equity.

Answers

1. a ($500 × 6% × 60/360 = $5)

2. c

3. a ($500 − $300 = $200 expense)

4. c

Chapter Summary

Promissory notes were analyzed in considerable depth from the point of view of both the maker (who has a liability called "notes payable") and the payee (who has an asset called "notes receivable"). A promissory note typically includes interest over the life of the note. Both the face value and the interest are ordinarily paid on the note's maturity date. Interest accrues throughout a note's life. Therefore, if the maker's and the payee's accounting periods end prior to the note's maturity date, an adjusting entry must be recorded by each for the accrued interest.

Prepaid expenses are classified as current assets on a balance sheet. They become expenses when a company receives benefits from using the prepaid items. Period-end adjusting entries are recorded to recognize the expense portion of these assets.

A brief introduction to payroll accounting was provided in the chapter. This introduction included examples of the journal entries required by a company each pay period for its salaries expense and for its payroll taxes expense.

The last topic discussed was *long-term liabilities*: debts of a company due for payment beyond a one-year time period. A common type of long-term liability in a corporation is from the sale of bonds.

To illustrate the financial statement location of the major accounts discussed in this chapter, the 1983 income statement and balance sheet of the Royer Company are presented in Exhibits 6-2 and 6-3. The new items from this chapter are designated by *arrows* (the dollar figures are assumed).

Chapter Problem

The solution to the problem is given in the appendix. However, the reader is urged first to attempt to work the problem on his own and then to check his work against the given solution.

Exhibit 6-2

Royer Company
Income Statement
For the Year Ended December 31, 1983

Sales				$40,000
Less: Sales returns and allowances			$ 800	
Sales discounts			700	1,500
Net sales				$38,500
Cost of merchandise sold:				
Merchandise inventory, January 1			$10,000	
Plus: Purchases	$20,000			
Transportation in	900			
	$20,900			
Less: Purchase returns and allowances	$500			
Purchase discounts	400	900		
Net purchases			20,000	
Cost of merchandise available for sale			$30,000	
Less: Merchandise inventory, December 31			11,000	
Cost of merchandise sold				19,000
Gross profit on sales				$19,500
Operating expenses				
Administrative expenses:				
⟶ Administrative payroll taxes expense	$ 500			$ 500
Administrative salaries expense	7,500			
Rent expense	3,000			
Insurance expense	1,200			
⟶ Office supplies expense	580			
Utilities expense	500	$13,280		
Selling expenses:				
⟶ Selling payroll taxes expense	$ 300			$ 300
Selling salaries expense	3,700			
Uncollectible accounts expense	300			
Advertising expense	240	4,540		
Total operating expenses				$17,820
Income from operations ⟵———				$ 1,680
⟶ Nonoperating items				
⟶ Add: Interest earned				420
				$ 2,100
⟶ Deduct: Interest expense				300
Net income				$ 1,800

Exhibit 6-3

Royer Company
Balance Sheet
December 31, 1983

ASSETS			*LIABILITIES & OWNER'S EQUITY*		
Current assets:			Current liabilities:*		
Cash (includes			→ Accounts payable	$17,685	
petty cash			Salaries payable	300	
fund of $100)	$15,000		→ FICA tax payable	100	
Accounts			→ State unemployment		
receivable $9,000			compensation tax		
Less: Allow-			payable	50	
ance for un-			→ Federal unemployment		
collectibles 450	8,550		compensation tax		
			payable	10	
			→ Employees federal in-		
Notes receivable ←			come tax payable	800	
(due in six			→ Accrued interest		
months)	700		payable	200	
Accrued interest			Notes payable (due in		
receivable ←	300		→ five months)	500	
			Total current liabilities		$19,645
Merchandise			→ Long-term liabilities:		
inventory (on a			Bonds payable		
LIFO cost basis)	11,000		→ (due in 20 years)	$20,000	
Office supplies ←	600		Notes payable		
Prepaid expenses ←	500		→ (due in 3 years)	5,000	
			Total long-term liabilities:		25,000
			Total liabilities:		$44,645
			Owner's equity:		
			Royer, capital		
Total current assets		$ 36,650	Jan. 1, 1983	$63,205	
Long-term assets:			Plus: Net income		
Land	$13,000		for 1983	1,800	
Building	60,000		Royer, capital		
Total long-term assets		73,000	Dec. 31, 1983		65,005
			Total liabilities and		
Total assets		$109,650	owner's equity		$109,650

---

*A $1025 contingent liability exists on the note of Mark Simkin discounted with recourse at the 1st Center Bank on December 20, 1983. The note's maturity date is January 18, 1984.

Problem Situation

The Shipley Furniture Company sells household furniture items (sofas, bedroom sets, etc.). The company closes its accounting records annually on December 31 in order to prepare financial statements. Since each merchandise inventory item has a rather large wholesale cost, the Shipley Furniture Company utilizes a perpetual inventory system (with a specific identification costing method). The company does not allow its customers any cash discounts on the purchase of furniture. However, it does give the customers one month after the date of sale to pay for the furniture without charging them any interest.

Problem Requirements

Part A

Assume that you are the accountant for the Shipley Furniture Company (which uses a perpetual investment system). Presented below are some financial transactions that occurred during the years 1983 and 1984. You are required to prepare the necessary entries in the Shipley Furniture Company's journal for these financial transactions.

1. On July 1, 1983, the Shipley Furniture Company sold a sofa to the Burton Company at a retail price of $1200. The wholesale cost of this sofa was $800. Following its normal sales policy, the Shipley Furniture Company allowed the Burton Company one month (from the July 1 sale date) to pay for the sofa without charging any interest. Prepare the entry (or entries) in the Shipley Furniture Company's journal for the July 1, 1983 sale to the Burton Company.

2. On August 1, 1983 (the date the $1200 payment was due), the owner of the Burton Company visited the Shipley Furniture Company. He indicated that because of financial difficulties, it would be impossible to immediately pay the $1200 owed on the July 1 sofa purchase. However, the Burton Company owner was willing to immediately pay $200 cash and then pay the remaining $1000 in six months. The owner of the Shipley Furniture Company agreed to this payment plan under the condition that the Burton Company sign a six-month note at a 9 percent yearly interest rate for the $1000. The Burton Company was favorable toward this arrangement. Prepare the entry in the Shipley Furniture Company's journal for the receipt of the $200 cash and the $1000 note from the Burton Company on August 1, 1983.

3. On December 31, 1983, the Shipley Furniture Company wants to prepare its yearly financial statements. The company's accountant is currently recording the necessary adjusting entries to update the accounting records. Prepare the adjusting entry required on December 31, 1983 relating to the August 1, 1983 note transaction with the Burton Company.

4. On February 1, 1984 (the due date of the six-month, $1000 note from the Burton Company), the Shipley Furniture Company receives a check from the Burton Company in full payment of the principal and interest on the note. Prepare the February 1, 1984 entry in the Shipley Furniture Company's journal for the collection of the $1000 note.

Part B

Assume that you are the accountant for the Burton Company. This company also closes its accounting records annually on December 31. Referring back to Part A of the problem requirements, prepare all the necessary entries in the Burton Company's journal for its financial transactions with the Shipley Furniture Company during the years 1983 and 1984.

Problem Objectives and Solution Approach

Objectives:

1. To understand the accounting process involved for the sale of merchandise inventory (from both the seller's and buyer's point of view).

2. To analyze a note transaction from both the maker's and payee's point of view.

Solution Approach:

Part A

1. Record the Shipley Furniture Company's journal entries for the sale and cost of merchandise sold relating to the sofa.

2. Record the Shipley Furniture Company's journal entry to replace its previous account receivable from the Burton Company with a note receivable.

3. Record the Shipley Furniture Company's adjusting entry for the accrued interest earned on the note for the period August 1 to December 31, 1983.

4. Record the Shipley Furniture Company's journal entry for the note collection on its maturity date.

Part B

1. Record the Burton Company's journal entry for the sofa purchase.

2. Record the Burton Company's journal entry to replace its previous account payable to the Shipley Furniture Company with a note payable.

3. Record the Burton Company's adjusting entry for the accrued interest expense on the note for the period August 1 to December 31, 1983.

4. Record the Burton Company's journal entry for the note payment on its maturity date.

7

Financial Statement Analysis
Long-Term Assets

Chapters 7 and 8 conclude the analysis of assets by discussing two major categories of long-term assets: (1) plant and equipment, and (2) intangibles. The common characteristic of all long-term assets is their expected utilization beyond a one-year time period. An additional common trait of most long-term assets is that each one typically has a significant dollar cost.

The term *term and equipment* refers to all types of tangible, long-term assets that are normally utilized in the operating activities of an organization. These assets are not purchased with the intent of their being sold to customers. Tangible assets are those having physical existence. Examples of tangible plant and equipment assets are land, buildings, machinery, automobiles, and office equipment such as typewriters, desks, and calculators. Another term often used in accounting to mean the same thing as plant and equipment is *fixed assets*. This term implies that the assets are of a long-term nature and that the organization plans to use them in operating its business.

Basis of Valuing Plant and Equipment Assets

The generally accepted accounting method for valuing plant and equipment assets (as well as the intangible assets discussed in Chapter 8) is at their *cost*. The cost of a plant and equipment asset includes all the expenditures incurred to get the asset into operational use.

159

Assume that the Wayne Kelley Sporting Goods Company purchased a piece of machinery from the Dator Company at a list price of $1000. A 2 percent cash discount was received as a result of the Kelley Company's paying for the machine within 10 days of the purchase date. In addition, the Kelley Company made the following expenditures: sales tax of 5 percent, $100 freight to have the machine delivered, and $40 to Ted Rankin for installing the machine.

Based upon this information, the *actual* cost of the purchased machine is computed as follows:

List price of machinery		$1000
Less: Cash discount (2% × $1000)*		20
Net cash price of machinery		$ 980
Plus: Sales tax (5% × $1000 list price)	$ 50	
Freight cost	100	
Installation cost	40	190
Total cost of machinery		$1170

*A discount is subtracted directly from the machine's list price; thus, no separate accounting is utilized for the discount.

The 2 percent cash discount is *subtracted* from the $1000 list price to determine the machine's net cash price. Before the machine could be used by the Kelley Company, three additional costs were incurred: $50 sales tax was paid to the Dator Company on the machine purchase, $100 was paid to a freight company for delivering the machine, and $40 installation charges were paid. After these three additional costs are added to the $980 net cash price, the $1170 actual cost of the purchased machine is determined.

If it is assumed that all the above costs are paid immediately, the following journal entry is recorded by the Kelley Company for the machine acquisition:

Machinery	1170	
Cash		1170

There are no separate accounts established for the sales tax, freight cost, or installation cost on the purchased machine. Since these three expenditures are all part of acquiring the machine and making it operational to the Kelley Company, they are debited directly to the long-term tangible asset account called "machinery."

Two additional long-term assets are *land* and *buildings*. As with machinery, the cost of these assets includes all the expenditures incurred to acquire and make these assets operational. For example, assume that a company intends to construct a new factory building on a purchased tract of land. A separate long-term asset account called "land" is debited for all the costs incurred in acquiring and preparing the land for the building construction. The following expenditures are thus charged to the land account: the land purchase price, the commission to the real estate agent selling the land, any legal fees associated with the land acquisition, and the costs of clearing, grading, and landscaping the property. Once the land has been prepared for construction, a long-term asset account called "building" is then debited for all the factory construction costs. These expenditures include the following: the cost of a building permit, the fee to architects, the cost of insurance during the construction period, the cost of building materials (concrete, steel, lumber, etc.), and the salaries of construction laborers.

Depreciation on Plant and Equipment Assets

The total cost of a machine or a building represents an asset at the time of acquisition. These items are economic resources having current and future value to a company and thus meet the definition of assets from Chapter 1. A piece of machinery and a building have value because of the benefits that can be received from them. For example, a building's present and future benefits result from the fact that a company can use the facilities to operate its business and, it is hoped, earn an income each year.

The term *depreciation* means the allocation of the total actual cost of a long-term tangible asset over its estimated useful life as an *expense*. If a company buys a piece of machinery for $5000, this machine is an asset because it represents "a bundle of service potentials" to the company. As the machine is utilized by the company in its daily business operations, an expense (called *depreciation*) should be recognized each accounting period for the service benefits received from this asset.

Depreciation expense on a plant and equipment asset is determined at the end of every accounting period in order to achieve a better matching of revenues earned against expenses incurred on the income statement. Assume for a moment that a company bought a $6000 machine on January 1, 1983 and recognized the entire cost as a 1983 expense. If the company expects to utilize this machine for five years, the recognition of the $6000 cost as a 1983 expense causes an improper matching of revenues and expenses on its income statement for each year from 1983 through 1987. A five-year useful life means that the company plans to receive service benefits from the machine during the next five years. Therefore, depreciation expense should be recognized every year of this five-year period. If the entire $6000 cost is recognized as a 1983 expense, the company's 1983 expenses on its income statement would be overstated (and the resultant net income understated), because only one year's worth of the machine's five years of service benefits is actually received during 1983. Also, in each year from 1984 through 1987, the expenses would be understated (and the net income overstated), since service benefits are received from the machine during these years but no depreciation expense is recognized. Thus, the objective of depreciation accounting is to determine, for each period, the portion of a plant and equipment asset's total cost that should be recognized as an expense. In this manner a better matching is achieved on the income statement.

Before depreciation expense on plant and equipment assets is computed, several important *estimations* are required:

1. An *estimate* must be made of the asset's expected *useful life.* The expected useful life represents the time period during which a company plans to receive service benefits. Therefore, this estimation is necessary to determine the number of years that depreciation expense will be recognized on the asset. The Internal Revenue Service publishes depreciation tax guide lines recommending useful lives for different categories of plant and equipment assets. Many companies follow these guide lines, even though their use is not required by the Internal Revenue Service. As long as the useful life selected for depreciating a plant and equipment asset appears reasonable, the Internal Revenue Service ordinarily accepts a company's own estimation.

2. An *estimate* must be made of the asset's expected *salvage value* (also called *scrap value* or *residual value*). The salvage value represents the amount of money that a company expects to receive from selling the plant and equipment asset at the end of its useful life. Depreciation expense is not recognized on the salvage value, since this portion of the asset's original cost will be recovered when sold. Only the portion of the asset's total cost that is not expected to be recovered (the original cost minus the estimated salvage value) at the end of its useful life is recognized as depreciation expense.

In addition to depreciation expense being caused by the *use* of plant and equipment assets each accounting period, it also occurs as a result of asset *obsolescence.* With new technological developments in the market, a company's long-term assets may become obsolete (outdated). This causes the current and future service benefits from the assets to be reduced.

It is extremely difficult to measure *quantitatively* each period's depreciation expense caused by obsolescence. Even though no direct measurement is made of the depreciation expense due to obsolescence, the reader should understand that obsolescence is a factor in the overall concept of depreciation. Furthermore, when an organization attempts to estimate the useful life of a plant and equipment asset, the effect of obsolescence is considered.

The only plant and equipment asset that is not depreciated is *land.* A company's land does not wear out from use and is assumed to have an infinite life. Consequently, depreciation expense is not recognized on this long-term asset.

An organization often makes improvements to its land (such as a fence) which are subject to depreciation. However, no depreciation expense can be recognized on improvement costs if they are debited to the land account, because of the accounting principle that any dollar costs included in the land account are undepreciable. Therefore, many companies maintain a separate plant and equipment asset account called "land improvements." This account is debited for improvement expenditures to land, allowing these expenditures to be depreciated over the estimated useful life of the improvements.

Depreciation Methods for Plant and Equipment Assets

The discussion in Chapter 5 indicated that any of the inventory costing methods (FIFO, LIFO, etc.) can be utilized for determining an organization's period-end inventory and cost of merchandise sold expense. Once a particular costing method has been selected, it should be *consistently* used each accounting period.

There are four major methods for computing depreciation expense on plant and equipment assets. The consistency concept also applies to depreciation methods. When a company makes a decision to use a particular depreciation method on a plant and equipment asset, this method should be consistently used during the asset's estimated useful life. The company can, however, utilize different depreciation methods for other plant and equipment assets within its organization.

Depreciation Methods Based Upon Time Passage Rather Than Actual Usage

A depreciation method based upon the passage of time means that depreciation expense on a plant and equipment asset is recognized at the end of each period regardless of the quantity of use obtained from the asset. The criterion for recognizing depreciation is the passage of days, weeks, months, etc., during the asset's estimated useful life.

There are three major depreciation methods based upon time passage: the *straight-line method*, the *sum-of-the-years'-digits method*, and the *declining-balance method*. Each of these methods is discussed and illustrated on the basis of the following situation:

> The Wayne Kelley Sporting Goods Company purchased a piece of machinery on January 1, 1983 at a total cost of $1000. The machine has an estimated useful life of five years and an estimated salvage value of $100 at the end of the fifth year.

Straight-line Depreciation Method

This is the simplest of all the depreciation methods. It *assumes* that an organization obtains equal benefits in each accounting period from a plant and equipment asset. Therefore, an equal dollar amount of depreciation expense is recognized for every period.

The computations below and in Exhibit 7-1 reflect the annual depreciation expense on the Kelley Company's $1000 machine. The "accumulated depreciation" account and the term "book value of a plant and equipment asset" are shown in Exhibit 7-1 and will be discussed shortly.

Total cost of machine on January 1, 1983	$1000
Less: Estimated salvage value of machine at the end of its expected five-year useful life	100
Depreciable basis of machine	$ 900
Estimated useful life of machine	5 years

$$\text{Depreciation expense each year} = \frac{\text{depreciable basis of machine}}{\text{estimated useful life of machine}}$$

$$= \frac{\cdot \$900}{5 \text{ years}} = \$180 \text{ per year}$$

Exhibit 7-1

YEAR	DEPRE-CIATION EXPENSE EACH YEAR	BALANCE OF ACCU-MULATED DEPRECIA-TION ACCOUNT AT THE END OF EACH YEAR	BOOK VALUE OF PLANT AND EQUIP-MENT ASSET AT THE END OF EACH YEAR
1983	$180	$180	$820 ($1000 – $180)
1984	180	360 ($180 + $180)	640 ($1000 – $360)
1985	180	540 ($360 + $180)	460 ($1000 – $540)
1986	180	720 ($540 + $180)	280 ($1000 – $720)
1987	180	900 ($720 + $180)	100 ($1000 – $900)
	$900		

Machine's total
depreciation expense
during five-year
estimated useful life

Machine's estimated *salvage value* at the end of the fifth year

The following *adjusting entry* is recorded each December 31 of years 1983 through 1987 to recognize the annual depreciation expense under the straight-line method:

Depreciation expense	180	
Accumulated depreciation—machinery		180

This adjusting entry assumes that the Kelley Company closes its books only once a year to prepare financial statements. If the company has a monthly closing, then each month's adjusting entry for depreciation is $15 ($180 yearly depreciation ÷ 12 months).

The first step in determining the annual depreciation expense is to compute the machine's *depreciable basis*. It represents the dollar portion of the asset's total cost that will be depreciated during the estimated useful life. Since the *salvage value* is expected to be recovered at the end of the asset's estimated life, it is *subtracted* from the total cost to determine the depreciable basis ($900 for the Kelley Company's machine).

Remember, the straight-line depreciation method results in an equal dollar amount of depreciation expense each period during a plant and equipment asset's estimated useful life. Therefore, *dividing* the asset's depreciable basis by its estimated useful life gives the yearly depreciation expense ($180 per year for the Kelley Company's machine). The column of the depreciation schedule titled *"Depreciation Expense* Each Year" indicates the $180 annual expense in years 1983 through 1987. To understand the column called "Balance of *Accumulated Depreciation* Account at the End of Each Year," return to the annual adjusting entry for depreciation.

The debit is to an income statement account called "depreciation expense." This account is classified as an operating expense on the income statement and is closed to the owner's equity account in the same manner as other expense accounts at the end of an accounting period. The credit is to a special account called "Accumulated depreciation—machinery." It is a balance sheet *contra* account to the machine asset being depreciated. As with all balance sheet accounts, the accumulated depreciation account is not closed at the end of the accounting period. Rather, its balance *increases* each period because of the depreciation adjusting entry.

Exhibit 7-2 presents the Kelley Company's two general ledger balance sheet accounts for the $1000 machine during its five-year estimated useful life (for simplification, posting reference numbers are excluded).

The machinery account is debited for $1000 when the asset is purchased. Then, at the end of each year, the accumulated depreciation—machinery account is credited for the period's depreciation. Under the straight-line depreciation method, this account is credited $180 every December 31 during the machine's five-year estimated useful life.

The column of the depreciation schedule (see Exhibit 7-1) labeled *"Book Value* of Plant and Equipment Asset at the End of Each Year" represents the difference between the asset's original total cost and the accumulated depreciation account balance. For example, the machine's book value at the end of 1984 is $640 ($1000 cost minus $360 accumulated depreciation account balance). Book value is the portion of a plant and equipment asset's

Exhibit 7-2

Account: Machinery   Account No.   15

DATE	ITEM	POSTING REFERENCE	DEBIT	DATE	ITEM	POSTING REFERENCE	CREDIT
1983 Jan. 1	Purchase of Machine		1000				

Account: Accumulated Depreciation–Machinery   Account No.   16

DATE	ITEM	POSTING REFERENCE	DEBIT	DATE	ITEM	POSTING REFERENCE	CREDIT
				1983 Dec. 31	Adjusting entry		180
				1984 Dec. 31	Adjusting entry *(360)*		180
				1985 Dec. 31	Adjusting entry *(540)*		180
				1986 Dec. 31	Adjusting entry *(720)*		180
				1987 Dec. 31	Adjusting entry *(900)*		180

total cost that has not yet been depreciated. That is, since the "accumulated depreciation" account balance indicates the depreciated portion of the asset's cost, its subtraction from the asset's total cost gives the undepreciated cost (called the *book value*).

Another approach to understanding the term *book value* is to simply analyze the two words—*book* and *value*. These words indicate what the accounting records (often called the *books*) show as the value of a plant and equipment asset. It should be emphasized, however, that "book value" and "market value" do not mean the same thing. The latter is the price that could be received by selling the asset to someone outside the organization. A plant and equipment asset's market value is typically different from what the organization's accounting records indicate as its book value.

At the end of 1987 the accumulated depreciation account has a $900 balance (see Exhibit 7-2). The machine's book value is therefore $100 ($1000 cost *minus* $900 accumulated depreciation balance). A $100 salvage value was estimated when the machine was purchased on January 1, 1983.

Since the salvage value reflects the machine's worth at the end of its useful life, the $100 book value on December 31, 1987 represents the company's salvage value estimation.

A partial balance sheet illustrating a company's plant and equipment assets is presented below with assumed dollar figures. The heading "Plant and Equipment" could also be called "Long-Term Assets."

Plant and Equipment

Land		$20,000
Building	$100,000	
Less: Accumulated depreciation	30,000	70,000
Machinery	$ 20,000	
Less: Accumulated depreciation	15,000	5,000
Total plant and equipment assets		$95,000

As discussed previously, depreciation is not recognized on land. Therefore, an accumulated depreciation account for this asset does not exist. A separate accumulated depreciation account is utilized for each plant and equipment asset with its dollar balance subtracted from the related asset. The building's book value is $70,000, and the machinery has a $5000 book value.

Review Questions

At this point, answer the following multiple-choice questions to test your knowledge of the previous reading material. The solutions are given below.

1. Which financial item is not a plant and equipment asset?
   a. Land.
   b. Office supplies.
   c. Machinery.
   d. Typewriter.

2. The Zipp Company purchased a machine on Jun 1, 1983 at a list price of $500. The following monetary items relate to the machine acquisition:

Cash discount received	$10
Sales tax on purchase	$25
Installation cost for machine	$30

   The machine's total cost is
   a. $500.
   b. $515.
   c. $545.
   d. $565.

3. The Porter Company bought a $400 typewriter during 1983 and estimated its useful life to be six years. The $400 expenditure was recognized as a 1983 operating expense rather than the asset's cost being depreciated over its·six-year life. What effect will this have on the company's 1984 income?
   a. Overstated.
   b. Understated.
   c. No effect.

4. What is the best definition of *book value*?
   a. A plant and equipment asset's estimated salvage value.
   b. A plant and equipment asset's market value.
   c. A plant and equipment asset's total cost minus its accumulated depreciation account balance.
   d. A plant and equipment asset's depreciation expense balance minus its accumulated depreciation account balance.

Answers

1. b

2. c ($500 – $10 + $25 + $30)

3. a

4. c

Accelerated Depreciation Methods

There are two depreciation techniques that are called *accelerated* methods. As compared to straight-line depreciation, these methods cause larger depreciation expense deductions during the early years of a plant and equipment asset's useful life and smaller expense deductions in later years.

Under the straight-line method, each period's depreciation expense is the same; equal benefits from a plant and equipment asset are assumed for every accounting period throughout the asset's estimated useful life. The underlying *assumption* of accelerated depreciation methods is that more benefits are received from a plant and equipment asset during the early years of its estimated life than in later years. Therefore, each period's depreciation expense is larger in the early years.

Sum-of-the-years'-digits Method

The steps involved when depreciation is computed under this accelerated method (using the data from the Kelley Company's January 1, 1983 machine purchase on page 163) are as follows:
   1. As the title of this method indicates (the "sum of the years' digits"), you first add the total digits in the asset's estimated

useful life. The sum of the digits for the Kelley Company's five-year-estimated-life machine is 15 (5 + 4 + 3 + 2 + 1 = 15). This number represents the denominator in each year's fraction for computing depreciation expense.

2. The numerator of each year's depreciation fraction is the number of years remaining in the asset's estimated useful life at the beginning of the particular year for which depreciation is being computed. The Kelley Company's 1983 fraction is 5/15, since 5 years remain in the machine's estimated useful life at the beginning of 1983. The depreciation fractions for the subsequent years are: 4/15 in 1984, 3/15 in 1985, 2/15 in 1986, and 1/15 in 1987.

3. The fractions determined from steps 1 and 2 are multiplied each year by the asset's depreciable basis (total cost minus estimated salvage value) to compute the yearly depreciation expense. Remember, the depreciable basis of the Kelley Company's machine is $900.

By the sum-of-the-years'-digits method, the Kelley Company's depreciation computational schedule for its machine is shown in Exhibit 7-3.

Exhibit 7-3

YEAR	DEPRECIATION EXPENSE EACH YEAR	BALANCE OF ACCU-MULATED DEPRE-CIATION ACCOUNT AT THE END OF EACH YEAR	BOOK VALUE OF PLANT AND EQUIP-MENT ASSET AT THE END OF EACH YEAR
1983	$300 (5/15 × $900)	$300	$700 ($1000 – $300)
1984	240 (4/15 × $900)	540 ($300 + $240)	460 ($1000 – $540)
1985	180 (3/15 × $900)	720 ($540 + $180)	280 ($1000 – $720)
1986	120 (2/15 × $900)	840 ($720 + $120)	160 ($1000 – $840)
1987	60 (1/15 × $900)	900 ($840 + $ 60)	100 ($1000 – $900)
	$900		

Machine's total *depreciation*
expense during five-year
estimated useful life

Machine's estimated *salvage*
value at the end of the
fifth year

A comparison of this depreciation schedule with Exhibit 7-1 (where the straight-line method is used) shows that both the sum-of-the-years'-digits and the straight-line methods result in $900 depreciation expense during the machine's five-year estimated useful life. Further analysis of the

two methods reveals that the sum-of-the-years'-digits causes larger depreciation expense deductions in the early years of the machine's life (1983 and
1984) and smaller deductions in the later years (1986 and 1987). The Kelley
Company will record an adjusting entry each December 31 during the
machine's five-year life, debiting "depreciation expense" and crediting "accumulated depreciation—machinery" for the dollar amounts in the above
schedule.

When an asset is depreciated under the sum-of-the-years'-digits
method, the summation of the yearly fractions equals *one*. For example, the
fractions for the Kelley Company's machine are 5/15 + 4/15 + 3/15 + 2/15 +
1/15 = 1. Since the depreciable basis is multiplied by each of the fractions
during the asset's useful life, the total depreciable basis will always be recognized as depreciation expense over the life of the asset. The following formula
can be used to determine the denominator for each year's fraction: $n(n + 1)/2$,
where n equals the estimated number of years in the asset's life. The reader
should recognize the usefulness of this formula when the estimated life of a
plant and equipment asset is quite large. For example, the denominator
computation for a building with a 100-year estimated life is

$$\frac{n(n + 1)}{2} = \frac{100(100 + 1)}{2} = 5050$$

Declining-balance Method

This technique is typically the most accelerated of the depreciation
methods, since it normally results in the largest depreciation expense being
recognized during a plant and equipment asset's early years. The multiplica-
tion of a fixed percentage by the asset's *undepreciated cost* (another term for
book value) gives the yearly depreciation expense under the declining-balance
method. For depreciating tangible personal property (machinery and other
types of equipment), the Internal Revenue Service allows a maximum fixed
percentage of twice (200 percent of) the asset's straight-line rate. On real estate property such as a building, the maximum fixed percentage that can be
used is 1-1/2 times (150 percent of) the asset's straight-line rate. If the declining-balance method is used, the Internal Revenue Service permits a company to ignore the estimated salvage value of its plant and equipment asset
when computing each period's depreciation expense. However, even with this
special provision, an asset cannot be depreciated below its expected salvage
value.

The declining-balance method is now demonstrated by returning
to the Kelley Company's machine acquisition on January 1, 1983. Since the
machine's estimated useful life is 5 years, the straight-line depreciation rate
would be 20 percent each year (5 years = 1/5 per year = 20 percent). Under
the declining-balance method, the maximum fixed percentage depreciation
rate is therefore 40 percent (20 percent × 2).

Exhibit 7-4 is the five-year depreciation schedule for the Kelley
Company's machine.

Exhibit 7-4

YEAR	DEPRECIATION EXPENSE EACH YEAR	BALANCE OF ACCUMU-LATED DEPRECIATION ACCOUNT AT THE END OF EACH YEAR	BOOK VALUE (UNDE-PRECIATED COST) OF PLANT AND EQUIPMENT ASSET AT THE END OF EACH YEAR
1983	$400.00 ($1000 × 40%)*	$400.00	$600.00 ($1000 – $400.00)
1984	240.00 ($600 × 40%)†	640.00 ($400.00 + $240.00)	360.00 ($1000 – $640.00)
1985	144.00 ($360 × 40%)	784.00 ($640.00 + $144.00)	216.00 ($1000 – $784.00)
1986	86.40 ($216 × 40%)	870.40 ($784.00 + $ 86.40)	129.60 ($1000 – $870.40)
1987	29.60‡	900.00 ($870.40 + $ 29.60)	100.00 ($1000 – $900.00)
	$900.00		

Machine's total *depreciation expense* during five-year estimated useful life

Machine's estimated *salvage value* at the end of the fifth year

* For the first-year depreciation computation, the 40 percent declining-balance rate is multiplied by the machine's $1000 total cost (salvage value is ignored). Since depreciation has not previously been recognized, the machine's total cost is the same as its undepreciated cost.

† In 1984, the fixed percentage (40 percent) is multiplied by the undepreciated cost ($600).

‡In 1987, the depreciation expense is $29.60. Remember, a plant and equipment asset cannot be depreciated below its estimated salvage value. Since the machine's undepreciated cost is $129.60 at the end of 1986 and the estimated salvage value is $100, only $29.60 ($129.60–$100.00) depreciation can be recognized during 1987.

The $900 total depreciation expense recognized on the machine is the same as under the straight-line method (see Exhibit 7-1) and the sum-of-the-years'-digits method (see Exhibit 7-3). This depreciation technique is called the *declining-balance method* because each period's depreciation expense is determined through the process of multiplying a fixed percentage rate by an asset's declining balance (the undepreciated cost). Based upon the above depreciation schedule for the machine's five-year life, an adjusting entry will be recorded every December 31 debiting "depreciation expense" and crediting "accumulated depreciation—machinery" for the specific amount indicated in the schedule.

Comparison of Three Depreciation Methods Based Upon the Passage of Time

Presented in Exhibit 7-5 is a summarized schedule of the depreciation expense recognized on the Kelley Company's machine under the three depreciation methods discussed in this chapter.

Exhibit 7-5

Depreciation Expense

YEAR	STRAIGHT-LINE METHOD	SUM-OF-THE-YEARS'-DIGITS METHOD	DECLINING-BALANCE METHOD
1983	$180.00	$300.00	$400.00
1984	$180.00	240.00	240.00
1985	180.00	180.00	144.00
1986	180.00	120.00	86.40
1987	180.00	60.00	29.60
	$900.00	$900.00	$900.00

Total *depreciation expense*
recognized during machine's
five-year estimated life

These depreciation methods have two important common characteristics:

1. Each period's depreciation expense is unaffected by *actual usage*. Rather, the depreciation expense computed under any of the three methods is based upon time passage (a month, a year, etc.).

2. Under generally accepted accounting procedures as well as Internal Revenue Service requirements, the maximum depreciation expense that can be recognized during a plant and equipment asset's useful life is its total cost minus estimated salvage value. For the Kelley Company's machine, each of the three illustrated methods resulted in a total $900 depreciation expense ($1000 asset cost minus $100 salvage value).

Income Tax Advantage from Accelerated Depreciation Methods

An organization's taxable income is determined by subtracting its business expenses from the earned revenues. The total depreciation expense (which is tax deductible) recognized during a plant and equipment asset's estimated useful life is the same, regardless of which depreciation method is used. As discussed previously, an accelerated depreciation method, as compared to the straight-line method, causes larger depreciation expense deductions in the early years of an asset's life and smaller deductions in later years. Consequently, if an accelerated depreciation method is used, the taxable income and the resultant taxes paid to the government will be smaller during these early years and larger thereafter.

The advantage of paying less taxes in the early years of an asset's estimated life is that a company thereby *defers* this portion of the tax payment to future years. The deferred tax money can then be used within the company rather than its being paid immediately to the government. For example, assume that an organization's 1983 tax liability is reduced $300 from using the declining-balance depreciation method instead of the straight-line method. Even though the organization's tax liability will be larger in subsequent years, it has the opportunity currently to use the $300 tax reduction money and earn a favorable return. At a minimum, the organization can deposit this $300 in a bank savings account and earn approximately 5-1/2 percent interest.

Because of the tax benefits from accelerated depreciation methods, many organizations utilize them even when there is no theoretical justification. We have indicated that the straight-line depreciation method assumes equal benefits each period from a plant and equipment asset, whereas the accelerated methods assume more benefits during the asset's early years. From a *practical* point of view, however, it is rather difficult to quantitatively measure the periodic benefits obtained. As long as a depreciation method is consistently used, once it is selected for a particular asset, an organization is not required to theoretically justify the method.

An exception to the consistency principle exists for income tax purposes. The Internal Revenue Service permits a company to switch from the declining-balance depreciation method to the straight-line method at any time during a plant and equipment asset's estimated useful life.

Depreciation Method Based Upon the Actual Usage of Plant and Equipment Assets Rather Than the Passage of Time

Previous depreciation methods discussed in this chapter recognize each period's depreciation expense based upon time passage. The *units-of-output* method causes the periodic depreciation expense to be affected by the *actual usage* of a plant and equipment asset.

To illustrate the units-of-output depreciation method, the Kelley Company's $1000 machine purchase is again utilized. Under this depreciation method, however, the actual usage (output) from an asset must be estimated rather than the number of years in the asset's useful life. For its machine, the Kelley Company estimates that 22,500 hours of usage will be obtained. The units-of-output depreciation rate is then determined as follows:

$$\frac{\text{Depreciable basis of asset}}{\text{Estimated output from asset}}$$

$$= \frac{\$1000 \text{ cost of machine} - \$100 \text{ estimated salvage value}}{22,500 \text{ Estimated Hours}}$$

$$= \frac{\$900}{22,500} = \$.04 \text{ per hour depreciation rate}$$

Dividing the machine's depreciable basis by its estimated output gives a depreciation rate per hour of activity. Each period's depreciation expense is determined by multiplying the actual hours of machine usage by the $.04-per-hour depreciation rate. If the Kelley Company's machine is operated 6000 hours during 1983, the depreciation expense for 1983 is $240 (6000 hours × $.04). The December 31, 1983 adjusting entry to recognize depreciation on the machine would be

Depreciation expense	240	
Accumulated depreciation—machinery		240

Assume that the Kelley Company did not utilize its machine throughout 1984. Therefore, under the units-of-output method, the 1984 depreciation expense would be zero (0 hours × $.04).

Depreciation for a Portion of a Year

In the year that a plant and equipment asset is purchased or sold, depreciation expense should be recognized for only the portion of the year the asset is owned. For example, a company purchased a $3000 machine on October 1, 1983. This machine has a three-year estimated useful life and an expected salvage value of $300 at the end of the third year. The company chooses the straight-line depreciation method for the machine. Presented below is the computation of the 1983 depreciation expense:

Total cost of machine on October 1, 1983	$3000
Less: Estimated salvage value	300
Depreciable basis of machine	$2700

$$\text{Depreciation expense each year} = \frac{\$2700}{3 \text{ years}} = \$900 \text{ per year}$$
(under straight-line method)

$$\text{Depreciation expense for 1983} = \frac{3 \text{ months (from Oct. 1 through Dec. 31)}}{12 \text{ months}}$$

$$\times \$900 = 1/4 \times \$900 = \underline{\$225}$$

The depreciation expense for a full year is $900. However, since the machine was purchased on October 1, 1983, the company owned it for only three months during 1983. Therefore, three months' (1/4 of a year) depreciation expense should be recognized in 1983.

If a plant and equipment asset is disposed of during a year, depreciation expense should be recorded in that year for the time period the asset was owned. For example, the sale of a plant and equipment asset on February 1, 1983 results in only one month's (January) depreciation expense being recognized on this asset during 1983.

A practical rule often followed when a plant and equipment asset is purchased on a day other than the first of the month is to recognize a full month's depreciation if the asset is acquired on any day from the first through the fifteenth and no depreciation in that month if the purchase is made after the fifteenth. For a plant and equipment asset sale, the rule would be to recognize a full month's depreciation if the asset is sold on the fifteenth or thereafter and no depreciation for that month if it is sold before the fifteenth. Since estimates are involved in periodic depreciation calculations (the useful life and salvage value are estimated), it would be rather meaningless to compute depreciation for the specific number of days that an asset is owned. Furthermore, if the above rules are used, a company's annual depreciation expense will not be significantly affected.

Fallacy Surrounding Depreciation

People who are not accountants often think—wrongly—that the function of periodic depreciation recognition is to determine a plant and equipment asset's decreased value. Rather, depreciation accounting is an *allocation* technique, not a valuation technique. By recognizing periodic depreciation, a long-term asset's total cost (less estimated salvage value) is allocated as an expense to the periods receiving benefits from the asset's utilization. On a company's income statement, this allocation process achieves a better matching during each accounting period of revenues earned against expenses incurred. The adjusting entry for depreciation reflects the portion of a plant and equipment asset's total cost that has become an expense during the period.

Review Questions

At this point, answer the following multiple-choice questions to test your knowledge of the previous reading material. The solutions are given below.

1. What is the major advantage of an accelerated depreciation method?
   a. A more accurate matching of revenues earned against expenses incurred on each period's income statement.
   b. Less income tax is paid during the early years of a plant and equipment asset's useful life.
   c. Less income tax is paid during the later years of a plant and equipment asset's useful life.
   d. A plant and equipment asset's market value is better reflected.

2. A $600 machine was purchased by the Haven Company on January 1, 1983. This machine has a $100 estimated salvage value and a five-year useful life. Under the declining-balance method, the company's 1983 depreciation expense is
   a. $100.
   b. $120.
   c. $200.
   d. $240.

3. Which depreciation method is based upon each period's actual usage of a plant and equipment asset?
   a. Straight-line method.
   b. Units-of-output method.
   c. Sum-of-the-years'-digits method.
   d. Declining-balance method.

4. The Lee Company purchased a $700 office calculator on December 1, 1983. The calculator's estimated salvage value is $100 at the end of its five-year useful life. The company plans to depreciate the calculator by the straight-line method. The 1983 depreciation expense is
   a. $ 10.00.
   b. $ 11.67.
   c. $120.00.
   d. $140.00.

Answers

1. b

2. d ($600 × 40%)*

3. b

4. a ($700 – $100 salvage value = $600 depreciable basis *divided by* 5 years = $120 per year depreciation × 1/12 = $10 depreciation during 1983 for one month asset owned)

*5 year life = 20 percent straight-line rate × 2 = 40 percent declining-balance rate. Salvage value is ignored when 1983 depreciation expense is computed.

Chapter Summary

The "plant and equipment" long-term asset category was discussed in this chapter. The process of allocating a plant and equipment asset's total cost (less expected salvage value) over its estimated useful life is called *depreciation accounting*.

There are three major depreciation methods based upon the passage of time: the *straight-line* method, the *sum-of-the-years'-digits* method, and the *declining-balance* method. The actual usage of a plant and equipment asset is considered under the *units-of-output* depreciation method.

The sum-of-the-years'-digits and declining-balance methods are called *accelerated depreciation methods*, since the depreciation expense amounts (compared to the depreciation expense amount under the straight-line method) are larger during the early years of the asset's estimated useful life. This causes a company to pay less income taxes in the asset's early years.

Theoretically, the straight-line depreciation method should be used when an organization expects to receive equal benefits each year from a plant and equipment asset. An accelerated depreciation method is theoretically justified when more benefits are expected during the early years than in the later years of an asset's useful life. Because of the difficulty of measuring the periodic benefits from a plant and equipment asset, a company is not required to give theoretical justification for the depreciation method it selects. However, the depreciation method adopted for a plant and equipment asset must be consistently used for each accounting period during the asset's useful life.

Chapter Problem

The solution to the problem is given in the appendix. However, the reader is urged first to attempt to work the problem on his own and then to check his work against the given solution.

Problem Situation

The Lester Company began business on January 1, 1981 to manufacture and sell prefabricated garages for homeowners. The company closes its accounting books each December 31 and prepares annual financial statements. To manufacture the prefabricated garages, a $6000 machine was purchased on January 1, 1981. Its estimated useful life is four years, and the company expects to sell the machine for $1000 at the end of the fourth year. The sum-of-the-years'-digits method was selected for depreciating the piece of machinery.

On January 1, 1981, the Lester Company also purchased a truck to deliver its sold garages. It cost $4500 and has a $500 estimated salvage value. A decision was made to depreciate the truck based upon the actual miles driven every year. The company plans to drive the truck 40,000 miles before replacing it with a new one.

Presented below is the plant and equipment asset section of the Lester Company's balance sheet on January 1, 1983 (two years after the start of business)

Plant and equipment:

Machinery	$6000	
Less: Accumulated depreciation	3500	$2500
Truck	$4500	
Less: Accumulated depreciation	1500	3000
Total plant and equipment assets		$5500

Problem Requirements

Part A

Assume that the current date is December 31, 1983. The Lester Company must, therefore, record adjusting entries for 1983 in order to have its accounting records updated before preparing the financial statement.

1. On the basis of the information in this problem, compute the correct 1983 depreciation expense for the Lester Company's machine and then prepare the December 31, 1983 adjusting entry to reflect the year's depreciation on the machinery.

2. Using the information in this problem and assuming that the Lester Company's delivery truck was driven 8000 miles during 1983, compute the 1983 depreciation expense for the truck and then prepare the December 31, 1983 adjusting entry to reflect the year's depreciation on the delivery truck.

Part B

Assuming that the Lester Company's 1983 adjusting entries for depreciation on its machine and truck have already been recorded and posted, prepare the plant and equipment asset section of the company's December 31, 1983 balance sheet in order to disclose the updated book values of these assets.

Part C

For illustrative purposes, assume that the Lester Company uses the *straight-line* depreciation method rather than the sum-of-the-years'-digits method for its $6000 machine acquired January 1, 1981. Compute the 1983 depreciation expense for its machine under this assumption.

Problem Objectives and Solution Approach

Objectives:

1. To correctly utilize the sum-of-the-years'-digits, units-of-output, and straight-line methods in computing a company's annual depreciation expense on plant and equipment assets.

2. To understand the relationship between plant and equipment asset accounts and their contra "accumulated depreciation" accounts by preparing a partial balance sheet that discloses the plant and equipment asset section.

Solution Approach:

1. Since two years' depreciation has already been recognized on the machine as of December 31, 1983, determine the correct sum-of-the-years'-digits fraction for 1983. Using this fraction, compute and record the year-end adjusting entry to reflect the 1983 depreciation on the company's machine.

2. Two years' depreciation has also been recorded on the truck as of December 31, 1983 under the units-of-output method (a per mile depreciation rate being used). The company's depreciation rate per truck mile would have been previously determined when the truck was purchased on January 1, 1981. Since the rate was not given in the problem, it must now be computed. By using this depreciation rate along with the 1983 actual mileage driven, the company's 1983 truck depreciation can be determined followed by the correct year-end adjusting entry.

3. The January 1, 1983 "accumulated depreciation" account balances for the machine and truck are provided. After computing the machine and truck depreciation for 1983 in prior parts of this problem, *add* these amounts to their respective January 1 accumulated depreciation account balances. The December 31, 1983 plant and equipment asset section of the balance sheet can then be prepared.

4. Using the straight-line method, compute the 1983 depreciation expense for the company's machine.

8

Financial Statement Analysis

Long-Term Assets (Concluded)

Several additional accounting aspects of plant and equipment assets are analyzed in this chapter. Another category of long-term assets, called *intangible assets*, is also discussed.

Plant and Equipment (Continued)

Revenue Versus Capital Expenditures on Plant and Equipment Assets

A maintenance program should exist for an organization's plant and equipment assets in order to keep them operating efficiently. For example, machinery should be inspected and cleaned at regular intervals during the year so that better operational performance is obtained from the machines. In essence, we are talking about *preventive maintenance*; that is, a program of regular maintenance on a company's machinery should prevent breakdowns and premature physical deterioration. Another important aspect of a good maintenance program is proper training of the employees responsible for operating the various machines. Training procedures reduce the risk of improper use of a machine and the resultant decrease of efficiency.

The ordinary repair and maintenance costs on plant and equipment assets represent operating expenses that are often called *revenue expenditures*. The term "revenue expenditure" indicates that a particular cost incurred on a plant and equipment asset should be recognized as an expense to be subtracted from the revenues on a company's income statement. Thus, an account called "repair and maintenance expense" is debited for the ordinary expenditures under a plant and equipment asset maintenance program.

The opposite of a plant and equipment revenue expenditure is a *capital expenditure*. It represents an incurred cost that is debited to a plant and equipment asset account rather than to an expense account. In fact, we sometimes use the phrase "to capitalize an incurred cost" to indicate that an asset account should be debited for the expenditure. The basic difference between a *capital* and *revenue* expenditure is that the former results in a valuable economic resource (the basic definition of an *asset*). The latter, on the other hand, merely maintains a plant and equipment asset in good working order without increasing its useful life. When, for example, a company purchases a machine having current and future value, its cost is a capital expenditure that should be debited to an asset account. The subsequent costs each year to clean and oil this machine are revenue expenditures that should be debited to the repair and maintenance expense account.

A *betterment cost* incurred on a plant and equipment asset has the effect of increasing the asset's useful life beyond the original life estimation. This type of cost should be treated as a capital rather than a revenue expenditure, since the asset's value is being increased as a result of its estimated useful life's being extended. An example of a betterment is the cost of replacing a machine's old motor with a new one. Since the new motor should increase the machine's useful life, its cost represents a capital expenditure that is debited to the machinery account. The original cost and the accumulated depreciation on the old motor as of its replacement date should ideally be eliminated from the accounts, since this motor is no longer used. However, from a practical point of view, it is usually quite difficult to identify the portion of a machine's total cost and the related accumulated depreciation that applies to a replaced motor. Because of these practical difficulties, the cost and related depreciation on the replaced portion of a plant and equipment asset do not require elimination from the accounts. Rather, a betterment cost is debited to the plant and equipment asset account affected. Depreciation is then recognized on this cost as well as the undepreciated cost of the asset (on the date the betterment expenditure is made) over its remaining estimated useful life.

Disposal of Plant and Equipment Assets

A plant and equipment asset will ordinarily wear out or become obsolete after it has been used for several years. An organization may decide to dispose of its asset in one of the following ways:

1. *Discard* the asset.

2. *Sell* the asset.

3. *Trade* the asset for a new one.

Whenever a plant and equipment asset is disposed of, the two balance sheet accounts relating to the asset must be eliminated from a company's accounting records. For example, if a piece of machinery is sold, both the machinery and accumulated depreciation—machinery accounts for this asset are eliminated. Since the company no longer owns the machine, the balance sheet accounts for the disposed asset are removed.

The accounting process involved in discarding, selling, or trading a plant and equipment asset is now discussed.

Discarding a Plant and Equipment Asset

A plant and equipment asset is typically discarded (thrown away) when an organization has fully utilized the asset and it cannot be sold or traded to anyone. In essence, the asset is worthless for further use, since no additional value can be received from it.

For example, assume that the Wayne Kelley Sporting Goods Company purchased $800 worth of *office equipment* on January 1, 1973. It was estimated at the time of purchase that the office equipment would have a ten-year useful life and a $100 salvage value. Under the straight-line method, the asset's book value as of January 1, 1983 (ten years from the purchase date) is $100 [$800 cost - $700 accumulated depreciation account balance ($800 cost - $100 estimated salvage value = $700 depreciable basis ÷ 10-year useful life = $70 annual depreciation × 10-years' depreciation recognized = $700)]. Thus, on January 1, 1983, the office equipment's book value is equal to its $100 estimated salvage value, indicating that the asset has been fully depreciated. On this date, however, the Kelley Company realizes that excessive use of the office equipment during the past ten years has caused it to become completely worthless. As a result, the equipment cannot be sold at the $100 estimated salvage value or at any price. Also, because of the equipment's poor condition, no other company will accept it as a trade-in on new office equipment. A decision is therefore made on January 1 by the

Kelley Company's management to discard the office equipment. The following journal entry reflects this decision:

Accumulated depreciation—office equipment	700	
Loss on disposal of plant and equipment assets	100	
Office equipment		800

Since $700 depreciation has been recognized on the discarded office equipment during the past ten years, the debit to "accumulated depreciation—office equipment" eliminates this $700 from the company's accounting records. The $800 credit to "office equipment" eliminates the original cost of the discarded equipment from this asset account.

When a plant and equipment asset is disposed of, it is necessary to determine the dollar gain or loss from the transaction. It is computed by comparing the disposed asset's book value (cost less accumulated depreciation) to the value received. A company, when selling a plant and equipment asset after several years' use, typically receives cash. If the cash from the asset disposal is greater than the value sold (the asset's book value), a *gain* occurs. As illustrated later, this gain is credited to the revenue account "gain on disposal of plant and equipment assets." The disposal of a plant and equipment asset for less cash than the asset's book value causes a *loss*. The expense account "loss on disposal of plant and equipment assets" is then debited for this dollar loss.

As discussed in Chapter 6, "nonoperating items" appear at the bottom of an income statement. These revenue and expense items do not result from a company's normal operating activities and are thus disclosed separately on the income statement. Plant and equipment assets are acquired for use in a company's daily operating activities, not for disposal at a gain or loss. Therefore, any gain or loss from a plant and equipment disposal transaction should be reported under "nonoperating items." A gain represents nonoperating revenue and a loss is a nonoperating expense.

The $100 loss from discarding the Kelley Company's office equipment on January 1, 1983 is computed as follows:

Total cost of office equipment	$800	
Less: Accumulated depreciation as of January 1, 1983	700	
Book value of office equipment on January 1, 1983		$100
Compared to: Cash proceeds received (that is, the *value* received from the asset disposal)		0
Loss from discarded office equipment		$100

Since the equipment has a $100 book value but nothing is received from disposing of the asset, the company incurs a $100 loss. This loss is debited to the nonoperating expense "loss on disposal of plant and equipment assets."

Review Questions

At this point, answer the following multiple-choice questions to test your knowledge of the previous reading material. The solutions are given below.

1. The annual maintenance on a company's machinery is called a:
   a. Capital expenditure.
   b. Nonoperating expense.
   c. Betterment expenditure.
   d. Revenue expenditure.

2. The cost of replacing a machine's old motor with a new one should be debited to a (an):
   a. Operating expense account.
   b. Nonoperating expense account.
   c. Asset account.
   d. Operating revenue account.

3. On January 1, 1983, the updated account balances relating to a company's machine are

Machinery	$1000
Accumulated depreciation—machinery	800

   Since no further use can be received from the machine, a decision is made on this date to discard it. The January 1 journal entry reflecting the disposal transaction is:

   a. Accumulated depreciation—machinery   800
      Loss on disposal of plant and equipment assets   200
           Machinery   1000
   b. Machinery   1000
           Accumulated depreciation—machinery   800
           Gain on disposal of plant and equipment assets   200
   c. Loss on disposal of plant and equipment assets   1000
           Machinery   1000
   d. Accumulated depreciation—machinery   800
      Cash   200
           Machinery   1000

4. If a company disposes of a plant and equipment asset at a gain, this gain should be reported as:
   a. An operating revenue on the income statement.
   b. A nonoperating revenue on the income statement.
   c. A decrease in owner's equity on the balance sheet.
   d. A decrease in assets on the balance sheet.

Answers

1. d

2. c

3. a ($1000 cost − $800 accumulated depreciation = $200 book value *compared to* $0 cash proceeds = $200 loss)

4. b

Selling a Plant and Equipment Asset

Rather than discarding a plant and equipment asset, a company may be able to sell it to someone. The sale of a long-term asset at a *gain*, a *loss*, and *no gain* or *loss* is now discussed.

Each of the three illustrated sales is based upon the following situation:

A company purchased a $500 piece of machinery on January 1, 1980. Straight-line depreciation is used on the machine. It is estimated to have a four-year useful life and a $100 expected salvage value. If it is assumed that the company closes its accounting books each December 31, the annual depreciation expense is $100 ($500 total cost minus $100 estimated salvage value = $400 depreciable basis divided by 4-year estimated life = $100 per year depreciation expense). As of January 1, 1983 (after three years' depreciation has been recognized), the two balance sheet accounts relating to the piece of machinery appear as shown in Exhibit 8-1. (Posting reference numbers are excluded.)

Sale of the Plant and Equipment Asset at a Gain

Assume that on July 1, 1983 the piece of machinery is sold for $250 cash. An adjusting entry for depreciation was last recorded on this machine on December 31, 1982. Since December 31, the machine has been utilized an additional six months (January 1 to July 1, 1983) with no depreciation recognition during this time period. Therefore, before the machine sale is recorded, the following adjusting entry is necessary on July 1 to update the asset's depreciation for the six-month period:

Depreciation expense	50	
Accumulated depreciation—machinery		50

The annual depreciation on the sold machine is $100. Thus, six months' depreciation is $50 (6/12 × $100). Whenever a plant and equipment asset is disposed of, an adjusting entry like the above is required to reflect depreciation for the time period since it was last recorded.

After the July 1 adjusting entry, the gain or loss from the machine sale is determined as follows:

Exhibit 8-1

Account: <u>Machinery</u>   Account No. <u>14</u>

DATE		ITEM	POSTING REFERENCE	DEBIT	CREDIT	DR (CR) BALANCE
1980 Jan.	1	Purchase of machine			500	500

Account: <u>Accumulated Depreciation–Machinery</u>   Account No. <u>15</u>

DATE		ITEM	POSTING REFERENCE	DEBIT	CREDIT	(DR) CR BALANCE
1980 Dec.	31	Adjusting Entry			100	100
1981 Dec.	31	Adjusting Entry			100	200
1982 Dec.	31	Adjusting Entry			100	300

Book value of machine on sale date		
Cost of machine		$500
Less: Updated balance of accumulated depreciation–		
machinery account on July 1, 1983		
Balance of accumulated depreciation		
account as of December 31, 1982	$300	
Plus: *Increase* in accumulated		
depreciation account balance		
from July 1 adjusting entry	50	350
Book value		$150
Compared to: Proceeds received from the sale of machine		250
Gain on sale of machine		$100

The $250 cash from selling the machine exceeds its $150 book value by $100. Therefore, the company has a $100 gain on the machine disposal. The July 1 journal entry to reflect this sale is

Cash	250	
Accumulated depreciation–machinery	350	
Machinery		500
Gain on disposal of plant and equipment assets		100

The $100 gain represents nonoperating revenue, which is reported under "nonoperating items" at the bottom of the company's income statement. The accumulated depreciation—machinery account has a $350 credit balance on July 1, 1983. Since the machine has been sold, this account is eliminated by a $350 debit. Finally, the $500 credit to the machinery account eliminates this account's previous debit balance.

Sale of the Plant and Equipment Asset at a Loss

Assume here that the company's machine is sold on July 1, 1983 for only $100 cash. As in the previous example, an adjusting entry is first required on July 1 to update the machine's depreciation for the period January 1 to July 1, 1983. This entry is

Depreciation expense	50	
Accumulated depreciation—machinery		50

The gain or loss on selling the machine is then computed in the following manner (the only change from the previous example is the amount of cash received):

Book value of machine on sale date			
	Cost of machine	$500	
Less:	Updated balance of accumulated depreciation—machinery account on July 1, 1983	350	
	Book value		$150
Compared to:	Proceeds received from sale of machine		100
	Loss on sale of machine		$ 50

The $100 cash selling price is less than the machine's $150 book value by $50. Therefore, the company incurs a $50 loss on the machine disposal. The following July 1 journal entry recognizes this sale:

Cash	100	
Accumulated depreciation—machinery	350	
Loss on disposal of plant and equipment assets	50	
Machinery		500

The $50 loss is a nonoperating expense, which appears under "nonoperating items" at the bottom of the company's income statement.

Sale of the Plant and Equipment Asset at No Gain or Loss

If the company's machine is sold for $150 cash, the July 1 adjusting entry to update the machine's depreciation is

Depreciation expense	50	
Accumulated depreciation—machinery		50

The gain or loss on this sale is computed as follows (again, the only change from the prior two examples is the cash amount):

Book value of machine on sale date		
Cost of machine	$500	
Less: Updated balance of accumulated deprecia-		
tion—machinery account on July 1, 1983	350	
Book value		$150
Compared to: Proceeds received from sale of machine		150
Gain or loss on sale of machine		$ 0

The $150 cash from the machine sale is identical to its $150 book value. As a result, no gain or loss occurs on this transaction. The July 1 sales entry is

Cash	150	
Accumulated depreciation—machinery	350	
Machinery		500

The above entry recognizes the $150 cash and also eliminates the "accumulated depreciation—machinery" and "machinery" account balances relating to the sold machine.

Trade-in of a Plant and Equipment Asset

The third major method of disposing of a plant and equipment asset is through trading the asset for another one.

To illustrate the accounting procedures for a trade-in, the $500 piece of machinery in the preceding example is again utilized. However, the assumption is now made that the company trades its machine for a new one on July 1, 1983. This new machine has a $700 list price. A company trading an asset typically receives a *trade-in allowance*. We shall assume that the trade-in allowance on the old machine is $120. Therefore, the cash to be paid for the new machine is $580 ($700 list price minus $120 trade-in allowance). As required in the three sales transactions of the previous section, the following adjusting entry is recorded on July 1 to update the old machine's depreciation for the six-month period from January 1 to July 1, 1983:

Depreciation expense	50	
Accumulated depreciation—machinery		50

After the depreciation has been updated, the July 1 journal entry to reflect the trade-in transaction is then recorded:

Machinery	700	
Accumulated depreciation—machinery	350	
Loss on disposal of plant and equipment assets	30	
Machinery		500
Cash		580

Since the new machine's list price is $700, the machinery account is debited for this amount. The $350 debit to accumulated depreciation—machinery and the $500 credit to machinery eliminates the dollar balances in these two accounts relating to the traded machine. The $580 "cash" credit represents the payment made to acquire the new machine.

The $30 loss from the asset trade is determined by the following computation:

Book value of traded machine (computed previously)	$150
Compared to: Trade-in allowance on machine	120
Loss on trade-in transaction	$30

The $120 trade-in allowance on the old machine is $30 less than its $150 book value. This causes a $30 loss, which is debited to the nonoperating expense "loss on disposal of plant and equipment assets." When a trade-in allowance exceeds an asset's book value, the resultant gain is credited to the nonoperating revenue account "gain on disposal of plant and equipment assets."

If a plant and equipment asset is traded for a similar one, the Internal Revenue Service does not allow the recognition of a gain or loss from the transaction when an income tax return is prepared. Under this tax stipulation, a newly acquired asset is recorded at the traded asset's book value plus any additional cash paid to purchase the new asset. Those readers interested in learning more about the tax method of handling trade-in transactions should consult an advanced accounting book.

Intangible Assets

Chapter 7 emphasized that plant and equipment assets are long-term tangible assets having physical existence (for example, a machine or a building). *Intangible assets* are also long-term assets. However, these assets have no physical existence. As will be discussed shortly, many intangible assets derive their value from legal rights (a contract, a governmental regulation, etc.). An "intangible assets" category appears on a company's balance sheet to disclose these assets. The intangible asset items are typically the last asset category reported on the balance sheet.

Intangible Assets Having a Limited Life

Depreciation is recognized each accounting period during a plant and equipment asset's estimated useful life in order that a better matching of revenues against expenses on periodic income statements may be achieved. For intangible assets with a limited life, their costs must also be allocated to periodic income statements as expenses. This process is called *amortization.* In accounting, the term "amortization" is considered to mean the same as "depreciation," except that the former applies to intangible long-term assets, whereas the latter applies to tangible long-term assets.

Patents

A patent is an exclusive right granted by the United States Patent Office for the production, use, or sale of an invention. It basically protects an inventor from theft of his ideas. A patent is issued for a 17-year period, which represents its legal life. Therefore, the maximum time period over which a company can amortize the costs incurred in developing or purchasing a patent is 17 years. If, however, the benefits from the patent are expected to last less than 17 years, then its costs should be amortized over this shorter time period. The costs of developing or purchasing a patent are debited to the long-term intangible asset "patent." Each period's amortization is recorded by a debit to "patent expense" and a credit to "patent." The straight-line method is used for amortizing a patent's cost. This causes an equal amount of amortization expense every period during the patent's useful life.

Copyrights

Another intangible asset with a limited life is a copyright. It represents an exclusive privilege granted by the federal government to publish and sell work of a literary or artistic nature. For example, an individual writing a book may apply for a copyright to prevent another person from later claiming the book material as his own work. The legal life of a copyright is 28 years with the option to renew it for an additional 28 years. However, since most copyrights are not expected to have an actual 28-year useful life, the costs of developing a copyright are typically amortized (under the straight-line method) over a shorter period. The amortization period selected will depend upon the estimated useful life of the benefits to be received from an artistic work.

Goodwill

The intangible asset goodwill results from a company's excess earning power over other companies in the same industry. For example, assume that the Sedan Company is an automobile manufacturer. If the average annual rate of return $\left(\dfrac{\text{net income}}{\text{total assets}} = \text{percentage rate of return} \right)$ for other organizations in the automobile industry is 9 percent and the Sedan Company's is 11 percent, then the latter has excess earning power called goodwill.

An organization's goodwill is due to such factors as: a superior business location resulting in more sales, an excellent business reputation from selling a high-quality product, and a skillfully trained management group operating the business. To have objective evidence that goodwill exists, it cannot be recognized in the accounting records until a company is sold. The objective evidence results from the purchaser's actually paying extra money to acquire the company. At that time, he debits the intangible asset "goodwill" for the portion of the acquisition price that represents the company's excess earning power.

The competitive nature of business causes most accountants to believe that goodwill does not last indefinitely. If other organizations within an industry increase their earnings during future years, the previously recognized goodwill of a company may disappear. Therefore, at the time goodwill is recorded, an attempt should be made to estimate the number of years that it will exist. The goodwill intangible asset is then amortized under the straight-line method as an operating expense over this time period. The computation of purchased goodwill can be quite complicated and is further discussed in advanced accounting books.

Intangible Assets Having an Unlimited Life

This type of intangible asset is considered valuable throughout an organization's life. Consequently, its total cost is debited to an asset account, and no amortization is recognized.

Trademarks

A trademark is a specific label or a unique phrase for a company's products. For example, the trademark of the Coca-Cola Corporation is "Things go better with Coke." A company's trademark can be protected permanently by registering it with the federal government. The costs incurred in developing a trademark are debited to the intangible asset "trademark." Since a registered trademark benefits a company indefinitely, the asset's cost is not amortized.

Organization Costs

The initial costs incurred by a company when starting business are called organization costs. One example is the attorney's fees for handling the legal aspects of establishing a business.

Most accountants agree that organization costs benefit a company indefinitely, since it could not have come into existence in the first place without incurring these costs. Thus, the value from the organization costs remain throughout a company's operating life. The long-term intangible asset "organization costs" is debited for these initial costs of creating a business, and no amortization expense is recognized on this account.

Concluding Comments

Hopefully, the reader better understands that a company's income computation is an estimating procedure after study of the estimates involved when periodic depreciation and amortization expense are calculated. Remember, the determination of depreciation and amortization expense on long-term assets is part of the adjusting entry process in order to achieve the best possible matching of revenues earned against expenses incurred on each period's income statement.

Review Questions

At this point, answer the following multiple-choice questions to test your knowledge of the previous reading material. The solutions are given below.

1. A company purchased a $2000 machine on January 1, 1978. As of December 31, 1983, the accumulated depreciation recognized on the machine was $1700. On this date, the company sold its machine for $500. The gain or loss from the sale was
   a. $200 gain.
   b. $500 gain.
   c. $200 loss.
   d. $500 loss.

2. Assume that the company in question 1 traded the machine on December 31, 1983 for a new one having a $2500 list price. The trade-in allowance on the old machine was $400. The gain or loss from this trade-in transaction was
   a. $100 gain.
   b. $400 gain.
   c. $400 loss.
   d. $800 loss.

3. Which of the following statements is *true* concerning an intangible asset with an unlimited life?
   a. The intangible asset's cost should be recognized as an operating expense in the year that the asset is acquired.

b. Amortization expense should be recognized on the basis of the intangible asset's legal life.

c. The intangible asset's cost should be amortized over a five-year period.

d. No amortization expense should be recognized on the intangible asset's cost.

4. The intangible asset resulting from an organization's excess earning power is called:
   a. Organization costs.
   b. Patents.
   c. Goodwill.
   d. Trademarks.

Answers

1. a ($2000 cost – $1700 accumulated depreciation = $300 book value compared to $500 proceeds = $200 gain)

2. a ($2000 cost – $1700 accumulated depreciation = $300 book value compared to $400 trade-in allowance = $100 gain)

3. d

4. c

Chapter Summary

This chapter concluded the discussion of plant and equipment assets and also analyzed intangible long-term assets.

The difference between *revenue* and *capital* expenditures on plant and equipment assets was discussed. The ordinary repair and maintenance costs that keep a plant and equipment asset operating efficiently are expenses called *revenue expenditures*. Those costs incurred to acquire a long-term asset or to increase its useful life represent *capital expenditures*, which are debited to the specific asset account affected.

Plant and equipment assets can be disposed of by discarding, selling, or trading them. Each of these disposal situations was discussed, along with the method for recognizing a gain or loss from the transaction. Any gain or loss on a plant and equipment asset disposal appears under the "nonoperating items" section at the bottom of a company's income statement.

Intangible assets are long-term assets without physical existence. They typically derive their value from legal rights. The intangible assets (patents, copyrights, and goodwill) discussed in this chapter have a *limited life* and are thus subject to amortization.

By recognizing periodic amortization, an intangible asset's cost is allocated as an operating expense over its estimated useful life. The amortization period for some intangible assets is based upon their legal life. Two intangible assets with an *unlimited life* and therefore not subject to amortization are trademarks and organization costs.

Chapter Problem

The solution to the problem is given in the appendix. However, the reader is urged first to attempt to work the problem on his own and then to check his work against the given solution.

Problem Situation

The Hector Company manufactures and sells transistor radios. The company closes its accounting records annually on December 31 to prepare financial statements. As of January 1, 1983, the Hector Company owns a piece of machinery (used for manufacturing its transistor radios) originally purchased on January 1, 1980 for $600. This machine has a five-year estimated useful life and a $100 expected salvage value at the end of the fifth year. The machine is depreciated under the straight-line method.

Exhibit 8-2 gives the January 1, 1983 general ledger accounts relating to the Hector Company's machine (posting reference numbers are excluded).

A new type of machine superior to the Hector Company's machine recently came on the market. Therefore, a decision was made to sell its present machine and purchase this new one. The Crandall Company was quite interested in buying the Hector Company's old machine, and after several discussions, the Crandall Company agreed to pay $300 cash for the Hector Company's machine. On April 1, 1983, the payment was received and the machine was delivered to the Crandall Company. The Hector Company owner planned to purchase the new machine within the next few days.

Problem Requirements

Part A

Using the information in this problem, prepare the necessary entry (or entries) in the Hector Company's journal on April 1, 1983 for the sale of its machine to the Crandall Company.

Exhibit 8-2

Account: Machinery   Account No. 17

DATE	ITEM	POSTING REFERENCE	DEBIT	DATE	ITEM	POSTING REFERENCE	CREDIT
1980 Jan. 1	Purchase of machine		600				

Account: Accumulated Depreciation–Machinery*   Account No. 18

DATE	ITEM	POSTING REFERENCE	DEBIT	DATE	ITEM	POSTING REFERENCE	CREDIT
				1980 Dec. 31	Adjusting Entry		100
				1981 Dec. 31	Adjusting Entry		100
				1982 Dec. 31	Adjusting Entry		100
					300		300

*The Hector Company's yearly depreciation expense under the straight-line method is

$$\frac{\text{Depreciation expense}}{\text{each year}} = \frac{\text{depreciable basis of machine}}{\text{estimated useful life of machine}}$$

$$= \frac{\$600 - \$100}{5 \text{ years}} = \$100 \text{ per year}$$

Part B

For illustrative purposes only, assume that the Hector Company sold its machine to the Crandall Company on April 1, 1983 at a cash price of $225 rather than $300. Using this figure and the same problem information given, prepare the necessary entry (or entries) in the Hector Company's journal on April 1, 1983 for the sale of its machine to the Crandall Company.

Problem Objective and Solution Approach

Objective:

To correctly compute a gain or loss on a machine sale and record the proper journal entries reflecting this sale.

Solution Approach:

Part A

1. It is first necessary to update the machine's depreciation for the period January 1 to April 1, 1983. Therefore, compute the depreciation for these three months and then record the April 1 depreciation adjusting entry.

2. Determine any gain or loss on the machine sale by comparing the machine's April 1 book value to the cash selling price.

3. Record the April 1 journal entry to recognize the sale.

Part B

Repeat the three steps in Part A, using a $225 cash selling price instead of $300.

9

Partnerships

Except for a brief presentation of partnerships and corporations in Chapter 1, the discussion has centered around the *proprietorship* form of business, owing to the more simplified nature of a proprietorship as compared to a partnership or corporation. By developing the conceptual and procedural aspects of accounting under a proprietorship, it was felt that the reader would be able to better understand accounting's important role in business.

The objective of this chapter is to introduce the reader to some of the major accounting aspects of partnerships. Chapter 10 will discuss corporation accounting. For a more extensive coverage of partnerships and corporations, it is recommended that the reader refer to an advanced accounting book.

Partnership Accounting

A *partnership* is a business organization owned by two or more individuals. The official definition of a partnership under the Uniform Partnership Act (which has been adopted by more than three-fourths of our states) is "an association of two or more persons to carry on as co-owners of a business for profit." Remember, a proprietorship is a business owned by *one* individual. A proprietorship owner wanting to expand his business may ask one or more people to invest assets into his company and thereby to become co-owners in a newly formed partnership.

The partnership form of business is frequently utilized by professionals such as lawyers, doctors, and accountants. The number of partnership owners is determined by the people forming the business. A partnership may have only two partners (the minimum number required), or it may have hundreds of partners. For example, some of the large accounting firms in the country have more than 500 partners.

The accounting concepts developed in prior chapters are also applicable to partnership accounting. Thus, the objective of the following discussion is to analyze some of the unique characteristics of accounting for partnerships.

The four specific stages in the life of a partnership are

> Stage 1. The *formation* of a partnership.
> Stage 2. The *operation* of a partnership.
> Stage 3. The *dissolution* of a partnership.
> Stage 4. The *liquidation* of a partnership.

The Formation of a Partnership

When two or more people form a partnership, a written contract called the *articles of partnership* should be prepared. The items within this contract include: the dollar investment of each partner, the method of distributing the periodic income or loss to each partner, the salaries paid to the partners, any limitations on withdrawing assets by the partners, and the procedure for the admission of new partners or the withdrawal of old partners.

Individuals are not required to have a written contract as a basis for operating a partnership. It can be formed by an oral agreement between the prospective partners. However, from the standpoint of good business, the specific partnership provisions should be in writing to avoid the possibility of future conflict. For example, one partner may argue that he is entitled to a $20,000 annual salary (based upon an oral agreement), whereas the other partners may insist that his salary is only $17,000. If the salary amount is formally stated in the articles of partnership, this dispute can be avoided.

A partnership agreement may be silent concerning each partner's percentage share of the periodic income or loss. When this happens, the legal requirement is that the income or loss be allocated equally to the partners. For example, in a three-person partnership, each partner is entitled to *one-third* of the periodic income or loss if there is no written statement of a percentage distribution. Furthermore, a net loss is always shared by the partners in the same percentage as a net income, unless the articles of partnership indicate a different allocation percentage for losses. For example, a partnership's written agreement states that each of the four partners will receive one-fourth of the periodic net income. If no mention is made of the percentage distribution for a net loss, then each partner must also be allocated one-fourth of any loss.

Before forming a partnership, the prospective partners should also be aware of the following important characteristics of this type of organization:

1. *Limited Life.* This characteristic will be discussed further under the "dissolution of a partnership" section of the chapter. The "limited life" concept basically means that whenever there is a specific change in the partners of an ongoing partnership, the life of that partnership ceases (it is *dissolved*), and a new one must be formed. Some of the reasons for dissolving a partnership are the resignation of a partner, the bankruptcy or death of a partner, or the admission of a new partner. It is important to understand, however, that the limited life concept does not require a partnership's having a change in its partners to actually discontinue business. Rather, it is necessary only to prepare new articles of partnership each time a change occurs. For example, assume that Jim Cantrell and Bill Morell are partners of a clothing store. After three years' operating activity, they decide to admit Harry Royer as a partner. This causes the original Cantrell and Morell partnership to be dissolved. New articles of partnership must then be prepared for the three partners. However, Royer's admission would not require the clothing store to interrupt its daily operating activities.

2. *Unlimited Liability.* This characteristic makes each partner personally liable to creditors for debts that the partnership is unable to pay. Also, an individual partner can be held responsible by creditors for the acts of his other partners. Using the previous example of the Cantrell, Morell, and Royer partnership, assume that Cantrell makes a bad business decision, causing a $20,000 partnership liability. If the partnership has insufficient assets to pay this liability when it is due, the creditor can take legal action against any of the three partners' *personal assets*, even though the debt was caused by Cantrell. Personal assets are assets not invested into the partnership (for example, a partner's family automobile or home).

   Partners' unlimited liability is a major disadvantage of operating a partnership rather than a corporation. The stockholders who own a corporation (discussed in Chapter 10) have *limited liability* to creditors. Their maximum liability is the dollar amount invested in the corporation. An individual with a large quantity of personal assets should carefully evaluate his prospective partners' capabilities before joining a partnership. A careless and inefficient partner could cause this individual's personal assets to be claimed by creditors. The owner of a proprietorship also has unlimited liability to his business creditors.

3. *Ownership of Partnership Property.* This aspect relates to property (land, building, equipment, etc.) invested into a partnership by any one of the partners. The property, after being invested, is automatically owned by all the partners. If Cantrell invests land into the Cantrell, Morell, and Royer partnership,

this land becomes a partnership asset co-owned by the three partners.

Having completed the analysis of a partnership's major characteristics, we shall now specifically discuss the *formation* stage (followed by the operation, dissolution, and liquidation stages). To help the reader grasp the basic concepts of partnership accounting, this discussion is centered around the following example:

Jack Golding has been operating a small hardware store (a proprietorship called the Golding Company) for the past three years. Presented in Exhibit 9-1 is his post-closing trial balance on December 31, 1982. (Remember, all the revenue and expense accounts have been closed to the owner's equity account, since a post-closing trial balance is the last stage in the accounting cycle.)

Exhibit 9-1

The Golding Company
Post-closing Trial Balance
December 31, 1982

Cash	$ 2,000	
Accounts receivable	3,000	
Allowance for uncollectibles		$ 500
Merchandise inventory	8,000	
Office equipment	1,000	
Accumulated depreciation— office equipment		600
Accounts payable		1,500
Jack Golding, capital		11,400
	$14,000	$14,000

Mr. Golding wants to expand his present business but has insufficient assets. Therefore, he asks Steve Bogle to invest some assets and form a partnership as of January 1, 1983. Bogle agrees and the articles of partnership are prepared. This written contract indicates that Bogle will invest assets equal in dollar value to Golding's January 1, 1983 capital account balance. The two partners agree that Golding's additional business experience entitles him to a larger share of the periodic income. Thus, the articles of partnership indicate that each year's net income or net loss will be distributed 60 percent to Golding and 40 percent to Bogle. Golding and Bogle further agree that before the periodic income or loss is distributed, each partner will receive a $12,000 annual salary and 8 percent interest every year on his January 1 capital account balance. (The allocation procedure for the salaries and interest is illustrated under the "operation of a partnership" section of this chapter.)

The same type of journals and ledgers discussed in previous chapters can also be utilized in maintaining a partnership's accounting information. However, a separate capital account is established for each partner to reflect his ownership equity. Based upon the Golding Company's December 31, 1982 post-closing trial balance and the agreement concerning Bogle's initial investment, the January 1, 1983 general journal entries to reflect the Golding and Bogle partnership formation are as shown in Exhibit 9-2. (Explanations will follow this exhibit.)

Exhibit 9-2

Cash	2,000	
Accounts receivable	2,750	
Merchandise inventory	8,500	
Office equipment	400	
Accounts payable		1,500
Allowance for uncollectibles		100
Jack Golding, capital		12,050
(To record the initial investment of Jack Golding into the partnership)		
Cash	7,050	
Land	5,000	
Steve Bogle, capital		12,050
(To record the initial investment of Steve Bogle into the partnership)		

Noncash assets (all assets other than cash) invested into a partnership should be recorded at dollar amounts agreed upon by the partners on the formation date. In most cases, these assets are reflected at their *current market values* (what they would cost if currently purchased in the market) as of the partnership formation date.

The $2000 cash reported on Golding's post-closing trial balance is transferred to the partnership's accounting records in the journal entry for his investment (see Exhibit 9-2). The only accounts receivables that should be transferred to a newly formed partnership are those that appear to be collectible in the future. Golding and Bogle believe that of the $3000 receivables reported on Golding's post-closing trial balance, only $2750 of them are subject to collection. Therefore, accounts receivable is debited $2750. The December 31, 1982 balance of Golding's allowance for uncollectibles account is $500. This balance is the result of three years' operating activity by Golding's proprietorship. When the new partnership is organized, an attempt should be made to estimate what portion, if any, of Golding's receivables invested into the partnership will not be eventually collected. Since the partners estimate the future uncollectible receivables to be $100, the allowance for uncollectibles account is credited for this amount in the January 1 entry for Golding's investment.

Golding's post-closing trial balance disclosed merchandise inventory of $1800. Because of inflation, the current market value of this asset is $8500 on the partnership formation date. Therefore, to reflect the current value of Golding's inventory investment into the partnership, the merchandise inventory account is debited $8500.

The post-closing trial balance indicates that Golding's office equipment has a $400 book value ($1000 cost minus $600 accumulated depreciation). The two partners agree that $400 represents a reasonable estimate of the equipment's current market value on January 1, 1983. The office equipment asset account is therefore debited $400 in the January 1 journal entry for Golding's partnership investment. The office equipment's remaining useful life must then be estimated so that depreciation can be recognized on this asset during future accounting periods.

The Golding Company has $1500 of accounts payable liabilities on its December 31 post-closing trial balance. The $1500 credit to accounts payable in the January 1 entry transfers these liabilities to the partnership.

Jack Golding's capital account is credited $12,050 to reflect his ownership interest in the partnership's assets. This amount is determined as shown in Exhibit 9-3.

Exhibit 9-3

Assets invested by Golding into the partnership		
Cash		$ 2,000
Accounts receivable	$2,750	
Less: Allowance for uncollectibles	100	
Net realizable value of receivables		2,650
Merchandise inventory		8,500
Office equipment		400
Total assets		$13,550
Less: Liabilities of Golding transferred to the partnership		
Accounts payable		1,500
Net value of assets invested into the partnership by Golding		$12,050

The articles of partnership specify that Steve Bogle must invest assets equaling Jack Golding's January 1, 1983 capital account balance. Therefore, Bogle's required asset investment is $12,050. The second journal entry on January 1 (Exhibit 9-2) recognizes Bogle's partnership investment. The only noncash asset contributed by Bogle is a piece of land having a $5000 current market value. Bogle also puts $7050 cash into the partnership to make his investment equal that of Jack Golding ($12,050 contributed by Golding minus $5000 worth of land contributed by Bogle = $7050 additional investment needed). The ownership equity account "Steve Bogle, capital" is then credited $12,050 for Bogle's interest in the partnership's assets.

Review Questions

At this point, answer the following multiple-choice questions to test your knowledge of the previous reading material. The solutions are given below.

1. The Four Hundred Club has three partners. Its "articles of partnership" do not indicate each partner's percentage share of the periodic net income or net loss. Therefore, every period's income or loss should be allocated:
   a. One-third to each partner.
   b. Based upon the cost of each partner's initial asset investment.
   c. Based upon the current market value of each partner's initial asset investment.
   d. One-half to each partner.

2. What is required every time a change occurs in the number of partnership owners?
   a. Nothing is required.
   b. The partnership must discontinue business.
   c. The partnership must be dissolved.
   d. The partnership must pay all its creditors.

3. The *unlimited liability* characteristic of a partnership means that:
   a. Each partner must invest more assets than liabilities when he joins the partnership.
   b. Each partner is free to incur unlimited debts in the name of the partnership.
   c. Each partner is personally liable to creditors if the partnership is unable to pay them.
   d. Each partner's maximum liability to creditors is based upon his initial partnership investment.

4. Tom Bradshaw operates a proprietorship and decides to convert his business to a partnership with Reginald King. The only asset Bradshaw invests into the partnership is merchandise inventory from his proprietorship

business. This inventory's cost under LIFO is $5000. The current market value of this inventory on the partnership formation date is $6000. The partnership's journal entry to reflect Bradshaw's inventory investment is:

a. Merchandise inventory   5000
        Tom Bradshaw, capital   5000
b. Merchandise inventory   6000
        Tom Bradshaw, capital   6000
c. Tom Bradshaw, capital   5000
        Merchandise inventory   5000
d. Tom Bradshaw, capital   6000
        Merchandise inventory   6000

Answers

1. a

2. c

3. c

4. b

The Operation of a Partnership

Once a partnership's formation has been completed, the second major stage begins, which is the day-to-day operating activities of the organization. The various accounting journals and ledgers utilized by a partnership for accumulating its financial information are basically the same as those discussed in prior chapters. Except for a few changes mentioned below, the accounting cycle steps performed on a partnership's financial data are identical to the cycle discussed in Chapters 2 and 3.

A major difference between maintaining proprietorship accounting records and maintaining those for a partnership is in the distribution of any net income or loss at the close of a period. For a proprietorship, the net income or loss is transferred in its entirety to the owner's capital account through the closing entry process. This same closing entry process is also necessary in a partnership. However, the net income or loss is closed to the partners' capital accounts according to the requirements in the articles of partnership.

When one is determining the periodic distribution of a net income or loss to the partners, consideration must also be given to any other stipulations in the articles of partnership that affect their ownership interests. The Golding and Bogle articles of partnership indicate that Golding is entitled to 60 percent and Bogle to 40 percent of each year's net income or net loss. In addition, the following two provisions exist:

1. Each partner receives a $12,000 annual salary.

2. Each partner receives yearly interest of 8 percent on his January 1 capital account balance.

Most accountants agree that partners' salaries and interest represent a distribution of income rather than operating expenses. The partners and their organization are the same legal entity. That is, the partnership would not exist without the partners. Therefore, if the owners' salaries and interest were recognized as expenses the partnership would, in effect, have expenses to itself.

Special owners' equity accounts called *drawing accounts* are utilized to record the salaries and interest of partners. A separate drawing account is established for each partner and debited for his salary and interest. The two drawing accounts in Exhibit 9-4 appear in the Golding and Bogle partnership.

Exhibit 9-4

Jack Golding, Drawing	Steve Bogle, Drawing

If Golding and Bogle receive their $12,000 yearly salaries at the rate of $1000 per month ($12,000 divided by 12 months), the following journal entry is recorded on the last day of each month:

Jack Golding, drawing	1000	
Steve Bogle, drawing	1000	
Cash		2000

The debits to the owner's equity drawing accounts reduce the partners' interests in their organization's assets. This is caused by each partner's receiving cash for his monthly salary. (The payment of interest to a partner on his capital account balance requires a debit to the partner's drawing account and a credit to the cash account.) The articles of partnership may also stipulate that the partners can withdraw noncash assets during the year. If, for example, Jack Golding takes $200 of partnership inventory for his personal use, this journal entry is recorded:

Jack Golding, drawing	200	
Merchandise inventory		200

Withdrawing noncash items also reduces a partner's ownership interest in his organization's assets. To reflect this, the partner's drawing account is debited for the asset's cost.

The drawing accounts established for partners are actually subdivisions of their capital accounts. In fact, some partnerships do not even utilize drawing accounts. Rather, partners' salaries, interest, and their withdrawal of noncash assets are debited directly to each partner's capital account. By having separate drawing accounts that disclose the partners' receipt of assets, better information is provided each partner as well as other interested parties concerning the distribution of partnership assets. When drawing accounts are used, their balances are closed into the partners' capital accounts at the end of an accounting period. This closing entry process is illustrated later in the chapter.

A proprietorship owner can also use a drawing account for his salary, interest, and any personal withdrawal of noncash assets from the business. The proprietor and his business are the same legal entity. Therefore, the owner of a proprietorship should also treat his salary and his interest on capital account balance as a distribution of income and not as operating expenses. If an owner's equity drawing account is debited for a proprietor's salary, interest, and withdrawal of noncash assets rather than his capital account's being debited, then the account balance of the former is closed into the latter account at period-end.

With this brief dicussion of drawing accounts completed, we now return to the Golding and Bogle partnership income distribution. Assume that the partnership's 1983 net income is $27,178. The schedule in Exhibit 9-5 (explanations will follow) discloses the distribution of this income to the two partners:

Exhibit 9-5

ITEM DISTRIBUTED	NET INCOME DISTRIBUTED TO		TOTAL NET INCOME DISTRIBUTED
	GOLDING	BOGLE	
Salary allowance	$12,000	$12,000	$24,000
Interest allowance	964	964	1,928
Remaining net income in the partners' income and loss sharing percentages	750	500	1,250
Total increase in partners' capital accounts	$13,714	$13,464	$27,178

Before Golding and Bogle are allocated their 60 percent and 40 percent respectively of the net income, the other articles of partnership provisions must first be satisfied. Each partner is allocated his $12,000 annual salary and the 8 percent interest on his January 1 capital account balance. The journal entries for the partnership formation (see Exhibit 9-2) reflect the partners' January 1 capital account balances. Since each partner has a $12,050 capital account credit balance from these entries, the interest allocation per partner is $964 (8% × $12,050). In every succeeding year, the partners' January 1 capital account balances of that year will be multiplied by 8 percent to determine their interest allowances.

After the salary and interest allowances have been allocated, any remaining net income (or net loss) is then distributed to the partners in their income and loss sharing percentages. Thus, $1250 is still available for distribution [$27,178 net income minus $25,928 already allocated ($24,000 salaries + $1928 interest)]. Golding is then allocated $750 (60% × $1250) and Bogle $500 (40% × $1250).

The income distribution schedule shows that Golding's share of the $27,178 net income is $13,714 and Bogle's is $13,464. As a result of the partnership's December 31, 1983 closing entry process, the individual revenue and expense account balances would have been transferred into the "income summary" account, causing its credit balance to be $27,178. Based upon the income distribution schedule computation, the income summary account balance is then transferred into the partners' capital accounts by the following closing entry:

Income summary	27,178	
Jack Golding, capital		13,714
Steve Bogle, capital		13,464

Each partner's capital account reflects his share of the 1983 net income after this closing entry is posted. Since the partner's drawing accounts are subdivisions of their capital accounts, the final closing entry required is to transfer the former account balances into the latter accounts. On December 31, 1983, Golding's drawing account has a $13,164 debit balance ($12,000 annual salary + $200 merchandise inventory withdrawn + $964 interest allowance). Bogle's drawing account shows a $12,964 debit balance on this same date for his $12,000 annual salary + his $964 interest allowance. The December 31 entry to close the drawing accounts is

Jack Golding, capital	13,164	
Steve Bogle, capital	12,964	
Jack Golding, drawing		13,164
Steve Bogle, drawing		12,964

Golding and Bogle's drawing account balances represent a reduction of their ownership interests in the partnership's assets. By closing these accounts through the above entry, each partner's reduced ownership interest is recognized in his capital account.

In the income distribution schedule (see Exhibit 9-5), the partnership's $27,178 net income was large enough to cover the $24,000 total salaries and the $1928 total interest allowance. After these allocations, $1250 net income was still available for distribution to Golding and Bogle in their income and loss sharing percentages. To illustrate the income distribution process when the net income is not sufficient to cover salary and interest allowances, assume that the Golding and Bogle partnership net income is only $24,928 in 1983. Based upon this assumption, the income distribution schedule in Exhibit 9-6 is prepared.

Exhibit 9-6

| | NET INCOME DISTRIBUTED TO | | TOTAL NET INCOME |
ITEM DISTRIBUTED	GOLDING	BOGLE	DISTRIBUTED
Salary allowance	$12,000	$12,000	$24,000
Interest allowance	964	964	1,928
Remaining net income in the partners' income and loss sharing percentages	(600)	(400)	(1,000)
Total increase in partners' capital accounts	$12,364	$12,564	$24,928

The salary and interest allowance to each partner is the same as in the income distribution schedule in Exhibit 9-5. After these two allocations, the net income remaining is a *negative* $1000 [$24,928 net income minus $25,928 already allocated ($24,000 salaries + $1928 interest)]. In this situation, the salary and interest allowances have exceeded the partnership's 1983 net income. The negative $1000 (which can be considered a type of net loss) is then allocated to Golding and Bogle in their income and loss sharing percentages. Therefore, Golding's share is $600 ($1000 × 60 percent) and Bogle's is $400 ($1000 × 40 percent). The allocation of this negative $1000 is shown in parentheses to indicate that it *reduces* each partner's share of the 1983 total income distribution.

The above illustration emphasizes that whenever the articles of partnership specify salary and interest allowances (or any other monetary allowance to each partner), these provisions must be met even if the partnership net income is insufficient. The negative income resulting from the allocations is then apportioned to the partners in their income and loss sharing percentages.

If a net loss occurs during the year, the partners are still entitled to their salary and interest allowances. Assume that the Golding and Bogle partnership reports a $2000 net loss for 1983. Following the $25,928 salary and interest allocation, a *negative* $27,928 ($2000 net loss + $25,928) is apportioned to each partner in his income and loss sharing percentage.

Depending upon a partnership's preference, the income distribution schedule can be shown as a separate financial statement accompanying the income statement and balance sheet, or it can be presented at the bottom of the income statement. A *capital statement* is also typically included as one of a partnership's period-end financial statements. It provides information concerning the various monetary items during the period that caused a change in each partner's ownership interest in the organization's assets. Based upon the 1983 activities of the Golding and Bogle partnership and the information from its income distribution schedule (Exhibit 9-5), the capital statement in Exhibit 9-7 is prepared on December 31, 1983. (Assume that Jack Golding invested an additional $5000 cash on June 1, 1983.)

Exhibit 9-7

Golding and Bogle
Capital Statement
For the Year Ended December 31, 1983

	JACK GOLDING	STEVE BOGLE	TOTALS
Capital, January 1, 1983	$12,050	$12,050	$24,100
Plus: Additional investment on June 1	5,000		5,000
	$17,050	$12,050	$29,100
Plus: Distributive share of partnership net income	13,714	13,464	27,178
	$30,764	$25,514	$56,278
Less: Withdrawal of assets	13,164	12,964	26,128
Capital, December 31, 1983	$17,600	$12,550	$30,150

The $12,050 capital balances on January 1 represent each partner's initial investment (see Exhibit 9-2). The entry recorded for Golding's June 1 cash investment was

Cash	5000	
Jack Golding, capital		5000

The effect of this investment is to increase Golding's ownership interest $5000. Therefore, it is added to his $12,050 capital balance.

The income distribution schedule (Exhibit 9-5) reports Golding's share of the 1983 net income as $13,714 and Bogle's as $13,464. Each partner's ownership interest is increased by his allocated portion of the income. This is reflected on the December 31 capital statement by adding the partners' distributive shares of income to their capital balances. The withdrawal of assets can be found in each partner's drawing account. It was previously determined that Golding and Bogle have December 31 drawing account balances of $13,164 and $12,964 respectively. Asset withdrawals cause a decrease in the partners' ownership interests and are, therefore, subtracted from their capital balances. A capital statement similar to this one can also be prepared by a proprietorship owner to analyze his equity changes in the company's assets.

The Dissolution of a Partnership

This major phase is based upon the limited life characteristic of partnerships discussed earlier in this chapter. Any change in the specific owners of an ongoing partnership causes its *legal life* to end. When this occurs, the partnership's daily operating activities continue unaffected. The end of a partnership's legal life from a change in its owners requires only that new articles of partnership be prepared. The newly written articles cause a dissolution of the old partnership (its articles of partnership are nullified) and the legal formation of a new one without any significant operating activity stoppage. Of course, the extreme case of dissolution happens when a partnership decides to sell all its assets, pay each creditor, and discontinue business. This is called *liquidation* and will be discussed shortly.

A common event causing dissolution is the admission of a new partner into an ongoing partnership. If all the legal considerations are ignored, an individual can become a partner in an existing partnership basically by having the approval of the current owners. This admission takes place in one of two ways:

1. He purchases a partnership interest from one or more of the current partners.

2. He invests assets into the partnership without any of the current partners' selling their interests.

Continuing with the Golding and Bogle partnership example from the previous section, a brief discussion is now presented of the accounting procedures when a new partner is admitted through purchase of part of the current partners' ownership interests.

Assume that Golding and Bogle's updated capital account balances July 1, 1984 are

> Jack Golding, capital $24,000 (credit balance)
> Steve Bogle, capital $15,000 (credit balance)

On this date, the two partners agree to sell one-third of their partnership interests to Archie Smith for $13,000 cash. This decision causes the dissolution of the Golding and Bogle partnership. New articles of partnership must be prepared for the Golding, Bogle, and Smith business entity. While these new articles are being written, the partnership operating activities continue uninterrupted. The July 1 journal entry for Archie Smith's admission into the newly formed partnership is

Jack Golding, capital	8000	
Steve Bogle, capital	5000	
Archie Smith, capital		13,000

Since each partner sold one-third of his ownership interest to Smith, Golding's capital account is debited $8000 (1/3 × $24,000 July 1 capital balance) and Bogle's $5000 (1/3 × $15,000 July 1 capital balance). These debits reflect the reduced ownership interests of Golding and Bogle in the organization's assets. The owner's equity account "Archie Smith, capital" is credited $13,000 for Smith's acquired interest in the partnership's assets. The $13,000 cash is not recognized in the journal entry, since this money is paid directly to Golding and Bogle. Thus, it does not represent a partnership asset. From the partnership's viewpoint, the only monetary effect is the one-third reduction of Golding and Bogle's ownership interests and the creation of Smith's new equity interest.

Smith actually paid $13,000 cash for his $13,000 partnership interest. If, however, the past operating activities of the Golding and Bogle partnership were highly successful, Smith might be willing to pay more than $13,000 for a $13,000 ownership interest. On the other hand, unsuccessful past operating activities and the eagerness to have Smith join the partnership might cause Golding and Bogle to sell Smith a $13,000 interest for less than $13,000 cash. The relevant point is that the agreed-upon payment is a *personal matter* between the present partners and the potential new partner and has no effect on the organization's assets. Regardless of how much cash Smith pays for his one-third interest, the same journal entry shown above is recorded in the partnership's accounting records.

A partnership must be dissolved when one of the partners *withdraws* because of retirement or some other reason. Should a partner die, dissolution of the partnership is also required.

The Liquidation of a Partnership

The final stage in a partnership's life occurs when a decision is made to terminate business. This is called *liquidation*, since all the noncash assets are sold (liquidated), the liabilities are paid, and any remaining assets are distributed to the partners on the basis of their capital account balances.

A major reason for partnership liquidation is the failure to operate the business successfully. Net operating losses may have resulted for several years, and the partners may see no hope for the future. Therefore, a decision is reached to end the business. A partner's retirement or death can also lead to liquidation. If the remaining partners choose not to continue business, the liquidation process then takes place.

The accounting procedures for liquidating a partnership are typically quite complicated and are not illustrated here. Detailed discussion of this subject matter can be found in advanced accounting books.

Review Questions

At this point, answer the following multiple-choice questions to test your knowledge of the previous reading material. The solutions are given below.

1. Jack Burns is a partner in the Tomato Works Company. He receives a $1500 monthly salary. The journal entry for his March salary is
   a. Salary expense   1500
        Cash   1500
   b. Administrative expense   1500
        Cash   1500
   c. Jack Burns, capital   1500
        Jack Burns, drawing   1500
   d. Jack Burns, drawing   1500
        Cash   1500

2. Rory Perry and Bill Cox are partners of the Bright Day Flower Shop. The income and loss sharing percentages are 70 percent to Perry and 30 percent to Cox. A $30,000 net income was earned during 1983. Each partner is entitled to salary and interest allowances totaling $10,000. What is Perry's distributive share of the 1983 net income?
   a. $7,000.
   b. $10,000.
   c. $15,000.
   d. $17,000.

3. Harry Benson and Ted Bunning are the owners of a partnership. Their updated capital account balances on December 1, 1983 are $2800 and $2000, respectively. On this date, the partners agree to sell Mark Mitchell one-fourth of their ownership interests for $1500 cash. The partnership's journal entry for this transaction is
   a. Cash   1500
        Mark Mitchell, capital   1500
   b. Harry Benson, capital   700
        Ted Bunning, capital   500
           Mark Mitchell, capital   1200

c. Harry Benson, capital	800	
Ted Bunning, capital	700	
Mark Mitchell, capital		1500
d. Cash	1500	
Harry Benson, capital	700	
Ted Bunning, capital	500	
Mark Mitchell, capital		2700

4. Partnership liquidation means:
   a. That the current partnership must be dissolved and a new one formed because of a change in its owners.
   b. That the partnership sells some of its old assets and purchases new ones to replace them.
   c. That the partners are paid their monthly salary and interest allowances with cash.
   d. That the partnership terminates business.

Answers

1. d

2. d [70% X ($30,000 net income – $20,000 salary and interest allowances to both partners) = $7000 share of income after salary and interest allowances + $10,000 salary and interest allowance to Perry = $17,000]

3. b (1/4 X $2800 = $700 ownership interest sold by Benson. 1/4 X $2000 = $500 ownership interest sold by Bunning. Mitchell's new ownership interest: $700 + $500 = $1200)

4. d

Chapter Summary

This chapter has given the reader a basic understanding of the partnership organization. Exhibit 9-8 illustrates the four major stages possible in a partnership's business life.

A partnership's formation should preferably be based upon a written contract called the *articles of partnership*. It includes the following items: each partner's initial investment, salary and interest allowances, the partners' income and loss sharing percentages, and any other provisions agreed to by the partners.

Upon completion of the partnership formation, stage 2 of its business life begins. This is the actual day-to-day operating activities. At the end of each accounting period, the net income or net loss is allocated to the partners

Exhibit 9-8

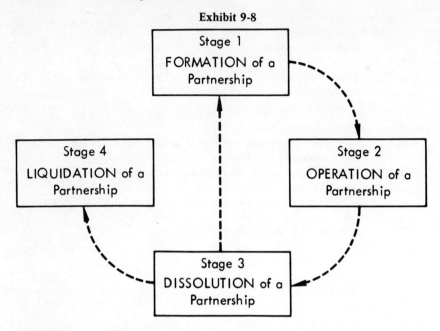

according to their income and loss sharing percentages agreed upon in the articles of partnership. Prior to this allocation, however, any salary and interest allowances disclosed in the articles are first apportioned to each partner. Thus, the articles of partnership developed in the *formation* stage are quite important during the *operation* stage.

Dissolution (stage 3) occurs whenever there is a change in the specific partners of an ongoing partnership. This change results from the admission or withdrawal of a partner. Exhibit 9-8 shows an arrow going from stage 3 to stage 1, emphasizing that dissolution does not necessarily cause liquidation. Rather, dissolution often results in the formation of a new partnership. The process requires only that new "articles of partnership" be written.

Partnership dissolution can, however, lead to *liquidation* (stage 4). This is the final business-life stage, since a partnership actually terminates its operating activities.

Chapter Problem

The solution to the problem is given in the appendix. However, the reader is urged first to attempt to work the problem on his own and then to check his work against the given solution.

Problem Situation

Tom Densey and Walter Brooks are medical doctors at the Canal Medical Center. For the past several months they have discussed the possibilities of establishing their own small medical clinic. The two doctors finally decide to resign from the Canal Medical Center and start their own clinic. Therefore, on March 14, 1983, Densey and Brooks officially resign and begin making plans for the opening of their clinic. Densey and Brooks are able to find a small office building that can be rented for $600 a month.

They decide to operate the clinic as a partnership and call it the Densey and Brooks Patient Care Center. Included within the articles of partnership are the following provisions:

1. The partnership will begin business operations May 1, 1983 and close its accounting records monthly in order to prepare financial statements. Initially, each partner will invest the following assets into the organization on May 1:

Densey		*Brooks*	
Cash	$5000	Cash	$3000
Office equipment (at the equipment's current market value)	$7000	Office equipment (at the equipment's current market value)	$5000

2. As a result of Densey's additional medical experience, the two doctors agree that the partnership's monthly net income or net loss will be allocated 55 percent to Densey and 45 percent to Brooks.

3. Before the income or loss is allocated, each partner will receive an $800 monthly salary (paid on the last day of the month) and 1 percent interest on his beginning of the month capital account balance. This interest will be credited to the partners' capital accounts on the last day of every month.

4. Each partner can withdraw a maximum of $50 noncash assets each month for his personal use.

Problem Requirements

Part A

Using the information provided, prepare the necessary May 1, 1983 entries in the Densey and Brooks Patient Care Center's journal for the two partners' initial investments.

Part B

1. During May the Densey and Brooks Patient Care Center pur-chases $100 of office supplies (stationery, envelopes, pens, and pencils). On May 20, Tom Densey takes some of these supplies costing $10 for his own personal use. Prepare the May 20 journal entry to reflect Densey's withdrawal of office supplies.

2. The partnership's cash account balance gets rather low during May from the large number of cash expenditures incurred. There-fore, Walter Brooks invests an additional $1000 cash into the partnership on May 29. Prepare the journal entry on this date for Brooks' investment.

Part C

It is now May 31, 1983, and the partnership's net income for the month is $1700. Perform the following accounting functions:

1. Prepare the May 31 journal entry for the payment of the two partners' monthly salaries.

2. Based upon the articles of partnership agreement, prepare an "income distribution schedule" on May 31 to determine the proper allocation of the May net income.

3. Each revenue and expense account balance has been closed into the income summary account. Prepare any remaining closing entry (or entries) required on May 31.

4. Prepare a May 31 "capital statement" to disclose the changes in the partners' capital account balances during the month.

Problem Objective and Solution Approach

Objective:

To understand some of the major accounting aspects involved in the *forma-tion* and *operation* stages of a partnership's "business life."

Solution Approach:

Part A

From the "articles of partnership" information, record the May 1 journal entries to recognize each partner's initial investment of assets.

Part B

1. Using an owner's equity drawing account, record the May 20 journal entry for the office supplies taken by Densey.

2. Record the May 29 journal entry for the $1000 cash investment by Brooks.

Part C

1. Using the articles of partnership information and owners' equity *drawing accounts*, record the May 31 journal entry for the partners' monthly salaries.

2. Referring to the "articles of partnership" agreement, perform the following steps to prepare the May 31 income distribution schedule:
   a. Allocate to each partner his salary allowance.
   b. Compute each partner's May interest allowance.
   c. *Subtract* the salary and interest allowances from the May net income and allocate this amount to each partner according to the income and loss sharing percentages.

3. Record the two additional closing entries necessary on May 31 relating to the income summary account and the partners' drawing accounts.

4. Based upon the May transactions affecting each partner's capital account balance, prepare the May 31 "capital statement" for the Densey and Brooks Patient Care Center.

10

Corporations

This chapter's objective is to acquaint the reader with another important type of organization called the *corporation*. Most advanced accounting books devote several chapters to corporations because of the many sophisticated accounting procedures involved. The current chapter will discuss the basic concepts of corporations without covering the more complicated aspects of corporate accounting.

Major Characteristics of Corporations

The majority of the large business organizations in the United States (for example, General Motors, General Electric, and United States Steel) operate as corporations. The following characteristics of a corporation explain why it is popular.

1. *Separate Legal Entity.* Proprietorships and partnerships are not considered separate legal entities from their owners. However, a corporation must be formally approved by the state where it operates, and it is a separate legal entity from the owners. This allows the corporation to purchase and sell property, to incur liabilities, etc., in its own name.

2. *Transferability of Ownership.* The owners of a corporation are called *stockholders*. An individual can obtain a corporate ownership interest by purchasing *stock certificates*. The certificates of many corporations are bought and sold on the New York Stock Exchange and the American Stock Exchange. People often invest in corporations by having a stockbroker handle their acquisitions. After owning a corporation's stock

for a certain time period, an investor may decide to sell his certificates in the market. This *transferability* of corporate stock ownership is a unique characteristic of corporations. Chapter 9 emphasized that proprietorships and partnerships must be dissolved each time the specific owners change because these organizations and their owners are the same legal entity. Since a corporation is a separate legal entity from its stockholders, dissolution is not required when there is an ownership change. This causes a corporation to have an *unlimited life* in terms of its owners. The specific stockholders can change daily without the corporation's continued existence being affected.

3. *Limited Liability of Stockholders.* If proprietorships and partnerships have insufficient assets to pay their liabilities, the creditors can claim the owners' personal assets. This is not true for a corporation. A major advantage of the corporate organization is the *limited liability* of its owners. Each stockholder's personal assets are safe from creditors should the corporation be unable to pay its debts. The stockholders' liability to creditors is limited to their investment of assets into the corporation. For example, assume that the Cooper Corporation obtains a $1000 loan from the bank. This transaction creates a legal contract between the corporate entity (not the stockholders) and the bank. If the Cooper Corporation is unable, later to pay its $1000 liability, the bank's only source of collection is the corporation's assets. The bank could force the corporation into bankruptcy to collect its money. If this happens, the maximum loss that the corporate stockholders could incur is their original investment. Because the corporation is a separate legal entity, the bank is prohibited from taking action against any stockholder's personal assets.

4. *Separation of Corporate Ownership and Management.* Proprietorship and partnership owners are usually involved in the daily operating decisions of their organizations. This is not ordinarily true of corporation owners. If an individual buys stock shares, he does not typically participate in his corporation's day-to-day operating activities. Rather, a professional group of managers is hired to supervise the business. Stockholders do, however, exercise indirect control over corporate management by electing a board of directors to represent their ownership interests. The directors have meetings during the year to discuss corporate objectives, elect management officers, declare stockholder dividends, and consider any additional relevant matters.

Accounting Aspects of Corporations

The basic accounting concepts and procedures discussed previously for proprietorships and partnerships are also applicable to corporations. The following analysis emphasizes the accounting methods that are unique to corporate organizations.

The Ownership Equity of Stockholders

The owners' equity section of a corporation's balance sheet differs significantly from that of a proprietorship or partnership. It is called the "stockholders' equity" and represents the interests of the stockholder owners in their corporation's assets. The two major sources of a corporation's stockholders' equity are

1. The investment of assets by stockholders (called *paid-in capital*).

2. The corporate operating activities causing a net income or net loss and the resultant payment of dividends to stockholders.

Source of Ownership Equity: Stockholder Investment (Paid-in Capital)

Individuals forming a corporation must apply for a corporate charter from the state in which they plan to do business. Since a corporation is a separate legal entity, its owners are required to have official state approval before operating activities can commence.

The specific procedures for applying for a corporate charter vary somewhat among the 50 states. In general, however, the following information must be included on the charter application form:

1. The name and address of the corporation.

2. The purpose for establishing the corporation (that is, what type of business activities it will be performing).

3. Since the ownership interests in a corporation are represented by shares of stock (often called *capital stock*), the corporation must disclose the total number of stock shares that it plans to sell. This is called the *authorized stock*, indicating the *maximum* shares that can be sold. If, at a later date, the corporation wants to sell more stock than originally authorized, it must again receive approval from the state.

Upon receiving an approved charter, a corporation can begin to sell its authorized stock. It may, however, decide not to sell all the authorized stock immediately. For example, assume that the Royal Corporation receives approval to sell 10,000 shares of stock. It immediately sells 7000 of these shares and decides to delay selling the remaining 3000 until a later time. The 7000 shares are called *issued* stock because they have been formally sold (and therefore *issued*) to stockholders. Occasionally, a corporation purchases from its stockholders previously issued shares. This reacquired stock is called *treasury stock*. All the capital stock shares currently owned by a corporation's investors are referred to as *outstanding stock*. The term "outstanding" indicates that the stock is not in the corporation's possession. Rather, it is "out" in the market being held by investors.

Assume that six months after the Royal Corporation sold the 7000 shares, it reacquires 500 of them. The following terminology describes the current status of the corporation's capital stock:

1. 10,000 shares of *authorized* capital stock.

2. 7000 shares of *issued* capital stock.

3. 3000 shares of *authorized, unissued* capital stock (10,000 authorized shares *minus* 7000 issued shares).

4. 500 shares of *treasury stock* (the reacquired shares).

5. 6500 shares of *outstanding* stock (7000 issued shares *minus* 500 treasury stock shares). Since treasury shares are no longer held by investors, they must be subtracted from the original issued shares to determine the outstanding stock.

Capital Stock Characteristics

The sale of a corporation's stock represents one major source of its ownership equity. Since investors "pay in" cash or noncash assets to acquire a corporate ownership interest, this equity source is called *paid-in capital*. The two major types of capital stock that a corporation can sell are *preferred* and *common* stock. If the corporation chooses to issue only one class of stock, it is automatically called *common stock*. However, many corporations offer both preferred and common stock (discussed shortly) in order to attract a larger number of investors. Automobile manufacturers, for example, produce several car models because of consumers' different tastes. People purchasing stock also have dissimilar needs with regard to the type of stock investment they desire. Therefore, a corporation typically sells different classes of stock to satisfy the investing public's varying demands.

Most states require a corporation to assign an arbitrary dollar amount to each share of stock. It is called the *par value* and is printed on every stock certificate issued to investors. The certificate represents evidence of stock ownership and, as discussed previously, is transferable from one investor to another. A corporation may also issue *no-par stock*. However, many states stipulate that no-par stock must have a *stated value* assigned to each share. In effect, this arbitrary stated value per share becomes the same as a par value. The corporate board of directors has the responsibility for knowing its state requirements and then deciding whether to issue par-value stock, no-par stock, or no-par stock with a stated value.

The major reason for assigning stock a par or stated value is to protect a corporation's creditors. The limited liability concept prohibits a creditor from claiming stockholders' personal assets if the corporation's assets should be insufficient to settle the debt. If, for example, a corporate organization is having financial difficulties, its stockholders may try to quickly withdraw the remaining assets. This would leave the creditors "out in the cold," unable to collect their money. To prevent such a situation, most states require that corporations designate a portion of their paid-in capital from stock sales as *legal capital*. The par or stated value of stock represents the legal capital. As long as a corporation has liabilities outstanding, the legal capital cannot be withdrawn by the stockholders. Rather, it must remain within the corporation to assure the creditors' payments.

Because the par or stated value of a corporation's stock is an arbitrary dollar amount determined by its board of directors, the stock's market selling price is typically different. There are several important factors affecting stock prices: the economic situation of the country, the corporation's past earnings record as well as its future earnings outlook, and the corporation's past history of paying dividends to stockholders. When each of these conditions is favorable, the corporation's stock is likely to sell at a higher market price.

As discussed above, one factor that determines a corporation's stock selling price is the payment of cash dividends. They represent a distribution of the corporation's net income to its stockholders. The corporate board of directors is responsible for determining how much of the earnings should be distributed to stockholders as a cash dividend. In proprietorships and partnerships, the periodic net income (or net loss) is automatically distributed to the owners. However, since a corporation is a separate legal entity from its stockholders, the corporation owns the net income until a decision is made by the board of directors concerning its disposition.

The directors typically have a year-end meeting to analyze the organization's operating activities. If present or future expansion programs are contemplated, the directors may decide to retain part of the income within the corporation. For example, plans may exist for the construction of a new factory. This project requires assets. One way to obtain a portion of these assets is through *external financing*, such as borrowing money from the bank or selling bonds. *Internal financing* can also be used to acquire the needed assets. This method involves the corporation's owners. Additional shares of stock may be sold to help finance the factory construction. Internal financing can also be achieved by using part of the corporation's earnings.

Since an earned net income increases the stockholders' interests in their corporation's assets, utilizing this income for expansion results in the corporate owners' financing the project.

After deciding what portion of the year's income will be retained within the corporation, the board of directors may then distribute the remaining income to its stockholders as a cash dividend. Many people invest their money in corporate stock with the major objective of receiving yearly dividends. However, a corporation has no legal obligation to pay dividends until they are formally declared by the board of directors.

Before declaring cash dividends to its stockholders, the directors must be familiar with the types of stock issued by the corporation. As previously mentioned, both preferred and common stock may be issued.

Preferred Stock. Investors owning "preferred stock" have *preference* over common stockholders in receiving cash dividends. Before dividends can be declared and paid on the common stock, all the preferred stockholders must first obtain their dividends. Also, in a corporate liquidation, owners of preferred stock are entitled to their share of the corporation's assets before the common stockholders. Preferred stock is typically sold with a *fixed percentage dividend rate*. For example, assume that a corporation's preferred stock has a $100 par value and a 9 percent annual dividend rate. If the board of directors declares a yearly dividend, each preferred stockholder is entitled to $9 for every share owned (9% $\times$ $100 par value). Cash dividends on preferred stock are ordinarily computed by *multiplying* the fixed dividend rate by the par or stated value of each share.

Preferred stock is more attractive to investors when additional features are included. For example, a corporation's authorized preferred stock may be sold with *cumulative* and *participating* provisions. Cumulative preferred stock stipulates that any prior years' undeclared cash dividends to preferred stockholders *accumulate* for those years and must eventually be paid (along with the current year's dividend) before common stockholders can receive any current year dividend. This accumulation of prior years' unpaid dividends is called "dividends in arrears." Investors buying *noncumulative* preferred stock are not entitled to receive any undeclared cash dividends from prior years. Therefore, a noncumulative provision is definitely less desirable, since dividends in arrears do not exist for this type of preferred stock.

A *participating* feature may also be included in preferred stock. As previously discussed, a corporation's preferred stock is usually issued with a fixed percentage dividend rate. The participating provision allows the preferred stockholders to share additional cash dividends with the common stockholders in excess of their regular preferred dividend rate. A *nonparticipating* clause limits the preferred stockholders to their fixed percentage dividend rate. There are many methods available for determining participative preferred stock cash dividends. The actual method selected would be stated in the contract between a corporation and its preferred stockholders.

The computational aspects of cumulative and participating preferred stock are not illustrated here. A detailed analysis of these special preferred stock provisions can be found in advanced accounting books.

Common Stock. Because of the preferences that preferred stock has over common stock, one may, at first glance, question an investor's decision to purchase the latter. The answer centers around the fact that even though both types of stock represent corporate ownership interests, the *common stockholders* are the "true" owners. Presented below are two of the reasons for this:

1. Only the common stockholders typically have *voting* rights on corporate matters (such as electing the board of directors). This permits common stock owners to exercise control over their corporation.

2. Preferred stockholders ordinarily are limited to a fixed dividend rate (except under the participating provision). This is not true for common stockholders. The cash dividend per share on common stock is determined each year by the board of directors. When an organization has highly favorable business operations, the owners should rightfully share this success. In general, preferred stock owners do not, since they will only receive their fixed dividend per share. Because the common stockholders are not controlled by a fixed dividend rate, these investors can directly share successful corporate operations by receiving larger cash dividends. For example, assume that a corporation's 1983 net income was $10,000 and the board of directors paid its common stockholders a 10¢ per share dividend. The corporation's earnings increased to $18,000 in 1984, causing the directors to pay its common stock investors a 15¢ per share dividend. Thus, the common stockholders directly shared the benefits of improved business operations by receiving larger cash dividends for 1984. In both years, however, the preferred stockholders received the same fixed dividend, even though the corporation experienced significant improvement during 1984.

Journal Entries for Corporate Stock Transactions

A corporation can sell its stock at a price *equal to, greater than,* or *less than* the par or stated value per share. To illustrate the journal entries when stock is sold, assume that the Moss Corporation receives authorization on January 1, 1983 to issue the following stock:

1000 shares of common stock with a $25 par value per share.

500 shares of 10 percent, cumulative, participating, no-par preferred stock with a $50 stated value per share.

Presented below are three stock sales transactions for the Moss Corporation and the journal entries required (explanations will follow):

January 5, 1983—sold 100 shares of common stock at $25 per share.

Cash	2500	
Common stock		2500

January 15, 1983—sold 200 shares of common stock at $30 per share.

Cash	6000	
Common stock		5000
Premium on common stock		1000

January 18, 1983—sold 100 shares of preferred stock at $45 per share.

Cash	4500	
Discount on preferred stock	500	
Preferred stock		5000

Since most stock sales are for cash, it is assumed that the Moss Corporation's three transactions are cash transactions. If, however, an individual purchases stock by investing noncash assets, the corporation should record these assets at their current market values as of the stock transaction date.

In the January 5 transaction, the current asset "cash" is debited for the $2500 proceeds from the stock sale (100 shares × $25). As discussed previously, the par or stated value per share of stock represents *legal capital*, which must be maintained in the corporation to protect creditors. For information purposes, this legal capital is reported in a separate stockholders' equity account. Since the 100 common shares are sold at a price equal to their $25 par value, the equity account "common stock" is *credited* for this $2500 legal capital. The $2500 credit increases the investors' interests in the corporation's assets.

These 100 common stock shares may have been purchased by several investors. They are issued stock certificates for the number of shares acquired. The Moss Corporation utilizes a "Stockholders' Register," which indicates each investor's name, address, and quantity of shares owned. When the board of directors declares a cash dividend, it refers to this register to ascertain the specific stockholders who are entitled to receive dividends.

For the January 15 stock sale, "cash" is debited $6000 (200 shares × $30). The "common stock" account is again credited for the legal capital from the stock issuance, $5000 (200 shares × $25 par value). This stock is sold at $5 per share more than its legal value ($30 selling price less $25 par value). The $5 per share excess over the stock's par value is called a *premium*. Therefore, the stockholders' equity account "premium on common stock" is *credited* $1000 for this premium (200 shares × $5 per share premium). Since the $1000 does not represent legal capital, it can eventually be distributed to the corporation's stockholders as a dividend. Another term commonly used to designate a stock sale premium is "paid-in capital in excess of par (or stated) value."

A $4500 "cash" debit is recorded for the January 18 preferred stock issuance (100 shares × $45). The "preferred stock" account is utilized in the same manner as the "common stock" account. Therefore, it is credited $5000 to reflect the legal capital from the stock sale (100 shares × $50 stated value). The preferred stock's selling price is $5 per share less than its legal value ($50 stated value less $45 sales price). This $5 per share below the stock's stated value is called a *discount*. The Moss Corporation recognizes the discount by debiting a stockholders' equity account "discount on preferred stock" for $500 (100 shares × $5 per share discount).

Issuing stock at a price below its par (or stated) value could be harmful to creditors, since the corporation receives fewer assets than the recorded legal capital. Remember, the purpose of legal capital is to protect creditors against the possibility of corporate owners' withdrawing all the assets. Selling discounted stock could eventually cause the corporation to have insufficient assets to cover its legal capital. Therefore, assets may not be available to pay the creditors. For this reason, some states do not allow the sale of stock at a discount. In those states where it is permitted, the investors purchasing discounted stock are often held *contingently liable* to creditors for this discount. If, for example, an investor purchases stock at a $10-per-share discount and the corporation has insufficient assets during liquidation to satisfy creditor claims, he may be required to pay the creditors $10 for each stock share owned.

If a corporation's authorized stock has neither a par nor stated value, it is called *no-par stock*. The entire issuance price of no-par stock must be recognized as legal capital for creditors' protection. Assume that the Ross Corporation sells 100 shares of no-par common stock at $20 per share. The journal entry reflecting this transaction is

Cash	2000	
Common stock		2000

Both the cash and common stock accounts are increased $2000 from the no-par stock sale (100 shares × $20).

Balance Sheet Presentation of Paid-In Capital From Stockholders' Investments

Exhibit 10-1 is the "Stockholders' Equity" section of a corporation's balance sheet illustrating the *paid-in capital* from the issuance of preferred and common stock. (The dollar figures are assumed.)

Exhibit 10-1

Stockholders' Equity

Paid-in capital

10 percent preferred stock, cumulative, participating, $40 par value (500 shares authorized, 300 shares issued)—dividends in arrears of $1,200	$12,000	
Plus: Premium on preferred stock	1,500	$13,500
Common stock, $20 par value (2000 shares authorized and issued)	$40,000	
Less: Discount on common stock	4,000	36,000
Total paid-in capital		$49,500

For information purposes, each class of stock is fully described on the balance sheet. The corporation did not declare a cash dividend last year to its preferred stockholders. Since this stock is *cumulative*, one year's "dividends in arrears" must be recognized ($40 par value X 10 percent annual dividend rate = $4.00 per share X 300 outstanding shares = $1,200). The *legal capital* from the preferred stock issuance is $12,000 (300 shares issued X $40 per share par value). The stock's selling price is $1500 *greater than* its par value. Therefore, this $1500 premium is *added* to the $12,000 par value in order to disclose the $13,500 total investment by the preferred stockholders.

The corporation's common stock has a $20 par value, and all 2000 authorized shares are issued. Therefore, the total *legal capital* is $40,000 (2000 shares issued X $20 per share par value). Since the stock is sold at $4000 *below* its par value, this discount is *subtracted* from the $40,000 par value. The resultant $36,000 represents the common stockholders' actual investment.

The $49,500 total paid-in capital indicates the *source* of the corporation's ownership equity resulting from the sale of its stock to investors.

Review Questions

At this point, answer the following multiple-choice questions to test your knowledge of the previous reading material. The solutions are given below.

1. A major characteristic of corporations is the *transferability of ownership*. This means that:
   a. Specific corporate owners can change without causing dissolution.
   b. Each current stockholder must approve the sale of additional shares to a new investor.

c. A stockholder maintains unlimited liability to creditors even when he sells part of his stock to another investor.

d. Corporate dissolution is required when a current stockholder sells his shares to another investor.

2. The stockholders' equity *source* resulting from the sale of stock is called:
   a. Retained earnings.
   b. Long-term assets.
   c. Paid-in capital.
   d. Dividend equity.

3. The following information is available concerning the Peck Corporation's common stock:

   Authorized shares 6000
   Treasury shares   200
   Issued shares   4000

   How many common stock shares does the corporation have outstanding?
   a. 1800.
   b. 2000.
   c. 3800.
   d. 4000.

4. The Baxter Corporation has $500 "dividends in arrears" on its preferred stock. This indicates that the preferred stock must have a:
   a. Participating provision.
   b. Nonparticipating provision.
   c. Cumulative provision.
   d. Noncumulative provision.

Answers

1. a

2. c

3. c (4000 issued shares – 200 treasury shares)

4. c

Source of Ownership Equity: Corporate Operating Activities

The accounting procedures for determining a corporation's net income (or net loss) are basically the same as in a proprietorship and partnership. The major difference is the technique of distributing the income. Proprietorship and partnership earnings belong to the owners and are therefore transferred to their equity accounts during the closing entry process at the end of each accounting period. This is not true for a corporation. Since it is a separate legal entity from the stockholder owners, the earned income belongs to the organization. The board of directors is then responsible for deciding how much of the corporate earnings will be distributed to the stockholders. Earnings distribution to stockholders is achieved through the formal declaration of a cash dividend by the directors.

At period end, a corporation's revenue and expense account balances are closed to the income summary account exactly as in a proprietorship or partnership. The income summary balance is then transferred to a special stockholders' equity account called "retained earnings." Assume that the Moss Corporation earns a $2000 net income in 1983. Its income summary account therefore has a $2000 credit balance after each revenue and expense account has been closed on December 31. The final closing entry is

Income summary	2000	
Retained earnings		2000

The above entry transfers the Moss Corporation's 1983 net income to its retained earnings account. As a result, the ownership interests of the stockholders are increased. If the Moss Corporation had incurred a $1000 net loss during 1983 rather than a net income, the income summary account would have a $1000 debit balance. The final closing entry would then be

Retained earnings	1000	
Income summary		1000

The retained earnings *debit* causes a $1000 reduction of the stockholders' interests in their corporation's assets.

The underlying reason for using the title "retained earnings" for this stockholders' equity account is

> When a net income is earned, the board of directors must decide what portion of this income will be retained within the corporation for present and future uses and what portion will be distributed to the stockholders as a dividend. The former causes an increase in the retained earnings account, and the latter causes a decrease (which is illustrated shortly). Since this account is increased by a credit and decreased by a debit, a credit balance reflects the portion of current and prior years' earnings that have been "retained" internally rather than distributed to stockholders.

To better understand the function of the retained earnings account, assume that the Orleans Corporation begins business January 1, 1983 and issues the following stock during 1983: 100 shares of 10 percent noncumulative, nonparticipating, $50 par value preferred stock and 200 shares of $40 par value common stock. The 1983 net income is $900, and the corporate board of directors declares the following cash dividend on December 31:

> ...a 10 percent per share dividend to preferred stockholders and a $1.00 per share dividend to common stockholders. This dividend

has a December 31, 1983 *declaration date*, a January 14, 1984 *record date*, and a January 28, 1984 *payment date*.

The above dividend information discloses three important dates. The first is the *declaration date* when the board of directors officially approves a cash dividend. Upon declaring this dividend, the corporation has a liability to its stockholders for the eventual payment. The *record date* is usually a few weeks later. On this date, the names of the specific investors who own the corporation's stock are obtained from the stockholders' register. Some investors may have purchased or sold stock shares between the declaration and record dates. Only those still owning stock on the date of record are eligible for a dividend. The stockholders receive their dividends a short time thereafter on the *payment date*.

The Orleans Corporation's December 31 closing entry process causes its $900 income to be reflected as a credit balance in the income summary account. The final closing entry is

Income summary	900	
Retained earnings		900

The above entry transfers the 1983 net income to the retained earnings account. The stockholders' interests in their corporation's assets are thus increased $900.

Based upon the declaration by the board of directors, the 1983 dividend is determined as shown in Exhibit 10-2.

Exhibit 10-2

COMMON STOCKHOLDERS		PREFERRED STOCKHOLDERS	
Number of shares		Par value per share	$ 50
outstanding	200	*Multiplied by:* Dividend rate	10%
Multiplied by: Dividend		Dividend per share	$ 5
per share	$1	*Multiplied by:* Number of	
Total cash dividend	$200	shares outstanding	✕100
		Total cash dividend	$500

The December 31 journal entry for the cash dividend declaration is

Retained earnings	700	
Cash dividends payable to common stockholders		200
Cash dividends payable to preferred stockholders		500

The $700 dividend represents a partial distribution of the corporation's income to its stockholders. It causes the corporate ownership interests to decrease. Therefore, the retained earnings account is debited for the declared dividend. Since the stockholders are not paid their dividend until January 28, 1984, the corporation has a liability to them as of December 31. Two separate current liability accounts are credited to reflect its obligation for eventual payment.

Exhibit 10-3 shows the retained earnings account on December 31 after the year-end journal entries have been posted. (The posting reference numbers are excluded.)

Exhibit 10-3

Account: Retained Earnings   Account Number: 32

1983			1983		
Dec. 31	Cash dividends declared	700	Dec. 31	Net income	900

The $200 credit balance represents the Orleans Corporation's earnings that have been retained within the organization and not distributed to its stockholders. This December 31 balance will be carried over to 1984 as the January 1 retained earnings account balance. At the end of 1984, the net income (or net loss) will again be closed to retained earnings and any declared dividends will be debited to this account. Thus, over a number of years, the retained earnings balance reflects the total historical earnings maintained within the corporate organization.

Financial statement readers normally want to know the causes for each period's change in the retained earnings account. Corporations provide this information by preparing a separate financial analysis called the "retained earnings statement." The Orleans Corporation's December 31, 1983 retained earnings statement is shown in Exhibit 10-4.

Exhibit 10-4

Orleans Corporation
Retained Earnings Statement
For the Year Ended December 31, 1983

Retained earnings, January 1, 1983	$ 0
Plus: Net income for year	900
	$900
Less: Cash dividends declared	700
Retained earnings, December 31, 1983	$200

Since 1983 is the first year of operating activity, the January 1 retained earnings balance is zero. The net income is added; then the declared dividends are subtracted to determine the updated December 31 retained earnings balance. It should be noted that the retained earnings statement provides the same information as the general ledger retained earnings account (see Exhibit 10-3). Financial statement readers do not, however, have the opportunity to see and analyze a corporation's general ledger retained earnings account. Thus, a formal retained earnings statement is a means of providing readers this relevant information.

Upon completion of the retained earnings statement, the period-end retained earnings balance is included under the stockholders' equity section of the balance sheet. Exhibit 10-5 is the Orleans Corporation's December 31, 1983 partial balance sheet showing the stockholders' equity section and its two major sources: paid-in capital and retained earnings. It is assumed that the preferred and common stock were originally sold at their par values. Consequently, no premium or discount exists on the stock issuances.

Exhibit 10-5
Stockholders' Equity

Paid-in capital:

10 percent preferred stock, noncumulative, nonparticipating, $50 par value (100 shares authorized and issued)	$ 5,000
Common stock, $40 par value (200 shares authorized and issued)	8,000
Total paid-in capital	$13,000
Retained earnings:	200
Total stockholders' equity	$13,200

The total paid-in capital from the sale of stock is $13,000. This includes $5000 worth of preferred stock (100 shares issued × $50 par value) and $8000 worth of common stock (200 shares issued × $40 par value). When the $200 retained earnings is added to the paid-in capital, the stockholders' interests in their corporation's assets are $13,200.

If a corporation has a net operating loss, it is debited to the retained earnings account in the closing entry process. This may cause retained earnings to have a debit balance rather than its usual credit balance. The debit balance represents a decreased ownership interest for the stockholders and is called a *deficit*. The stockholders' total equity is then determined by subtracting this deficit from the paid-in capital. A retained earnings debit balance indicates that earnings are not available for distribution to the stockholders. Therefore, many states do not allow a corporation to declare a cash dividend when a deficit exists in the retained earnings account.

To complete the analysis of cash dividends, we now return to the Orleans Corporation's $700 dividend declaration (see the December 31 journal entry on page 233). Since a cash dividend is a distribution of corporate earnings and not an operating expense, the retained earnings account is debited on December 31, and a current liability to each stockholder group is recognized. On the *record date* (January 14, 1984), the number of stock shares owned by every investor is ascertained from the stockholders' register. The only purpose of the record date is to "officially" determine those investors eligible to receive a cash dividend. As a result, no journal entry is required on this date. On the January 28 payment date, the following entry is recorded

```
Cash dividends payable to common stockholders      200
Cash dividends payable to preferred stockholders   500
   Cash                                                  700
```

The $700 credit represents the cash dividend payment to the stockholders. Consequently, the Orleans Corporation no longer has a liability to its investors. This is reflected by *debiting* the two current liability accounts initially established on the December 31 dividend declaration date.

Additional Corporate Accounting Topics

This section briefly analyzes a few important aspects of corporations not previously discussed. A more extensive coverage of these topics can be found in advanced accounting books.

Stock Dividends

The subject of cash dividends has already been discussed. They cause cash assets to leave the corporation. Because of unfavorable operating performance or the desire to maintain its assets internally for present and future expansion programs, a corporation's board of directors may not declare a cash dividend. However, the board can declare a *stock dividend*. It results in additional stock shares' being issued to the stockholders without distributing to them any assets. For example, the basic journal entry for a common stock dividend is

```
Retained earnings        XX
   Common stock               XX
```

This entry only affects stockholders' equity accounts with no assets leaving the corporation. The stock dividend causes a reclassification of the stockholders' equity section of the balance sheet. In other words, the retained earnings equity account is decreased by the same dollar amount that the common stock equity account is increased.

Earnings Per Share of Stock

Financial statement readers (especially current and potential investors) are interested in knowing how much of a corporation's periodic income applies to each share of outstanding stock. This is called the "earnings per share." Investors often analyze several corporations' earnings per share information before making their investment decisions.

Assume that the following data are available on December 31, 1983 for the Anderson Corporation:

> 100 shares of authorized and issued 8 percent non-cumulative, nonparticipating, $50 par value preferred stock
>
> 400 shares of authorized and issued $40 par value common stock
>
> 1983 net income—$2000

The Anderson Corporation's 1983 earnings per share on its preferred stock is computed as follows:

$$\frac{\text{Net income}}{\text{Number of preferred shares outstanding}} = \frac{\$2000}{100 \text{ shares}} = \underline{\$20} \text{ per share}$$

Each share of preferred stock earned $20 during 1983. The preferred stockholders do not, however, receive $20 for every share owned. They are entitled to an 8 percent annual cash dividend only if it is formally declared by the board of directors.

Since preferred stock owners have preference over the common stockholders in the distribution of corporate net income, the 1983 earnings per share on the Anderson Corporation's common stock is determined from the following computation:

$$\frac{\text{Net income available to common stockholders}}{\text{Number of common shares outstanding}}$$

$$= \frac{\text{Net income} - \text{cash dividend to preferred stockholders}}{\text{Number of common shares outstanding}}$$

$$= \frac{\$2000 - \$400 \left(\begin{array}{l} 8\% \text{ preferred dividend rate} \times \$50 \text{ par value} \\ = \$4 \text{ per share dividend} \times 100 \text{ shares outstanding} \end{array} \right)}{400 \text{ shares}}$$

$$= \underline{\$4} \text{ per share}$$

To compute the net income available to common stockholders, the preference of the preferred stockholders must be considered. This is accomplished by subtracting the $400 preferred dividends from the $2000 earnings. The remaining amount ($1600) is then divided by the 400 outstanding shares to determine the $4-per-share common stock earnings.

A corporation's earnings per share information is typically disclosed at the bottom of its income statement after the net income computation. This information has a major effect on the price at which the corporation's preferred and common stock is sold in the market. The market price is typically higher when stock has a favorable per-share earnings.

Review Questions

At this point, answer the following multiple-choice questions to test your knowledge of the previous reading material. The solutions are given below.

1. The Right Corporation incurred a $3000 net loss in 1983. All closing entries except the last one have been recorded. This final closing entry is
   a. Income summary   3000
         Common stock   3000
   b. Common stock   3000
         Income summary   3000
   c. Income summary   3000
         Retained earnings   3000
   d. Retained earnings   3000
         Income summary   3000

2. The following information is available on December 31, 1983 for the Power Corporation:

   Common stock balance December 31, 1983 $10,000
   Net loss for 1983 $ 500
   Cash dividend declared December 31, 1983 $ 600
   Retained earnings balance January 1, 1983 $ 2,000

The December 31, 1983 retained earnings account balance is
   a. $900.
   b. $1400.
   c. $1900.
   d. $2000.

3. The Pittsfield Corporation declared a $500 cash dividend to its preferred stockholders and a $400 cash dividend to its common stockholders. The corporation's journal entry on the record date is

a. Cash dividends payable to common stockholders 400
   Cash dividends payable to preferred stockholders 500
     Cash 900
b. Retained earnings 900
   Cash dividends payable to common stockholders 400
   Cash dividends payable to preferred stockholders 500
c. Retained earnings 900
   Cash 900
d. No journal entry required.

4. A stock dividend causes:
  a. The distribution of corporate assets to each current stockholder.
  b. No distribution of corporate assets to each current stockholder.
  c. An increase in the total stockholders' equity.
  d. A decrease in the total stockholders' equity.

Answers

1. d

2. a ($2000 January 1 balance – $500 net loss – $600 cash dividend declared)

3. d

4. b

Chapter Summary

This chapter has discussed the accounting aspects of corporations. The fact that a corporation is a separate legal entity from its stockholder owners allows ownership changes to occur without corporate dissolution being required. A major advantage of purchasing stock is that a stockholder's liability to creditors is limited to his asset investment into the corporation.

The two principal sources of the stockholders' equity in corporate assets are *paid-in capital* and *retained earnings*. The former results from stock sales transactions (both preferred and common stock) and the latter from corporate operating activities. Most states require a corporation to assign a legal value called the *par* or *stated value* to each stock share. This *legal capital* cannot be distributed to stockholders and therefore represents a protective device for the corporation's creditors.

Preferred and common stock may be sold at a price equal to, greater than (a premium), or less than (a discount) its par or stated value.

Preferred stock investors are typically paid a fixed percentage dividend rate and have preference over common stockholders in receiving their dividends. In the event of liquidation, the preferred stockholders also have preference in receiving any remaining corporate assets after the creditors are paid. Preferred stock is more attractive when it is sold with *cumulative* and *participating* features. Because common stockholders have voting privileges on corporate matters and can receive larger per share dividends when their organization is successful, these investors are considered the "true" corporate owners.

A corporation's period-end net income (or net loss) is closed into the stockholders' equity retained earnings account. These earnings belong to the corporate entity and are distributed to the stockholders only when the board of directors declares a *cash dividend*. A declared cash dividend reduces the stockholders' interests in their corporation's assets. This is reflected by debiting the retained earnings account.

The last section of this chapter briefly introduced two additional corporate accounting topics:

1. The concept of *stock dividends*. Rather than distributing assets to its investors in the form of a cash dividend, the board of directors may declare a stock dividend. This results in each investor's receiving additional shares of his corporation's stock.

2. The concept of *earnings per share of stock*. The preferred and common stock "earnings per share" data are typically disclosed at the bottom of a corporation's income statement. This information is highly important to current and potential investors in evaluating the corporation's operating activities.

Chapter Problem

The solution to the problem is given in the appendix. However, the reader is urged first to attempt to work the problem on his own and then to check his work against the given solution.

Problem Situation

The Henry Corporation began business on January 1, 1981. It manufactures and sells air conditioning units for homes, office buildings, and automobiles. The corporation closes its accounting records on each December 31 to prepare financial statements for its stockholders, management, creditors, and potential investors.

Exhibit 10-6 is the stockholders' equity section of the Henry Corporation's balance sheet on December 31, 1982.

Exhibit 10-6

Stockholders' Equity

Paid-in capital:

8 percent preferred stock, cumulative, nonparticipating, no-par stock with a $30 stated value (500 shares authorized, 300 shares issued)—		
dividends in arrears of $720	$ 9,000	
Plus: Premium on preferred stock	1,200	$10,200
Common stock, $20 par value (2000 shares authorized, 1560 shares issued)	$31,200	
Less: Discount on common stock	4,680	26,520
Total paid-in capital		$36,720
Retained earnings:		5,000
Total stockholders' equity		$41,720

The following accounting activities affected the corporation's stockholders' equity during 1983:

January 21   Sold 50 shares of common stock at $21 per share.

March 14   Sold 100 shares of preferred stock at $28 per share.

December 31   After the *revenue* and *expense* account balances are closed to the income summary account, this account has an $8000 *credit* balance (representing the 1983 net income).

December 31   The board of directors declared a cash dividend to its stock-holders. The common stockholders per share dividend is $1. This declared dividend has a January 10, 1984 record date and a January 20, 1984 payment date.

Problem Requirements

Using the above information, prepare *all* the Henry Corporation's 1983 journal entries affecting its stockholders' equity.

Problem Objective and Solution Approach

Objective:

To understand the accounting aspects of the *paid-in capital* and *retained earnings* stockholders' equity sources by recording transactions for the issuance of stock, for the transfer of corporate earnings to the stockholders' equity, and for the declaration of a cash dividend.

Solution Approach:

1. Prepare the January 21 journal entry for the common stock shares that are sold at a premium.

2. Prepare the March 14 journal entry for the preferred stock shares that are sold at a discount.

3. Prepare the final closing entry on December 31 for the $8000 net income.

4. In order to compute the December 31 declared cash dividend, first determine the number of preferred and common stock shares outstanding on this date. The outstanding shares include the issued stock as of December 31, 1982 plus the sold stock during 1983. Following this determination for each class of stock, the dollar dividend to the preferred and common stockholders can then be computed (remember, the preferred stock is cumulative). The final step is to record the December 31 journal entry for the cash dividend declaration.

11

Additional Relevant Accounting Topics

An important financial analysis called the "Statement of Changes in Financial Position" is discussed in this final chapter. Also, the use of a matrix accounting system for a small business is illustrated.

The Statement of Changes in Financial Position

An organization's *net working capital* is the dollar amount by which its current assets exceed its current liabilities. Since both current assets and current liabilities are short-term financial items, their monetary balances often change daily.

Assume that the Milton Corporation has $26,000 current assets and $9000 current liabilities on December 31, 1982. Its net working capital is, therefore, $17,000 ($26,000 - $9000). A year later, December 31, 1983, the corporation's current assets are $47,000 and its current liabilities are $14,000, resulting in $33,000 net working capital ($47,000 - $14,000). A comparison of these two years discloses that the Milton Corporation's net working capital increased $16,000 ($33,000 on December 31, 1983 - $17,000 on December 31, 1982).

A financial statement reader may be interested in knowing the specific monetary events that caused the $16,000 net working capital increase. Neither the income statement nor the balance sheet provides this information. Therefore, the Milton Corporation would prepare a separate financial analysis on December 31, 1983 called the "Statement of Changes in Financial Position" to explain its net working capital increase.

The three steps in preparing this statement of changes in financial position are now discussed.

Step 1. The corporation must first compute its total net working capital change from December 31, 1982 to December 31, 1983. The analysis in Exhibit 11-1 (utilizing the corporation's 1982 and 1983 balance sheet information) would have been prepared to compute the $16,000. (Explanations will follow.)

Exhibit 11-1

	DECEMBER 31, 1982	DECEMBER 31, 1983	EFFECT ON NET WORKING CAPITAL–INCREASE OR (DECREASE)
Current Assets			
Cash	$ 5000	$14000	$ 9000
Net accounts receivable*	8000	18000	10000
Merchandise inventory	12000	11000	(1000)
Office supplies	1000	4000	3000
Total current assets	$26000	$47000	$21000 increase
Current Liabilities			
Accounts payable	$ 4000	$10000	$ (6000)
Salaries payable	3000	1000	2000
Cash dividends payable to preferred and common stockholders#	2000	3000	(1000)
Total current liabilities	$ 9000	$14000	$ (5000) decrease
Net working capital (current assets minus current liabilities)	$17000	$33000	$16000 INCREASE

* The net accounts receivable represents the accounts receivable balance minus the allowance for uncollectibles balance.

\# Rather than separate liability accounts being established for preferred and common stockholders' dividends, only one is used in this illustration.

The last column indicates the effect of each current asset and current liability monetary change on the corporation's net working capital. Remember, the mathematical formula for computing net working capital is "current assets less current liabilities." Therefore, an *increase* in a current asset account balance from one period to the next causes net working capital to *increase*, and a current asset *decrease* causes a *decrease* in the net working capital. Since current liabilities are subtracted in the above formula, their periodic change has the opposite effect on net working capital. This means that a current liability account *increase* results in a net working capital *decrease*, whereas a *decrease* in any current liability balance causes a net working capital *increase*. For example, the Milton Corporation's accounts payable current liability increased by $6000 from December 31, 1982 to December 31, 1983. This $6000 increase causes a $6000 decrease in the net working capital.

The corporation's net working capital is increased $21,000 from the total current asset changes and decreased $5000 from the total current liability changes. Therefore, the overall effect on its net working capital is a $16,000 increase ($21,000 - $5000).

Step 2. After the total net working capital change has been determined, the next step is to ascertain the specific monetary events causing this change. An analysis is therefore made of the noncurrent accounts: plant and equipment assets, any additional long-term assets, long-term liabilities, and stockholders' equity. By analyzing these accounts, we determine the effect that their account balance changes have on the net working capital.

The Milton Corporation's noncurrent accounts with financial activity during 1983 are shown in Exhibit 11-2. Those inactive noncurrent accounts whose balances were unchanged in 1983 are excluded, since they would not have caused any part of the $16,000 net working capital increase. (The letters within the accounts are explained shortly.)

Exhibit 11-2

Machinery				Accumulated Depreciation—Machinery		
Jan. 1, 1983	7000					Jan. 1, 1983	3500
		(A)	6000	(A)	3000		
(C)	5000					(B)	2000

Land				Notes Payable (Long-Term)		
Jan. 1, 1983	6000					Jan. 1, 1983	1000
(D)	4000					(D)	4000

Common Stock				Retained Earnings		
		Jan. 1, 1983	30,000			Jan. 1, 1983	15,000
				(G)	3000		
		(E)	9,000			(F)	10,000

Step 3.   After the analysis of each noncurrent account has been completed, the statement of changes in financial position is then prepared (Exhibit 11-3). Letters rather than dates are shown in both the Milton Corporation's December 31, 1983 statement of changes in financial position and the above accounts. This is done in order to cross-reference each monetary item in the financial statement to its general ledger account. In the subsequent discussion of the individual items, these same letters are again used.

Exhibit 11-3

The Milton Corporation
Statement of Changes in Financial Position
For the Year Ended December 31, 1983

RESOURCES PROVIDED

Working capital from operations—		
net income	$10,000 (F)	
Add: Depreciation expense	2,000 (B)	
	$12,000	
Deduct: Gain on disposal of plant and equipment assets	1,000 (F)	
Total resources from operations		$11,000
Working capital from the sale of a long-term asset (machinery)		4,000 (A)
Working capital from the sale of common stock		9,000 (E)
Resources from the issuance of a long-term note payable (for the purchase of land)		4,000 (D)
Total resources provided		$28,000

RESOURCES APPLIED

Working capital used to purchase a long-term asset (machinery)	$ 5,000 (C)	
Working capital used for the declaration of a cash dividend to preferred and common stockholders	3,000 (G)	
Resources used for the purchase of land (through the incurrence of a long-term note payable)	4,000 (D)	
Total resources applied		12,000
Total increase in net working capital		$16,000

Explanation of Milton Corporation's Statement of Changes in Financial Position

A statement of changes in financial position includes two major sections—*resources provided* and *resources applied*. The resources of an organization are its assets. Therefore, the resources provided section discloses the sources from which the organization obtains its assets, and the resources applied section shows the manner in which the assets are used. The statement of changes in financial position can also be thought of as an "asset flow analysis." That is, resources provided reflect the flow of assets into an organization from financial transactions, whereas resources applied indicate the assets that flow out of the organization from financial transactions.

The monetary items on the Milton Corporation's statement of changes in financial position are now analyzed. This discussion centers around the *letters* reported on the corporation's financial statement (Exhibit 11-3) and its ledger accounts (Exhibit 11-2).

Letters F and B

An earned net income means that an organization's revenues exceed its expenses. Revenues cause a net working capital increase, since current assets (cash or accounts receivable) are typically received. On the other hand, expenses normally represent a net working capital decrease, because cash is either paid or a current liability is incurred. A net income is credited to the retained earnings account and reflects an increase in working capital from revenues exceeding expenses. Therefore, the Milton Corporation's $10,000 net income is reported under *resources provided* (see letter *F*) on its statement of changes in financial position. If an organization incurred a net loss (its expenses exceed revenues), this loss would cause a net working capital decrease and thus be reported under *resources applied* on the statement of changes in financial position.

The Milton Corporation's year-end adjusting entry for depreciation on its machinery was

Depreciation expense	2000	
Accumulated depreciation—machinery		2000

This $2000 depreciation was one of the operating expenses subtracted from the corporation's revenues to determine its $10,000 net income. However, the depreciation adjusting entry does not cause a change in net working capital, since neither the debit nor the credit is to working capital accounts (that is, current assets or current liabilities). Remember, the "accumulated depreciation—machinery" is a long-term *plant and equipment* asset account. To eliminate the effect of this depreciation from the corporation's net income, it is *added back* to the $10,000 (see letter *B*).

A $1000 gain on the sale of a machine is subtracted from the net income (also designated letter F). Its computation will be discussed under letter A below. This gain is already included in the $10,000 income computation, since it is a nonoperating item added at the bottom of the corporation's income statement (discussed in Chapter 8). However, the "working capital from operations" reported on the statement of changes in financial position should not include any nonoperating income or loss. The $1000 gain (previously added to the income and part of the $10,000 credit to the retained earnings account) is therefore subtracted from the net income to eliminate its effect. The resulting $11,000 represents the net working capital provided by corporate operating activities.

If an organization has a *nonoperating loss*, it is *subtracted* on the income statement. Then, to determine the working capital from operations for the statement of changes in financial position, this loss would be added back to the net income.

Letter A

The Milton Corporation's net working capital is increased by $4000 during 1983 from selling a piece of its machinery. As discussed in Chapter 8, a machine sale transaction requires the elimination of both the accumulated depreciation and the original cost relating to the disposed asset. This machine cost $6000 and had $3000 accumulated depreciation as of the sale date. The $4000 cash that was received from the machine disposal caused a $1000 gain ($6000 cost - $3000 accumulated depreciation = $3000 book value, compared to $4000 cash proceeds = $1000 gain). The journal entry reflecting the machine sale was

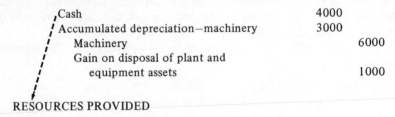

Cash	4000	
Accumulated depreciation—machinery	3000	
Machinery		6000
Gain on disposal of plant and equipment assets		1000

RESOURCES PROVIDED

On the basis of this entry, the noncurrent general ledger accounts for machinery and accumulated depreciation—machinery were updated (see Exhibit 11-2). The $1000 gain is included within the $10,000 net income credit to the retained earnings account (see letter F in Exhibit 11-2). The $4000 cash increases the Milton Corporation's net working capital (its current assets are increased) and is, therefore, reported as *resources provided* on the statement of changes in financial position.

Letter E

The Milton Corporation sold some common stock shares during 1983 at their $9000 par value (see the common stock account in Exhibit 11-2). The journal entry for this stock sale was

| Cash | 9000 | |
| Common stock | | 9000 |

RESOURCES PROVIDED

The $9000 cash represents resources provided on the corporation's statement of changes in financial position, since its net working capital is increased by this amount.

Letter D

Land costing $4000 was purchased by the Milton Corporation in 1983. To acquire this land, the corporation signed a three-year note. The following journal entry was recorded for the land transaction:

| Land | 4000 | |
| Notes payable (long-term) | | 4000 |

The general ledger accounts in Exhibit 11-2 reflect the above debit and credit. Since the land and notes payable (long-term) accounts are both noncurrent financial items, this transaction has no effect on the corporation's net working capital. However, the acquisition of land by incurring a long-term note liability is an important financial transaction that should be disclosed on the statement of changes in financial position. Therefore, it is reported as both *resources provided* and *resources applied*. The land asset acquired represents the resources provided from this transaction. Resources were applied to purchase the asset by signing a long-term note. Because the $4000 is included under resources provided as well as resources applied, its final effect on net working capital is zero.

Letter C

A $5000 piece of machinery was purchased (see the machinery account in Exhibit 11-2) by paying $1000 cash and incurring a 90-day note liability for the remainder. This transaction resulted in the following journal entry:

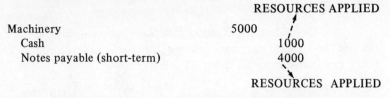

RESOURCES APPLIED

Machinery	5000
Cash	1000
Notes payable (short-term)	4000

RESOURCES APPLIED

Both credits cause a decrease in net working capital, since a current asset (cash) is decreased and a current liability (the short-term note payable) is increased. Therefore, the total net working capital decrease from the machine acquisition is $5000. It represents working capital resources used and is reported under *resources applied.*

The $4000 note liability was paid before the end of 1983. The corporation's journal entry at the time of this payment was

Notes payable (short-term)	4000	
Cash		4000

Only working capital accounts are affected in the above entry. That is, the current liability notes payable account and the current asset cash account are both decreased. As a result, the corporation's total net working capital is unchanged, and this transaction would not appear on the statement of changes in financial position. Whenever transactions involve only working capital accounts, the total net working capital is unaffected. These transactions cause a reclassification of monetary items within the current asset and/ or current liability accounts (a change in one is offset by the same change in another) but do not increase or decrease the total net working capital. Therefore, they are not reported on the statement.

Letter G

At the end of 1983, the Milton Corporation's board of directors declared a cash dividend to its preferred and common stockholders (see the $3000 debit to the retained earnings account in Exhibit 11-2). The journal entry on the cash dividend declaration date was

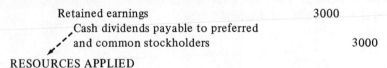

Retained earnings	3000	
Cash dividends payable to preferred and common stockholders		3000

RESOURCES APPLIED

The $3000 credit to the "cash dividends payable to preferred and common stockholders" current liability account causes the corporation's net working capital to decrease by this same amount. Thus, the declared cash dividend is reflected as *resources applied* on the statement.

When the Milton Corporation pays the cash dividend to its stockholders in 1984, the journal entry is

Cash dividends payable to preferred
and common stockholders   3000
    Cash   3000

Since this transaction does not cause the total net working capital to change
(only working capital accounts are affected), it would be excluded from the
1984 statement of changes in financial position.

Concluding Comments

The Milton Corporation's statement of changes in financial position (Exhibit 11-3) reveals that $28,000 in resources are provided from busi-
ness activities, while only $12,000 is applied. Therefore, more resources are
provided than applied ($28,000 - $12,000 = $16,000) during 1983. This
causes the corporation's net working capital to increase by $16,000.

The analysis of the individual changes in the Milton Corporation's
current assets and current liabilities from December 31, 1982 to December
31, 1983 (see Exhibit 11-1) also shows a $16,000 net working capital increase
during this time period. The statement of changes in financial position has
been prepared in order to explain the monetary causes of the $16,000 in-
crease. By including this statement along with the income statement and
balance sheet at the end of the accounting period, the Milton Corporation
provides its financial readers additional relevant information.

Review Questions

At this point, answer the following multiple-choice questions to
test your knowledge of the previous reading material. The solutions are given
below.

1. The purpose of a statement of changes in financial position is
   a. To analyze the changes in an organization's individual revenue and expense accounts from one accounting period to the next.
   b. To analyze the changes in an organization's individual plant and equipment asset accounts from one accounting period to the next.
   c. To analyze the causes for an organization's net working capital change
   from one accounting period to the next.
   d. To analyze the changes in an organization's individual owners' equity
   accounts from one accounting period to the next.

2. Presented below are some of the monetary balances of the Todder Corporation's financial items on December 31, 1983:

Plant and equipment assets	$100,000
Current liabilities	$ 25,000
Long-term liabilities	$ 20,000
Current assets	$ 50,000

The corporation's year-end net working capital is
a. $5,000.
b. $25,000.
c. $30,000.
d. $105,000.

3. The Bender Corporation received $5000 cash from the sale of its preferred stock. Where does the effect of this transaction appear on the corporation's statement of changes in financial position?
a. As *resources provided.*
b. As *resources applied.*
c. The transaction does not affect this financial statement.
d. As a net working capital decrease.

4. The Jackson Corporation's $2000 account receivable from George Harris was collected on December 10, 1983. What effect does this $2000 cash collection have on the corporation's net working capital?
a. Increased $2000.
b. Decreased $2000.
c. Increased $1000.
d. No change.

Answers

1. c

2. b ($50,000 current assets – $25,000 current liabilities)

3. a

4. d (Only working capital accounts are affected.)

A Matrix Accounting System

Most organizations use journals and ledgers for accumulating their accounting information. A small business can save time and effort in recording and classifying its financial transactions by having a *matrix accounting system* to replace the conventional journals and ledgers.

Assume that the Mike Por Company is a small proprietorship organization selling office supplies. Its January 1, 1983 trial balance is shown in Exhibit 11-4.

Exhibit 11-4

Mike Por Company
Trial Balance
January 1, 1983

Cash	$ 500	
Accounts receivable	400	
Merchandise inventory	2800	
Accounts payable		$1400
Mike Por, capital		2300
	$3700	$3700

The Por Company uses a perpetual inventory system. Its January transactions are

1. Sold merchandise on account at a $350 retail price. Cost of this merchandise to the Por Company, $140.

2. Paid the January store rent, $75.

3. Paid the January salary to part-time employee, $100.

4. Received $50 in payment of an account receivable.

5. Paid $200 of the accounts payable liabilities.

Based upon the January 1 trial balance and the above transactions, the matrix in Exhibit 11-5 is prepared. (Explanations will follow.)

The matrix columns are for recording debits, and the rows are for recording credits. Since a debit or credit may occur in each account, all of the accounts are listed in both columns and rows. The same debit and credit rules for increasing and decreasing accounts are used with a matrix accounting system: (1) asset and expense account increases are recorded in columns (debits) and decreases in rows (credits), and (2) liability, owner's equity, and revenue account increases are recorded in rows (credits) and decreases in columns (debits).

Each rectangular box within the matrix is called a *cell*. For discussion purposes, these cells are numbered. Based upon the Por Company's trial balance (see Exhibit 11-4), the January 1 account balances are entered in their proper cells. Since the asset accounts have debit balances, the cash, the accounts receivable, and the merchandise inventory balances are recorded in column cells 1, 2, and 3, respectively. The liability and the owner's equity accounts reflect credit balances and are, therefore, recorded in row cells 48 and 60, respectively.

After these account balances have been recognized, the January transactions (described above) are then recorded in the matrix cells. Each transaction is now discussed. (If period-end adjusting entries are required, they are recorded within the proper matrix cells in the same manner as the journal entries.)

Exhibit 11-5

COLUMNS FOR DEBITS

January 1, 1983 Account Balances	Assets (Increases)			Liabilities (Decreases)	Owner's Equity (Decreases)	Revenues (Decreases) and Expenses (Increases)				Row Totals	January 31, 1983 Account Balances
(12)	Cash (1)	Accounts receivable (2)	Merchandise inventory (3)	Accounts payable (4)	Mike Por, capital (5)	Sales (6)	Cost of merchandise sold (7)	Salaries expense (8)	Rent expense (9)	(10)	(11)
Cash (12) 500	(13)	(14)	(15)	(16) (5) 200	(17)	(18)	(19)	(20) (3) 100	(21) (2) 75	(22) 375	(23) —
Accounts receivable (24) 400	(25) (4) 50	(26)	(27)	(28)	(29)	(30)	(31)	(32)	(33)	(34) 50	(35) —
Merchandise inventory (36) 2800	(37)	(38)	(39)	(40)	(41)	(42)	(43) (1) 140	(44)	(45)	(46) 140	(47) —
Accounts payable (48) 1400	(49)	(50)	(51)	(52)	(53)	(54)	(55)	(56)	(57)	(58) 1400	(59) 1200
Mike Por, capital (60) 2300	(61)	(62)	(63)	(64)	(65)	(66)	(67)	(68)	(69)	(70) 2300	(71) 2300
Sales (72)	(73)	(74) (1) 350	(75)	(76)	(77)	(78)	(79)	(80)	(81)	(82) 350	(83) 350
Cost of merchandise sold (84)	(85)	(86)	(87)	(88)	(89)	(90)	(91)	(92)	(93)	(94) —	(95) —
Salaries expense (96)	(97)	(98)	(99)	(100)	(101)	(102)	(103)	(104)	(105)	(106) —	(107) —
Rent expense (108)	(109)	(110)	(111)	(112)	(113)	(114)	(115)	(116)	(117)	(118) —	(119) —
Column Totals (120)	(121) 550	(122) 750	(123) 2800	(124) 200	(125) —	(126) —	(127) 140	(128) 100	(129) 75	(130) —	(131) —
January 31, 1983 Account Balances (132)	(133) 175	(134) 700	(135) 2660	(136) —	(137) —	(138) —	(139) 140	(140) 100	(141) 75	(142) 4615	(143) 3850

ROWS FOR CREDITS
(Assets (Decreases); Liabilities (Increases); Owner's Equity (Increases); Revenues (Increases) and Expenses (Decreases); Column Totals; January 31, 1983 Account Balances)

254

Transaction 1.

In journal form, this transaction would have been recorded as

Accounts receivable	350	
Sales		350
Cost of merchandise sold	140	
Merchandise inventory		140

Cell number 74 reflects the first entry. This cell is in the accounts receivable debit column and sales credit row. Since the Por Company uses a perpetual inventory system, the second entry is also required. It is recorded in matrix cell number 43 (the cost of merchandise sold debit column and merchandise inventory credit row).

Transaction 2.

In journal form, this transaction would have been recorded as

Rent expense	75	
Cash		75

Cell number 21 represents this entry (the rent expense debit column and cash credit row).

Transaction 3.

In journal form, this transaction would have been recorded as

Salaries expense	100	
Cash		100

This salary payment is recorded in cell number 20 (the salaries expense debit column and cash credit row).

Transaction 4.

In journal form, this transaction would have been recorded as

Cash	50	
Accounts receivable		50

Matrix cell 25 reflects this entry (the cash debit column and accounts receivable credit row).

Transaction 5.

In journal form, this transaction would have been recorded as

Accounts payable	200	
Cash		200

This liability payment is recorded in cell number 16 (the accounts payable debit column and cash credit row).

When a conventional accounting system with journals and ledgers is used, the recorded journal entries are posted to general ledger accounts in order that each account balance can be determined. A matrix accounting system does not require all this work. Rather, an account balance is computed by adding the "column" and "row" monetary items for the account and then subtracting the smaller total from the larger one to determine its balance. For example, the cash column total is $550 (cell number 121) and the cash row total is $375 (cell number 22). The cash account therefore has a January 31 debit balance of $175 ($550 - $375). This is shown in cell number 133. The same process is followed to determine each account balance. Since matrix columns reflect debits, the monetary balances of the asset and expense accounts (having debit balances) appear in columns. The matrix rows represent credits. Thus, the dollar balances of the liability, owner's equity, and revenue accounts (having credit balances) are reported in rows. For example, the $1200 accounts payable liability balance is shown in matrix cell number 59 [$1400 row total (cell number 58) *less* $200 column total (cell number 124)].

The $4615 in cell number 130 is a "check figure" showing that the total of the column items (the debits) equals the total of the row items (the credits). Before preparing financial statements, a company should determine that its accounts with debit balances equal its accounts with credit balances. To accomplish this, a "trial balance" is prepared. Under a matrix accounting system, a separate trial balance is unnecessary, since the equality of debit and credit account balances can be ascertained directly from the matrix. Cell number 143 on the Por Company's matrix reflects its trial balance results. The January 31 *debit* account balances from the "column" financial items (asset and expense accounts) are added. Their total is $3,850. Then the January 31 *credit* account balances from the "row" financial items (liability, owner's equity, and revenue accounts) are added. Since this total is also $3850, the Por Company's trial balance is finished.

The financial statements can now be prepared. Based upon the account balances disclosed in the Por Company's January matrix, its month-end income statement and balance sheet are presented in Exhibits 11-6 and 11-7. The matrix cell number of each financial item is shown in parentheses.

The Por Company's February accounting transactions are recorded on a new matrix in the same manner as the January transactions. The January 31 asset and liability account balances are reported as the February 1 balances on this matrix. With a system of journals and ledgers, the revenue and expense account balances would have been closed into the owner's equity account at the end of January. Since journal entries are not utilized under a

Exhibit 11-6

Mike Por Company
Income Statement
For the Month Ended January 31, 1983

Revenues

Retail price of merchandise sold $350 (cell number 83)

Less: *Operating Expenses*

Cost of merchandise sold	$140 (cell number 139)	
Salaries expense	100 (cell number 140)	
Rent expense	75 (cell number 141)	
Total operating expenses		315
Net income		$ 35

Exhibit 11-7

Mike Por Company
Balance Sheet
January 31, 1983

ASSETS		*LIABILITIES & OWNER'S EQUITY*	
Current assets		Current liabilities	
Cash	$ 175 (cell #133)	Accounts payable	$1200 (cell #59)
Accounts receivable	700 (cell #134)	Owner's equity (cell #60)	
Merchandise inventory	2660 (cell #135)	Mike Por, capital, Jan. 1	$2300
		Plus: Net Income for Jan.	35
		Mike Por, capital, Jan. 31	2335
Total assets	$3535	Total liabilities and owner's equity	$3535

matrix system, the Por Company's January net income is added to the "Mike Por, capital" account. The resulting $2335 (see the owner's equity section of Exhibit 11-7) is then reflected as the February 1 balance of the "Mike Por, capital" account on the February matrix. Each revenue and expense account would have a zero balance to begin this new accounting period.

In the matrix accounting system example of Exhibit 11-5, only one transaction appeared within a particular cell. It should be noted, however, that more than one transaction (should the same transaction occur more than once during an accounting period) can be recorded in a specific matrix cell.

A matrix system is practical only for those organizations having a low volume of financial transactions. It eliminates the need for journals and ledgers, and is thus quite efficient for a small business. However, the simplicity of a matrix system would make its use impractical in a large organization. The high volume of transactions occurring in each accounting period would necessitate a system of journals and ledgers for this type of organization.

Review Questions

At this point, answer the following multiple-choice questions to test your knowledge of the previous reading material. The solutions are given below.

A partial matrix including some of the Brent Company's accounts is provided in Exhibit 11-8. Utilizing this matrix, answer the four questions.

Exhibit 11-8

	CASH (1)	ACCOUNTS RECEIVABLE (2)	ACCOUNTS PAYABLE (3)	RENT EXPENSE (4)
March 1 Account Balances ↓→	700	500		
CASH (5)	(6)	(7)	(8)	(9)
ACCOUNTS RECEIVABLE (10)	(11)	(12)	(13)	(14)
ACCOUNTS PAYABLE 400 (15)	(16)	(17)	(18)	(19)
RENT EXPENSE (20)	(21)	(22)	(23)	(24)

1. The Brent Company collected $200 during March from an account receivable customer. This transaction is recorded in matrix cell number.
   a. 7.
   b. 6.

c. 11.
d. 12.

2. The Brent Company paid its $150 March rent. This transaction is recorded in matrix cell number:
   a. 9.
   b. 6.
   c. 21.
   d. 24.

3. The Brent Company paid $100 of its accounts payable liabilities in March. This transaction is recorded in matrix cell number:
   a. 16.
   b. 18.
   c. 3.
   d. 8.

4. If there are no additional March transactions, the cash account row total is
   a. $200.
   b. $250.
   c. $650.
   d. $900.

Answers

1. c

2. a

3. d

4. b [$100 (cell number 8) + $150 (cell number 9)]

Chapter Summary

The statement of changes in financial position provides relevant information concerning the monetary activities that cause a change in an organization's net working capital (current assets less current liabilities) from one accounting period to the next. This financial statement is prepared by analyzing the increases and decreases in noncurrent accounts to determine what effect these changes have on the asset resources. The *resources provided* section of the statement of changes in financial position discloses the monetary transactions causing the flow of assets into an organization, and the *resources applied* section reports the asset flow out of the organization. A net working capital increase occurs when the resources provided exceed the resources applied. A statement of changes in financial position should be included along with an organization's income statement and balance sheet at the end of its accounting period.

This chapter also illustrated a matrix system for recording and classifying a small company's financial transactions. It eliminates the time-consuming function of recording transactions in a journal and posting them to general ledger accounts. A matrix system can be an efficient record-keeping method for those organizations having a relatively small volume of monetary transactions.

Concluding Comments

This book's objective has been to present a logical explanation of the basic accounting concepts and procedures. It is hoped that each reader has developed an appreciation of accounting's important role in business. Most of the topics in the book were discussed on an elementary level. Therefore, the author recommends the study of advanced books by those readers wanting to further their accounting education. Dynamic and challenging areas within the accounting field include cost accounting, income tax, budgeting, and systems analysis.

Chapter Problem

The solution to the problem is given in the appendix. However, the reader is urged first to attempt to work the problem on his own and then to check his work against the given solution.

Problem Situation

The Samantha Corporation sells billiard and pool tables. Its accounting records are closed each December 31 to prepare annual financial statements. The corporation's management is worried about the $10,000 net working capital decrease during 1983. The data regarding this decrease were obtained from the analysis in Exhibit 11-9.

Presented in Exhibit 11-10 are the Samantha Corporation's general ledger noncurrent accounts affected by financial transactions during 1983. The corporation's year-end adjusting and closing entries have already been recorded and posted (posting reference numbers are excluded).

Exhibit 11-9

	DECEM- BER 31, 1982	DECEM- BER 31, 1983	EFFECT ON NET WORKING CAPITAL– INCREASE OR (DECREASE)
Current assets			
Cash	$ 8,000	$ 3,000	$ (5,000)
Net accounts receivable*	7,000	8,000	1,000
Merchandise inventory	10,000	7,000	(3,000)
Office supplies	800	700	(100)
Total current assets	$25,800	$18,700	$ (7,100) decrease
Current liabilities			
Accounts payable	$ 5,000	$ 6,000	$ (1,000)
Salaries payable	2,000	900	1,100
Cash dividends payable to pre- ferred and common stockholders	1,000	4,000	(3,000)
Total current liabilities	$ 8,000	$10,900	$ (2,900) decrease
Net working capital (current assets *minus* current liabilities)	$17,800	$ 7,800	$(10,000) decrease

* The net accounts receivable represents the accounts receivable balance minus the allowance for uncollectibles balance.

Exhibit 11-10
General Ledger

Account: Equipment   Account No. 132

DATE	ITEM	POSTING REF.	DEBIT	DATE	ITEM	POSTING REF.	CREDIT
1983 Jan. 1 June 1	Balance Purchase of equipment for cash		8,000 6,000 *(12000)* 14 000	1983 May 1	Sale of equipment for $1000 Cash		 2000

Account: Accumulated Depreciation–Equipment   Account No. 133

DATE	ITEM	POSTING REF.	DEBIT	DATE	ITEM	POSTING REF.	CREDIT
1983 May 1	Elimination of accumu- lated depre- ciation on equipment sold		 400	1983 Jan. 1 Dec. 31	Balance Yearly adjusting entry *(3600)*		3000 1000 4000

Account: ___Land___   Account No. ___138___

DATE		ITEM	POSTING REF.	DEBIT	DATE	ITEM	POSTING REF.	CREDIT
1983								
Jan.	1	Balance		5,000				
Sept.	10	Purchase of land for cash		7,650				
Dec.	20	Purchase of land by incurring a 2-year note		1,000				
				(13650)				
				13650				

Account: ___Notes Payable (Long-term)___   Account No. ___206___

DATE	ITEM	POSTING REF.	DEBIT	DATE		ITEM	POSTING REF.	CREDIT
				1983				
				Jan.	1	Balance		3000
				Dec.	20	Purchase of land		1000
						(4000)		4000

Account: ___Common Stock___   Account No. ___300___

DATE	ITEM	POSTING REF.	DEBIT	DATE		ITEM	POSTING REF.	CREDIT
				1983				
				Jan.	1	Balance		15,000
				April	10	Sale of stock for cash		500
						(15500)		15500

Account: ___Premium on Common Stock___   Account No. ___301___

DATE	ITEM	POSTING REF.	DEBIT	DATE		ITEM	POSTING REF.	CREDIT
				1983				
				Jan.	1	Balance		1000
				April	10	Premium on April 10 stock sale		50
						(1050)		1050

Account: ___Retained Earnings___   Account No. ___308___

DATE		ITEM	POSTING REF.	DEBIT	DATE		ITEM	POSTING REF.	CREDIT
1983					1983				
Dec.	31	Cash dividend declared to preferred and common stockholders			Jan.	1	Balance		12,000
					Dec.	31	Net income for 1983		4,500
				4000			(12500)		16500

The Samantha Corporation's summarized income statement for the year ended December 31, 1983 is

Net sales	$14,100*
Less: Operating expenses	9,000†
Income from operations	$ 5,100
Nonoperating items	
Deduct: Loss on disposal of plant	
and equipment assets	600‡
Net income	$ 4,500

* The $14,100 net sales represents the sales minus the sales returns and allowances and minus the sales discounts.

† Included within the $9000 operating expenses is $1000 depreciation expense.

‡ The $600 loss resulted from the sale of equipment on May 1, 1983.

Problem Requirements

The Samantha Corporation's management wants to know the causes for the $10,000 net working capital decrease in 1983. Therefore, prepare a statement of changes in financial position on December 31, 1983.

Problem Objective and Solution Approach

Objective:

To correctly analyze the changes in an organization's noncurrent accounts in order to prepare its financial statement called the "statement of changes in financial position."

Solution Approach:

1. Analyze the noncurrent accounts (as well as the income statement information) to determine what effect the monetary activities within each account have on the corporation's resources provided and resources applied.

2. Using the information obtained from 1, prepare the statement of changes in financial position to explain the causes of the $10,000 net working capital decrease.

Appendix

Solutions to Chapter Problems

The solutions to the problems from Chapters 1 through 11 are presented in this appendix. Explanatory comments are in italic to distinguish them from the actual solutions.

Chapter 1

Part 1.

The River Company
Income Statement
For the Month Ended November 30, 1983

Revenues		
Retail price of merchandise sold		$2500
Less: *Expenses*		
Cost of merchandise sold	$1550	
Rent on the store and office facilities	275	
Salaries to employees	625	
Total expenses		2450
Net income		$ 50

The River Company
Balance Sheet
November 30, 1983

ASSETS		*LIABILITIES & OWNERS' EQUITY*		
Cash	$ 200	Liabilities:		
Accounts receivable	**200**	Accounts payable		$ 450
Merchandise inventory	1300	Owners' equity:		
Office supplies	100	Owners' equity,		
		November 1, 1983	$1300	
		Plus: **Net income for**		
		the month of November	**50**	
		Owners' equity,		
		November 30, 1983		1350
		Total liabilities and		
Total assets	$1800	owners' equity		$1800

The $200 accounts receivable is determined by using the balance sheet equation. The total assets excluding the accounts receivable are $1600 ($200 cash + $1300 merchandise inventory + $100 office supplies). Since a company's assets must equal its liabilities + owners' equity (which is the balance sheet equation), and the River Company's liabilities + owners' equity totals $1800, the unknown accounts receivable must therefore be $200 ($1800 minus $1600) in order to make the balance sheet equation "balance."

The $50 comes from the income statement computation above and is added to the November 1 owners' equity in order to determine the updated November 30 owners' equity.

Part 2.

a. Percentage interest of outside parties (that is, the liabilities) =

$$\frac{\text{Total liabilities}}{\text{Total assets}} = \frac{\$ 450}{\$1800} = 25 \text{ percent}$$

Outsiders therefore have a 25 percent interest in the River Company's total assets.

b. Percentage interest of internal parties (that is, the owners) =

$$\frac{\text{Owners' equity}}{\text{Total assets}} = \frac{\$1350}{\$1800} = \underline{\text{75 percent}}$$

> *Owners therefore have a 75 percent interest in the River Company's total assets.*

Chapter 2

Journal

Page 5

DATE		DESCRIPTION	POSTING REFERENCE	DEBIT	CREDIT
1983 Oct.	1	Rent expense Cash (Payment of October rent on law office)	500 100	100	 100
	5	Cash Accounts receivable (Received payment from client for legal services performed last month)	100 101	50	 50
		Since the legal services were performed for the client last month, the revenue from legal services was, therefore, recognized last month along with the establishment of an accounts receivable against the client. The transaction on October 5 involves the collection of this receivable.			
	8	Accounts receivable Revenue from legal services (Sent bill to client for services performed)	101 400	200	 200

DATE		DESCRIPTION	POSTING REFERENCE	DEBIT	CREDIT
1983 Oct.	12	Accounts payable Cash (Payment of liability owed from last month)	200 100	25	 25
	20	Land Accounts payable (Purchased a piece of land with payment due next month)	103 200	300	 300
		The law firm did not have a "land" *account on its September 30, 1983* *balance sheet. This indicates that no* *land was owned at the end of Sep-* *tember. Therefore, a new account* *for "land" must be established in* *the law firm's general ledger so that* *this transaction can be posted to* *the land asset account.*			
	25	Cash Revenue from legal services (Received payment from a client for legal services performed)	100 400	300	 300
	28	Utilities expense Cash (Payment of the elec- tricity and water bill for the month of October)	501 100	50	 50
	31	Wages expense Cash (Payment of the month- ly wages to the part- time secretary)	502 100	200	 200

DATE		DESCRIPTION	POSTING REFERENCE	DEBIT	CREDIT
1983 Oct.	31	Office supplies expense	503	50	
		Office supplies	102		50
		(Recognition of the office supplies used during the month of October)			
		The $100 worth of office supplies on the September 30, 1983 balance sheet is an asset. During October, $50 worth of these supplies were used. Therefore, this $50 represents an expense of the law firm. Also, the utilization of the office supplies causes a reduction in the office supplies asset account.			

General Ledger*

Account: Cash   Account No. 100

DATE		ITEM	POSTING REFERENCE	DEBIT	DATE		ITEM	POSTING REFERENCE	CREDIT
1983 Sept.	30	Balance	✓	500	1983 Oct.	1		5	100
Oct.	5		5	50		12		5	25
	25		5	300		28		5	50
			⟨475⟩	___		31		5	200
				850					*375*

Account: Accounts Receivable   Account No. 101

DATE		ITEM	POSTING REFERENCE	DEBIT	DATE		ITEM	POSTING REFERENCE	CREDIT
1983 Sept.	30	Balance	✓	200	1983 Oct.	5		5	50
Oct.	8		5	200					
			⟨350⟩	*400*					

Account: Office Supplies   Account No. 102

DATE		ITEM	POSTING REFERENCE	DEBIT	DATE		ITEM	POSTING REFERENCE	CREDIT
1983 Sept.	30	Balance	✓	100	1983 Oct.	31		5	50
			⟨50⟩						

*The "balancing-down process" for accounts is not illustrated here.

Account: <u>Land</u>   Account No. <u>103</u>

DATE	ITEM	POSTING REFERENCE	DEBIT	DATE	ITEM	POSTING REFERENCE	CREDIT
1983 Oct. 20		5	300				

Account: <u>Accounts Payable</u>   Account No. <u>200</u>

DATE	ITEM	POSTING REFERENCE	DEBIT	DATE	ITEM	POSTING REFERENCE	CREDIT
1983 Oct. 12		5	25	1983 Sept. 30 Oct. 20	Balance (375)	✓ 5	100 300 *400*

Account: <u>Wages Payable</u>   Account No. <u>201</u>

DATE	ITEM	POSTING REFERENCE	DEBIT	DATE	ITEM	POSTING REFERENCE	CREDIT

There were no monetary transactions affecting this liability account during the month of October.

Account: <u>Harry Jungbluth, Capital</u>   Account No. <u>300</u>

DATE	ITEM	POSTING REFERENCE	DEBIT	DATE	ITEM	POSTING REFERENCE	CREDIT
				1983 Sept. 30	Balance	✓	700

Account: <u>Revenue from Legal Services</u>   Account No. <u>400</u>

DATE	ITEM	POSTING REFERENCE	DEBIT	DATE	ITEM	POSTING REFERENCE	CREDIT
				1983 Oct. 8 25	(500)	5 5	200 300 *500*

Account: <u>Rent Expense</u>   Account No. <u>500</u>

DATE	ITEM	POSTING REFERENCE	DEBIT	DATE	ITEM	POSTING REFERENCE	CREDIT
1983 Oct. 1		5	100				

Account: Utilities Expense _____   Account No. 501 ___

DATE	ITEM	POSTING REFERENCE	DEBIT	DATE	ITEM	POSTING REFERENCE	CREDIT
1983 Oct. 28		5	50				

Account: Wages Expense _____   Account No. 502 ___

DATE	ITEM	POSTING REFERENCE	DEBIT	DATE	ITEM	POSTING REFERENCE	CREDIT
1983 Oct. 31		5	200				

Account: Office Supplies Expense _____   Account No. 503 ___

DATE	ITEM	POSTING REFERENCE	DEBIT	DATE	ITEM	POSTING REFERENCE	CREDIT
1983 Oct. 31		5	50				

Harry Jungbluth Law Firm
Trial Balance
October 31, 1983

		DEBIT	CREDIT
1	Cash	$ 475	
	Accounts receivable	350	
	Office supplies	50	
	Land	300	
	Accounts payable		$ 375
	Harry Jungbluth, capital		700
2	Revenue from legal services		500
	Rent expense	100	
	Utilities expense	50	
	Wages expense	200	
	Office supplies expense	50	
		$1575	$1575

[1] *The balance sheet accounts from the general ledger are presented first (the assets, then all liabilities, and finally, the owner's equity). It should be noted that there is no merchandise inventory asset account. This is so because the law firm does not sell a physical product to customers. Rather, it provides legal services to clients.*

[2] *The income statement accounts from the general ledger are presented after the balance sheet accounts (the revenue item followed by the expenses).*

Harry Jungbluth Law Firm
Income Statement
For the Month Ended October 31, 1983

Revenues
From legal services to clients		$ 500

Less: Expenses

Rent expense	$100	
Utilities expense	50	
Wages expense	200	
Office supplies expense	50	
Total expenses		400
Net income		$100

Harry Jungbluth Law Firm
Balance Sheet
October 31, 1983

ASSETS		*LIABILITIES & OWNER'S EQUITY*		
Cash	$ 475	Liabilities		
Accounts receivable	350	Accounts payable		$ 375
Office supplies	50	Owner's equity		
Land	300	**Harry Jungbluth,**		
		capital, Oct. 1, 1983	**$700**	
		Plus: **Net income for**		
		the month of October	**100**	
		Harry Jungbluth,		
		capital, Oct. 31, 1983		800
		Total liabilities and		
Total assets	$1175	owner's equity		$1175

The $700 balance in the owner's equity account "Harry Jungbluth, capital" is taken from the October 31, 1983 trial balance, but is actually the October 1, 1983 account balance (since the net income or net loss for October has not yet been transferred to the owner's equity account). The $100 October net income increases Harry Jungbluth's interest in the law firm's assets and is, therefore, added to the $700 in order to determine Jungbluth's $800 updated account balance on October 31, 1983.

Chapter 3

1. a.   1983
         Oct. 31   Wages (or salaries) expense   4000
                        Wages (or salaries) payable   4000
                        (Wages owed to the employees
                        at the close of the accounting
                        period)

*Since the employees worked four of the five work days in the week (that is,
Monday through Thursday) as of October 31, the Kool Playhouse has an expense (the debit to the wages expense account) and a liability (the credit to
the wages payable account) of $4000* $\left(\dfrac{4 \; days \; worked \; by \; employees}{5 \; days \; in \; work \; week} \times \$5000 \right)$.

1. b.   1983
         Nov. 1   Wages (or salaries) payable   4000
                   Wages (or salaries) expense   1000
                        Cash   5000
                        (Payment of the employees'
                        weekly wages)

*Of the $5000 salaries paid to the employees on November 1, $4000 relates
to the Kool Playhouse's liability established on October 31. Thus, the wages
payable liability account is now debited $4000. The wages expense account is
debited for the one day's work (that is, Friday) by the employees in the
November accounting period (1/5 × $5000 = $1000). Remember, the wages
expense for the first four days of the week was recognized in the Playhouse's
adjusting entry on October 31.*

2. a.   1983
         Oct. 1   Prepaid rent   2400
                        Cash   2400
                        (Payment of one year's
                        rent on the leased building)

*"Prepaid rent" is an asset account, since it represents one year's rental bene-
fits to be received by the Kool Playhouse as a result of the $2400 advance
payment.*

2. b.   1983
         Oct. 31   Rent expense   200
                        Prepaid rent   200
                        (Recognition of the October
                        rent expense)

One month's rental benefits have been received by the Kool Playhouse as of October 31. Therefore, one of the twelve months' prepaid rent now represents rent expense (1/12 × $2400 = $200). Also, the prepaid rent asset account is reduced by the $200 rental benefits from October.

	1983			
3. a.	Oct. 7	Cash	6000	
		Unearned ticket revenues		6000
		(Cash received from drama series ticket sales for five future plays)		

The liability account "unearned ticket revenues" is credited since as of October 7, the Kool Playhouse has not performed any of the five plays for which the $6000 cash was received. Therefore, the Playhouse has a liability to its customers eventually to perform these five plays.

	1983			
3. b.	Oct. 31	Unearned ticket revenues	2400	
		Earned ticket revenues		2400
		(Recognition of the revenue earned from the performance of plays A and B in October)		

As of October 31, the Kool Playhouse has performed two of the total five plays in the drama series. Therefore, $2400 of the $6000 cash originally re-

$$\frac{2 \; plays \; actually \; performed}{5 \; plays \; in \; drama \; series} \times \$6000 \; .$$

Also, the Kool Playhouse's liability to its customers is reduced $2400 as a result of these two plays having been performed.

	1983			
4. a.	Oct. 31	Rent receivable	450	
		Rent revenue		450
		(Recognition of the October rent earned on the office building)		

The $450 October rent has been earned by the Kool Playhouse (thus, the rent revenue account is credited), even though payment will not be received until November 1. The Playhouse also debits the rent receivable account to recognize its asset claim against the Plymouth Company for October's rent.

4. b.   1983
          Nov. 1   Cash   900
                        Rent receivable   450
                        Rent revenue   450
                    (Collection of the October
                    and November rent on the
                    office building)

The $900 cash represents the rent paid by the Plymouth Company for October and November. Of this $900, only the $450 relating to the November rent is earned revenue in November. Thus, the rent revenue account is credited for this amount. The $450 cash for the October rent was already recognized as October earned revenue in the October 31 adjusting entry. This payment of October's rent requires the elimination of the rent receivable asset claim established against the Plymouth Company on October 31. Therefore, the rent receivable account is credited $450.

5. a.   1983
          Oct. 9   Office supplies   500
                        Cash   500
                    (Purchase of office supplies)

5. b.   1983
          Oct. 31   Office supplies expense   200
                        Office supplies   200
                    (Recognition of office
                    supplies used during October)

The $200 worth of office supplies used during October represents an expense to the Kool Playhouse. Thus, the office supplies expense account is debited $200. Also, as a result of these supplies' having been used, the Kool Playhouse's office supplies asset is reduced. Therefore, the office supplies account is credited $200.

Chapter 4

Part 1.

The Elmwood Company
Bank Reconciliation Statement
April 30, 1983

Balance per bank statement,		Balance per Elmwood	
April 30	$473	Company's records, April 30	$500

Add: **Deposit in Transit—** Deposit of April 29, not recorded by the bank in April.	200 $673	

Deduct: **Outstanding checks—**		
Check No. 133	$ 75	
Check No. 136	125	
Check No. 137	25	225

Adjusted balance per bank
statement, April 30   **$448**

Deduct:
NSF check for $50 from
the Aztec Company charged
to the Elmwood Company's
account on April 28. $50

Bank service charge for
the month of April.   2   52

Adjusted balance per Elmwood
Company's records, April 30   **$448**

To determine any deposits in transit on April 30, a comparison must be made of the bank deposits reported in the Elmwood Company's accounting records during April with the bank deposits that are actually recorded on the April bank statement. Also, it must be determined whether the $50 deposit in transit from the Elmwood Company's March 31 bank reconciliation statement is recorded on the April bank statement. Since the $200 April 29 deposit is not shown on the bank statement, it is the only deposit in transit as of April 30.

To determine any outstanding checks on April 30, a comparison must be made of the cash disbursement checks written by the Elmwood Company during April (reported in its accounting records) with the checks that actually cleared the April bank statement. In addition, it must be determined whether the outstanding checks from the Elmwood Company's March 31 bank reconciliation statement (check numbers 131 and 133) have cleared the April bank statement. Since check numbers 133, 136, and 137 are not shown on the bank statement, they represent the outstanding checks as of April 30.

Part 2.

1983			
April 30	Accounts receivable	50	
	Cash		50
	(To reestablish an accounts receivable against the Aztec Company, whose check was determined bad on April 28)		
30	Bank service charge expense	2	
	Cash		2
	(To recognize expense for April bank service charge)		

Journal entries are recorded only for those bank reconciliation items that affect the "Balance per Elmwood Company's records, April 30." The reconciliation items that affect the "Balance per bank statement, April 30" have already been recognized in the Elmwood Company's accounting records (that is, the April 29 deposit in transit and the three outstanding checks), and, therefore, do not require journal entries. It is the bank's responsibility to record the $200 deposit in transit when it arrives at the bank. Also, the three outstanding checks will be recorded by the bank when they are presented for payment.

Chapter 5

Part A

Since the Sunshine Dress Shop owners believe that the per unit purchase costs of their merchandise inventory items will continue to increase during 1983, the dress shop should utilize the LIFO inventory costing method. Under LIFO, the most recent inventory items purchased are assumed to be sold first. In an inflationary period with rising per unit costs, these most recently purchased items would have a larger unit cost than earlier purchased items. LIFO would thus cause a larger cost of merchandise sold expense. The subtraction of this larger expense from revenues would result in a smaller net income amount. The dress shop would, therefore, pay less income taxes to the government at year's end.

LIFO computation of the Sunshine Dress Shop's January 31, 1983 merchandise inventory asset account balance (relating only to the inventory of blouses) and the January, 1983 cost of merchandise sold expense (relating only to the blouses sold during January):

Total blouses available for sale during January—
January 1 purchase	6 blouses	
+ January 23 purchase	4 blouses	
Total		10 blouses

Less : Total blouses sold during January—
January 20 sale	3 blouses	
+ January 28 sale	1 blouse	
Total		4 blouses

January 31 inventory of blouses to be costed under LIFO · · · · · · · · · · · 6 blouses

Computation of January 31, 1983 merchandise inventory under LIFO; 6 blouses to be costed

From January 1 purchase (the earliest purchase of blouses)

<u>6</u> blouses at $2 per blouse =   <u>$12</u>

Total blouses	*Total dollar cost*
accounted for in	*of 6 blouses in*
Jan. 31 inventory	*Jan. 31 merchandise*
	inventory

Since the most recent merchandise inventory items purchased are assumed to be sold first under LIFO, the January 31 inventory is priced at the $2 per blouse cost from January 1.

Computation   of January 1983 cost of merchandise sold expense
under LIFO

Total cost of blouses available for sale during January:

January 1 Purchase	6 blouses at $2 per blouse	= $12
+ January 23 Purchase	4 blouses at $2.25 per blouse =	9
Total		$21

Less: Cost of January 31 merchandise inventory of blouses
(computed above)   12

January 1983 cost of merchandise sold (relating to blouses only)   <u>$ 9</u>

Part B

FIFO computation   of the Sunshine Dress Shop's January 31, 1983 merchandise inventory asset account balance (relating only to the inventory of blouses) and the January 1983 cost of merchandise sold expense (relating only to the blouses sold during January):

Computation   of January 31, 1983 merchandise inventory under FIFO;
6 blouses to be costed (computed in Part A)

From January 23 purchase (the most recent purchase
of blouses)   4 blouses at $2.25 per blouse = $ 9

From January 1 purchase (the next most recent purchase
of blouses)   <u>2</u> blouses at $2 per blouse   =   <u>4</u>
                           <u>6</u>   <u>$13</u>

Total blouses	*Total dollar cost*
accounted for in	*of 6 blouses in*
Jan. 31 inventory	*Jan. 31 merchandise*
	inventory

Since the earliest inventory items purchased are assumed to be sold first under FIFO, the January 31 inventory consists of the most recently purchased items. Thus, four of the six blouses are priced at the $2.25-per-blouse cost *from January 23, and the remaining two blouses are priced at the $2-per-blouse cost from January 1.*

Computation of January 1983 cost of merchandise sold expense under FIFO

Total cost of blouses available for sale during January (computed in Part A)	$21
Less: Cost of January 31 merchandise inventory of blouses (computed above)	13
January 1983 cost of merchandise sold (relating to blouses only)	$ 8

Average cost computation of the Sunshine Dress Shop's January 31, 1983 merchandise inventory asset account balance (relating only to the inventory of blouses) and the January 1983 cost of merchandise sold expense (relating only to the blouses sold during January):

Weighted average cost per blouse

$$= \frac{\text{total cost of blouses available for sale during January}}{\text{total blouses available for sale during January}}$$

$$= \frac{\$21 \text{ (computed below)}}{10 \text{ blouses (computed below)}} = \underline{\$2.10} \text{ per blouse weighted average cost}$$

Remember, under a periodic inventory system, the average inventory cost per unit is called a "weighted average cost."

Total quantity and cost of blouses available for sale during January:

January 1 purchase	6 blouses at $2 per blouse	=	$12
+ January 23 purchase	4 blouses at $2.25 per blouse=		9
	10		$21

Total blouses available for sale during January   *Total cost of blouses available for sale during January*

Computation of January 31, 1983 merchandise inventory under Average cost; 6 blouses to be costed

6 blouses × $2.10 weighted average cost per blouse = $12.60

Computation of January 1983 cost of merchandise sold expense under average cost

Total cost of blouses available for sale during January	$21.00
Less: Cost of January 31 merchandise inventory of blouses	12.60
January 1983 cost of merchandise sold (relating to blouses only)	$ 8.40

Chapter 6

Part A

1. 1983

July	1	Accounts receivable	1200
		Sales		1200

(To recognize the sale of a sofa to the Burton Company)

	1	Cost of merchandise sold	800
		Merchandise inventory		800

(To recognize the cost of merchandise sold and the inventory reduction for the sofa sale to the Burton Company)

2. 1983

Aug.	1	Cash	200
		Notes receivable	1000
		Accounts receivable		1200

(To recognize a six-month note at 9 percent annual interest and $200 cash from the Burton Company to replace its July 1 accounts receivable)

The $1200 accounts receivable asset claim against Burton Company is now eliminated since the Shipley Furniture Company receives $200 cash and a $1000 note from the Burton Company.

3. 1983

Dec.31	Accrued interest receivable	37.50
	Interest earned		37.50

(To record the adjusting entry for accrued interest on the Burton Company's $1000 note)

Computation of accrued interest on December 31, 1983:

Principal of note	*$1000*
Multiplied by interest rate	*× .09*
	$ 90 per year interest on the note.

The note from the Burton Company is only a six-month note (half of a year). Thus, the total interest earned by the Shipley Furniture Company on this note would be $45 (1/2 of $90). As of December 31, five months of the note's life have passed (from August 1 through December 31). This results in five months' accrued interest income at year end—5/6 × $45 = $37.50.

4. 1984

Feb. 1 **Cash** 1045.00

        Notes receivable **1000.00**

        Accrued interest receivable **37.50**

        Interest earned **7.50**

        (To recognize the principal and interest
collection on the Burton Company's
note)

The cash collected on the note's February 1 maturity date is the $1000 principal plus the $45 interest.

Since the note's principal and interest are now collected, the two asset claims against the Burton Company must be eliminated. This results in credits to the notes receivable account (recognized August 1) and to the accrued interest receivable account (recognized December 31). The interest earned credit reflects the Shipley Furniture Company's interest income on this note for January (1/6 × $45 = $7.50).

Part B

1. 1983

July 1 **Office furniture** 1200

        Accounts payable 1200

        (To recognize the purchase of a sofa
from the Shipley Furniture Company)

The "office furniture" account would be reported under long-term assets on the Burton Company's balance sheet, since the company plans to use the sofa for longer than one year.

2. 1983

Aug. 1 Accounts payable 1200

        Cash **200**

        Notes payable **1000**

        (To recognize a six-month note liability at 9 percent annual interest and a $200 cash payment to the Shipley Furniture Company to replace its July 1 accounts payable)

The $1200 accounts payable liability to Shipley Furniture Company is now eliminated, since the Burton Company pays $200 cash and issues a $1000 note to the Shipley Furniture Company.

3. 1983

Dec.31 Interest expense   37.50

          Accrued interest payable   37.50

(To record the adjusting entry for accrued interest on the $1000 note lia-
bility to the Shipley Furniture
Company)

*This accrued interest is determined in exactly the same manner as previously
computed by the Shipley Furniture Company in its December 31 adjusting
entry. However, this $37.50 represents five months' interest expense to the
Burton Company.*

4. 1984

Feb. 1 **Notes payable**   1000.00

    Accrued interest payable   37.50

    Interest expense   7.50

        Cash   **1045.00**

(To recognize the principal and interest
payment on the August 1 note issued to
the Shipley Furniture Company)

*Since the note's principal and interest
are now paid, the two liabilities to
Shipley Furniture Company must be
eliminated. This results in debits to
the notes payable account (recognized August 1) and to the accrued
interest payable account (recognized
December 31). The interest expense
debit reflects the Burton Company's
January expense for interest on this
note (1/6 × $45 = $7.50).*

*The cash paid on the note's Feb-
ruary 1 maturity date is the $1000
principal plus the $45 interest. This
interest is identical in amount to
that previously computed for the
Shipley Furniture Company.*

Chapter 7

Part A

*1. In addition to disclosing the 1983 decpreciation on the Lester Company's
machine, the schedule below also shows the 1981 and 1982 depreciation
computation as well as the "accumulated depreciation–machinery" balance
and the book value (cost – accumulated depreciation balance) for each of
these three years.*

Year	Depreciation Expense Each Year	Balance of Accumulated Depreciation–Machinery Account at the End of Each Year	Book value of machine at the End of Each Year
1981	$2000 (4/10 × $5000)	$2000	$4000 ($6000 – $2000)
1982	1500 (3/10 × $5000)	3500** ($2000 + $1500)	2500** ($6000 – $3500)
1983	1000 (2/10 × $5000)	4500 ($3500 + $1000)	1500 ($6000 – $4500)

**The $3500 "accumulated depreciation–machinery" balance and the $2500 book value on December 31, 1982 appear on the Lester Company's January 1, 1983 partial balance sheet provided in this problem. Remember, the monetary balances reported at the end of a year are the beginning balances in the subsequent year.

Each year's depreciation fraction is computed as follows: Since the machine's estimated useful life is four years, the sum of the years' digits is 10 (4 + 3 + 2 + 1). This number represents the denominator for each year's fraction. The machine was purchased on January 1, 1981. Thus, at the beginning of 1981, there are 4 years remaining in the asset's estimated life. The 1981 depreciation fraction is therefore, 4/10. The 1982 fraction is 3/10 (three years remain in the machine's useful life on January 1, 1982, and the 1983 fraction is 2/10. Each year's fraction is then multiplied by the asset's $5000 depreciable cost ($6000 cost – $1000 estimated salvage value) to determine the annual depreciation expense.

The Lester Company's December 31, 1983 adjusting entry is
(See above depreciation schedule for $1000 computation.)

    1983
    Dec. 31   Depreciation expense   1000
                    Accumulated depreciation–
                    machinery   1000
                    (To record the yearly adjusting
                    entry for depreciation on the machine)

2.   1983
    Dec. 31   Depreciation expense   800
                    Accumulated depreciation–
                    truck   800
                    (To record the yearly adjusting
                    entry for depreciation on the
                    delivery truck)

Computation of the delivery truck depreciation:
        Depreciation rate per mile (determined on January 1, 1981 when the delivery truck was purchased)

$$= \frac{\textit{depreciable basis of truck}}{\textit{estimated mileage output from truck}}$$

$$= \frac{\$4500 \text{ truck cost} - \$500 \text{ estimated salvage value}}{40,000 \text{ estimated miles}}$$

$$= \frac{\$4000}{40,000 \text{ estimated miles}} = \$.10 \text{ per mile depreciation rate}$$

1983 depreciation expense = *the number of actual miles driven during the year multiplied by the depreciation rate per mile*

= *8000 miles* × *$.10 per mile depreciation rate*

= *$800*

Part B

Partial balance sheet of the Lester Company, December 31, 1983

Plant and equipment

Machinery	$6000	
Less: Accumulated depreciation	4500	$1500
Truck	$4500	
Less: Accumulated depreciation	**2300**	**2200**
Total plant and equipment assets		$3700

This $4500 accumulated depreciation balance is determined by adding the $1000 increase from the December 31, 1983 adjusting entry to the $3500 balance on January 1, 1983. The subtraction of this updated accumulated depreciation balance from the machine's $6000 cost gives the $1500 book value.

This $2300 accumulated depreciation balance is determined by adding the $800 increase from the December 31, 1983 adjusting entry to the $1500 balance on January 1, 1983. The subtraction of this updated accumulated depreciation balance from the truck's $4500 cost gives the $2200 book value.

Part C

Under the straight-line method, an equal dollar amount of depreciation expense is recognized each year during the machine's estimated useful life. This annual expense is computed as follows:

Depreciation expense each year

$$= \frac{depreciable\ basis\ of\ machine}{estimated\ useful\ life\ of\ machine}$$

$$= \frac{\$6000\ machine\ cost - \$1000\ estimated\ salvage\ value}{4\ years}$$

$$= \frac{\$5000}{4\ years} = \$1250$$

Therefore, the Lester Company's 1983 depreciation expense on its machine is $1250.

Chapter 8

Part A

1983
April 1   Depreciation expense   25
                 Accumulated depreciation—
                  machinery   25
                 (To update the sold machine's de-
                 preciation for the period January 1
                 to April 1)

A depreciation adjusting entry was last recorded on this sold machine on December 31, 1982. Therefore, on the April 1 sale date, an adjusting entry is required for three months' depreciation (January, February, and March). This expense is $25 (3/12 × $100 per year depreciation).

1983
April 1   Cash   300
                 Accumulated depreciation—
                 machinery   325
                      Machinery   600
                      Gain on disposal of plant and
                      equipment assets   25
                 (To recognize the sale of the machine
                 to the Crandall Company)

Computation of $25 gain on machine sale:
*   Balance of machinery account (original cost of*
*   machine)—see general ledger account in chap-*
*   ter problem*   *$600*
Less: Updated balance of accumulated deprecia-
*   tion—machinery account on April 1, 1983*
*   Balance of accumulated depreciation account*
*   as of December 31, 1982—see general ledger*
*   account in chapter problem*   *$300*
*   Plus: Increase in accumulated depreciation*
*   account from April 1 adjusting entry*   *25*   *325*
Book value of machine on date of sale   *$275*
Compared to: Proceeds received from sale of machine   *300*
*   Gain on sale of machine*   *$ 25*

Since the Hector Company sold its machine, the monetary balances of the two general ledger accounts reflecting the machine's book value must be eliminated. The "machinery" *The Hector Company's normal operating activities are manufacturing and selling transistor radios. Therefore, this $25 gain would be reported as nonoperating revenue on the* *account has a $600 debit balance on the sale date and is therefore eliminated by a $600 credit. The "accumulated depreciation–machinery" account has an April 1 credit balance of $325. This balance is eliminated by a $325 debit.*

company's income statement and added to its "income from operations."

Part B

	1983			
	April 1	Depreciation expense	25	
		Accumulated depreciation–machinery		25
		(To update the sold machine's depreciation for the period January 1 to April 1)		

This adjusting entry is identical to the one recorded in Part A.

	1983			
	April 1	Cash	225	
		Accumulated depreciation–machinery	325	
		Loss on disposal of plant and equipment assets	50	
		Machinery		600
		(To recognize the sale of the machine to the Crandall Company)		

Computation of $50 loss on machine sale:

Balance of machinery account (original cost of machine)–see general ledger account in chapter problem	*$600*
Less: Updated balance of accumulated depreciation–machinery account on April 1, 1983 (see computation in Part A)	*325*
Book value of machine on date of sale	*$275*
Compared to: Proceeds received from sale of machine	*225*
Loss on sale of machine	*$ 50*

The explanation for eliminating the "machinery" and the "accumulated depreciation–machinery" accounts is identical to that in Part A.

This $50 loss would be reported as a nonoperating expense on the Hector Company's income statement and subtracted from its "operating income."

Chapter 9

Part A

```
1983
May  1    Cash                              5,000
          Office equipment                  7,000
                Tom Densey, capital                   12,000
          (to record Tom Densey's initial
          partnership investment)

May  1    Cash                              3,000
          Office equipment                  5,000
                Walter Brooks, capital                 8,000
          (to record Walter Brooks' initial
          partnership investment)
```

The office equipment invested by each partner is recorded at its current market value.

Part B

```
1.   1983
     May 20   Tom Densey, drawing            10
                   Office supplies                        10
              (To recognize Densey's with-
              drawal of office supplies)
```

Densey's drawing account is debited $10 to reflect his reduced ownership interest in the partnership's assets.

```
2.   1983
     May 29   Cash                          1000
                   Walter Brooks, capital                1000
              (To recognize Brooks' additional
              cash investment)
```

This $1000 credit increases Brooks' ownership interest in the partnership's assets.

Part C

```
1.   1983
     May 31   Tom Densey, drawing            800
              Walter Brooks, drawing         800
                   Cash                                 1600
              (To recognize the partners'
              monthly salaries)
```

The debits to each partner's drawing account reduce their ownership interests in the partnership's assets.

2.

Densey and Brooks Patient Care Center
Income Distribution Schedule
For the Month Ended May 31, 1983*

	NET INCOME DISTRIBUTED TO		TOTAL NET INCOME
ITEM DISTRIBUTED	*DENSEY*	*BROOKS*	*DISTRIBUTED*
Salary allowance	$800	$800	$1600
Interest allowance	120	80	200
Remaining net income in the partners' income and loss sharing percentages	(55)	(45)	(100)
Total increase in partners' capital accounts	$865	$835	$1700

*This schedule is based upon the following articles of partnership provisions:

Salary allowance $800 per month to Densey
                          $800 per month to Brooks

Interest allowance   1 percent monthly to each partner computed on his beginning of month capital account balance. Since the partnership began business May 1, the partners' asset investments on this date (see Part A) represent their beginning of month account balances. Therefore, Densey's interest allowance is $120 (1% × $12,000 May 1 capital balance) and Brooks' $80 (1% × $8000 May 1 capital balance).

Remaining net income   The partners' salary and interest allowances total $1800 ($1600 + $200). Since the May net income is only $1700, a negative $100 ($1800 – $1700) must be allocated to Densey and Brooks in their income and loss sharing percentages of 55 percent and 45 percent, respectively. Therefore, Densey's allocation of the negative $100 is $55 (55% × $100) and Brooks' is $45 (45% × $100). These allocations are subtracted in the above schedule, because they reduce each partner's share of the May income distribution.

Densey's total allocation of the $1700 May net income is $865 and Brooks' is $835.

3.   1983

May 31   Income summary   1700

                 Tom Densey, capital   865

                 Walter Brooks, capital   835

                 (To close the income summary

                 account into the partners' capital

                 accounts)

Before this closing entry, the income summary account has a $1700 credit balance reflecting the May net income. The income summary debit transfers this income to the partners' capital accounts. Each partner's share of the income is determined from the May income distribution schedule (see 2 above).

          1983

May 31   Tom Densey, capital   **930**

                 Walter Brooks, capital   **880**

                 Tom Densey, drawing   **930**

                 Walter Brooks, drawing   **880**

                 (To close the partners' drawing

                 accounts into their capital

                 accounts)

Before this closing entry, Densey's drawing account has an $930 debit balance ($10 office supplies withdrawn May 20 + $800 salary May 31 + $120 interest allowance May 31) and Brooks' an $880 debit balance ($800 salary May 31 + $80 interest allowance May 31). The above entry transfers each partner's drawing account balance to his capital account.

4.

Densey and Brooks Patient Care Center
Capital Statement
For the Month Ended May 31, 1983

	DENSEY	*BROOKS*	*TOTALS*
Capital, May 1, 1983	$12,000	$8,000	$20,000
Plus: Additional investment (see Part B, number 2)		1,000	1,000
	$12,000	$9,000	$21,000
Plus: Distributive share of partnership net income (see income distribution schedule in Part C, number 2)	865	835	1,700
	$12,865	$9,835	$22,700
Less: Withdrawal of assets	930	880	1,810
Capital, May 31, 1983	$11,935	$8,955	$20,890

The Densey and Brooks Patient Care Center started business on May 1, 1983. Therefore, each partner's May 1 capital account balance results from his asset investment on this date (see Part A).

Each partner's asset withdrawals are reflected in his owner's equity drawing account.

Chapter 10

```
1983
Jan. 21   Cash                             1050
              Common stock                      1000
              Premium on common stock             50
          (To recognize the issuance of 50
          shares of common stock at $21
          per share)
```

"Cash" is debited $1050 (50 shares × $21 per share selling price), "common stock" is credited $1000 (50 shares × $20 per share par value), and "premium on common stock" is credited $50 [50 shares × $1 per share premium ($21 selling price – $20 par value)].

```
1983
Mar. 14   Cash                             2800
          Discount on preferred stock       200
              Preferred stock                   3000
          (To recognize the issuance of 100
          shares of preferred stock at $28
          per share)
```

"Cash" is debited $2800 (100 shares × $28 per share selling price), "discount on preferred stock" is debited $200 [100 shares × $2 per share discount ($30 stated value – $28 selling price)], and "preferred stock" is credited $3000 (100 shares × $30 per share stated value).

```
1983
Dec. 31   Income summary                   8000
              Retained earnings                 8000
          (To close the income summary
          account into the retained earn-
          ings account)
```

Before the above entry, the income summary account has an $8000 credit balance, reflecting the 1983 net income. This closing entry transfers the income into the stockholders' equity retained earnings account.

1983
Dec. 31   **Retained earnings**   3290

	Cash dividends payable to common stockholders	**1610**
	Cash dividends payable to preferred stockholders	**1680**

(To recognize the cash dividend declared by the Board of Directors; record date is Jan. 10, 1984, and payment date is Jan. 20, 1984.)

The retained earnings account is debited in order to reduce the stockholders' equity for this $3290 declared cash dividend.

Computation of Cash Dividend to the Henry Corporation's Preferred and Common Stockholders

	CASH DIVIDEND TO PREFERRED STOCK-HOLDERS	CASH DIVIDEND TO COMMON STOCK-HOLDERS	TOTAL DIVIDENDS
Dividends in arrears to preferred stockholders based upon the cumulative provision (see the stockholders' equity section of the December 31, 1982 balance sheet)	$ 720		$ 720
Regular 1983 dividend to preferred stockholders—$30 stated value per share × 8% dividend rate = $2.40 per share dividend × 400 outstanding shares (300 shares issued as of December 31, 1982 + 100 shares issued on March 14, 1983)	960		960
1983 dividend to common stockholders—$1 per share dividend × 1610 outstanding shares (1560 shares issued as of December 31, 1982 + 50 shares issued on Jan. 21, 1983)		$1610	1610
Totals	$1680	$1610	$3290

Chapter 11

Note: Letters are included by the various monetary items to facilitate the subsequent explanations.

The Samantha Corporation
Statement of Changes in Financial Position
For the Year Ended December 31, 1983

Resources provided
  Working capital from operations
    Net income $4,500
    Add: Depreciation expense $1,000

          Loss on disposal of plant and
          equipment assets   600   1,600

       Total resources from operations $ 6,100 (A)

Working capital from the sale of a
long-term asset (a piece of equipment)   1,000 (B)

Working capital from the sale of
common stock   550 (C)

Resources from the issuance of a long-
term note payable (for the purchase of
land)   1,000 (D)
       Total resources provided $ 8,650

Resources Applied

Working capital used to purchase a long-
term asset (a piece of equipment) $6,000 (E)

Working capital used to purchase a long-
term asset (a piece of land)   7,650 (F)
Working capital used for the declaration
of a cash dividend to preferred and com-
mon stockholders   4,000 (G)

Resources used for the purchase of land
(by incurring a long-term note payable)   1,000 (D)
       Total resources applied   18,650

Total decrease in net working capital $10,000 (H)

Explanations of the monetary items in the Samantha Corporation's statement of changes in financial position:

Letters (A) and (B)

The $1000 depreciation represents one of the operating expenses previously subtracted from the revenues to compute the corporation's 1983 net income. Since depreciation does not affect net working capital, this $1000 is eliminated from the income calculation by adding it back.

The May 1 journal entry for the equipment sale was

Cash	1000	
Accumulated depreciation–equipment	400	
Loss on disposal of plant and equipment assets	600	
Equipment		2000

The $600 loss is a nonoperating expense that was subtracted from the operating income to compute the corporation's final net income. Since the loss represents a nonoperating item, this $600 is added back to the $4500 net income to eliminate its effect.

After the depreciation and nonoperating loss have been added to the net income, the $6100 working capital from operations is determined (see letter A).

The $1000 cash from the May 1 equipment sale increases net working capital and is, therefore, reported under resources provided (see letter B).

Letter (C)

The Samantha Corporation received $550 cash from selling common stock. Its stockholders' equity accounts "common stock" and "premium on common stock" were credited $500 and $50, respectively, for this transaction. The $550 cash increases net working capital by this amount and, therefore, represents resources provided.

Letter (D)

The December 20 journal entry for the acquisition of land by incurring a two-year note liability was

Land	1000	
Notes payable (long-term)		1000

The corporation's net working capital is unaffected by the above transaction, since only noncurrent accounts are involved. However, the incurrence of a long-term note liability to purchase land is an important financial transaction that should be disclosed on the statement of changes in financial position. Consequently, this transaction is reported under both resources provided and resources applied.

Letter (E)

The corporation purchased equipment on June 1 by paying $6000 cash. This transaction causes net working capital to decrease and, therefore, represents resources applied.

Letter (F)

The $7650 cash payment on September 10 for the land purchase decreases net working capital and is reported as resources applied.

Letter (G)

The December 31 journal entry reflecting the $4000 declared cash dividend to the preferred and common stockholders was

Retained earnings	4000
Cash dividends payable to preferred and common stockholders	4000

Since the cash dividends payable to preferred and common stockholders account is a current liability, this transaction causes a net working capital decrease. Therefore, the $4000 represents resources applied.

Letter (H)

The Samantha Corporation's total resources applied ($18,650) exceeds its total resources provided ($8650) by $10,000. As a result, the net working capital decreases by this amount in 1983.

Index